Performing *the* GOSPEL

in liturgy and lifestyle

CHARLES SHERLOCK

Performing the Gospel—in liturgy and lifestyle

First published in 2017
by Broughton Publishing Pty Ltd
32 Glenvale CrescentMulgrave VIC 3170

Revised edition 2018

Copyright © Charles Sherlock 2017

All rights reserved. No part of this publication may be reproduced, stored in a retrieval system or transmitted, in any form or by any means electronic, photocopying, recording or otherwise, without the prior written permission of the publisher.

ISBN 978-0-9870458-6-7

Contents

Acknowledgements   v

Foreword   vii

Introduction   1

Chapter 1   *Liturgy and lifestyle: performing Christian worship*   17

Chapter 2   *Setting the scene: spaces for gospel performance*   39

Chapter 3   *Being 'upfront': performing and presiding*   69

Chapter 4   *The words of gospel performance*   97

Chapter 5   *Performing the gospel 'according to the scriptures'*   117

Chapter 6   *The sound of music in performing the gospel*   137

Chapter 7   *Seeing is believing? Liturgy on screen*   173

Chapter 8   *When we perform the gospel: times and seasons*   203

Chapter 9   *Common prayer? Planning to perform the gospel*   233

Further reading   262

Acknowledgements

Performing the Gospel brings together insights I began learning as a child. Each Sunday morning my mother Emily took us to Holy Communion from the *Book of Common Prayer* (1662)—Dad was presiding up front. She would invite 'different' people to join us, and was keen to make Sunday in a busy rectory enjoyable. Breakfast meant Milo on our cereal, a traditional roast followed Sunday School and Morning Prayer, and the afternoon was seasoned by 'Sunday surprises', while supper after Evensong included scones in the colours of the church year. Her sometimes-eccentric example of performing the gospel as a 'di-rector' laid foundations for my own living as a Christian.

A succession of wise organists and patient head servers put up with a teenager's questioning of the 'whys' of worship, while the Evangelical Union and Anglican Society at Sydney University widened my Christian experience. Lectures in 1966 by (later Archbishop) Donald Robinson on prayer book revision, just commencing for Australian Anglicans, whetted my appetite for more.

From 1969 I was a student and tutor at Ridley College. Principal Leon Morris engaged us deeply in the experiments going in prayer book revision, which would lead to the publication in 1978 of *An Australian Prayer Book (AAPB)*. A year later Dr Morris retired, and I was handed the baton of teaching 'Prayer Book' and 'Christian Worship'. Teaching without doubt helps you learn. I gladly acknowledge the influence of generations of students on my understanding: in my quarter-century at Ridley, they came from a hundred or more Anglican settings, besides other Christian traditions.

In 1989, General Synod began to explore the revision of *AAPB*, and when the Liturgy Commission was reconstituted, I was appointed as a member. The outcome was an intense five years of writing and meetings, leading to the adoption of *A Prayer Book for Australia* at the 1995 General Synod. Three members of that Commission were especially important for my ongoing learning: Lawrence Bartlett (Sydney), Evan Burge (Melbourne), and Ronald Dowling (Melbourne, Adelaide and Perth), each of whom has now departed this earthly life and fallen asleep in Christ. It was a privilege to work closely with them in the communion that is God's gift and being. Many of their insights, though not always accepted, have given focus and depth to this current book.

I cannot ignore the influence of Christians beyond the Australian or the Anglican tradition. Participation in the *Anglican-Roman Catholic International Commission* (ARCIC II), the *International Anglican Liturgical Consultation* (IALC), *Australian Academy of Liturgy* (AAL)—notably its Victorian chapter—and teaching at the United Faculty of Theology, has provided significant opportunities for dialogue, and to have developing ideas tested.

At a practical level, Robert Andersen of Broughton Books has been a constant encouragement, and I am very grateful to Robyn O'Sullivan for her editorial skills and insights. I thank Stephen Burns, Leigh Mackay, Peter Angelovski and Heather Marten for their invaluable feedback.

Finally, and most of all, I must acknowledge Peta Sherlock, with whom I have shared life, love, home and theology for a half-century. As a delightful writer, keen theologian, creative liturgist, insightful school chaplain, parish priest and cathedral dean, she embodies what this book is about.

Foreword

Charles Sherlock invites us to consider what it means for Christian people to perform the service that is our response to God, specifically the worship which is our due to the Holy Trinity. It is after all, the living God—Father, Son and Holy Spirit—'who initiates, enables and receives our worship'. Sherlock's book is a practical guide, but thoroughly steeped in the best theological understanding of what worship really is about and to whom it is offered. In an era when the choices of worship style are often presented as polar opposites to prove a point, Charles Sherlock offers a refreshing alternative to blind conservatism or deconstructionism. Identity and worship are always connected, and it is to be hoped that the application of the schema of this book will refresh and deepen the identity of the people of God in the one whom they worship.

I'm looking forward to parishes, theological colleges and worship committees taking up the challenge that is laid out in *Performing the Gospel—in liturgy and lifestyle*. It deserves wide attention.

The Most Reverend Dr Philip L Freier
Primate

Introduction

You have been approached about helping arrange a dramatic performance in church, and have a week to think about your response. You are excited about the idea, and take it very seriously. So you jot down some questions:
- Why is the performance being put on at this time and place?
- Who will be in the audience? How will they relate to the performance?
- Who is sponsoring the performance, and why? Are they looking for any particular outcomes, or 'product placements'?
- What do you make of the script? And, remembering a recent eco-feminist re-reading of Romeo and Juliet that impressed you, you wonder how open the script is to re-interpretation.
- Who will play the lead parts? How experienced do they need to be, or can fresh faces be tried? What choreography is needed, possible or desirable—and who will plan it?
- What about the set? How flexible is the space where the performance takes place? What lighting possibilities are there? Will the budget allow scene changes, and perhaps stretch to some professional props?
- Will there be background music? Performed music or songs? Will the audience be asked to join in singing — will it be like a 'sing along *Sound of Music*'?
- What do you want participants to feel, learn and respond to from the performance? Afterwards, what do you hope they will be talking about over coffee?

Your creative juices get going, and a day or so later you ask for some more details—in particular, when the performance is happening. To your surprise you find that it is next week; and that it has been put on every week for several years. Then it dawns on you: you are being asked to be part of the planning team for the regular Sunday service at your local church, for which your minister is encouraging a fresh look.

Worship—performing the gospel drama

Performance is a time-honoured way of thinking about what a Christian congregation does when it gathers. Christian services typically set out to have us take part in the great divine drama that revolves around Jesus Christ. As Robert Webber puts it, "worship is characterised by a dramatic re-telling" of God's action in the Christ-event and all that leads to and from it.[1] In the Eastern Orthodox tradition, the 'divine liturgy' is set out as a drama telling the story of incarnation, life, death and exaltation of the Lord Jesus, in which the congregation (through the Holy Spirit) again encounters Christ's risen presence.

Performance: some dangers

An important clarification must be made at this point. 'Performing' can be a vehicle for a person to show off, manipulate others, or just act out a role with little concern about its meaning or effect. Those involved in Christian worship face temptations like these, especially leaders whose spiritual authority is well accepted. Preachers can

---

[1] Robert E. Webber, *Worship is a Verb* (Waco: Word, 1985) 37-46. Other works that pick up the 'performance' motif include Marva J. Dawn, *A Royal "Waste" of Time* (Grand Rapids: Eerdmans, 1999), and (in relation to the interpretation of Holy Scripture), Frances Young, *The Art of Performance* (London: DLT, 1990).

focus on impressing the congregation with their wit, wisdom or knowledge of Hebrew vowels. Pentecostals can use their platform ministry to impose their views on social and political issues. Priests can enjoy 'turning it on' when presiding at the eucharist, drawing attention to themselves rather than to Christ. Musicians can want to 'put on a show' upfront, and/or control the songs chosen. Prayers can seek to impress by their long words, or abuse this ministry by spreading gossip.

In speaking of Christian worship as 'performance', the key focus is on what *God* is doing in our midst, through the ministry of the gospel in Word, sacrament, common prayer and common life. In the Christian tradition, grounded in the teaching of the scriptures, the responsibility and accountability for these ministries lies with those called to exercise them—churches are not 'democratic' in that anyone can do what they like.[2] And these ministers are called to *perform*, using their God-given skills to the fullest, entering into the roles they are assigned in the same way that an actor does. Their own personality must serve the part they are called to play, not dominate or displace it.[3]

That said, it is tempting to think that the performers are just the ministers and musicians, while the audience is the congregation,

---

2   As Article XXIII of the Thirty-Nine Articles, *Of Ministering in the Congregation*, states:

 It is not lawful for any man to take upon him the office of publick preaching, or ministering the Sacraments in the Congregation, before he be lawfully called, and sent to execute the same. And those we ought to judge lawfully called and sent, which be chosen and called to this work by men who have publick authority given unto them in the Congregation, to call and send Ministers into the Lord's vineyard.

 This issue is taken up more fully in Chapter Four.

3   So F.H. Brabant. 'The Art of Public Worship' in W.K. Lowther Clarke (ed), *Liturgy and Worship. A Companion to the Prayer books of the Anglican Communion* (London: SPCK, 1932) 29-31.

who join in only now and then. There are two problems here. First, performing the gospel is the calling of every Christian, whether in daily life or 'in church': how each person participates may differ, but all are 'performers'. Secondly, and far more problematic, the 'audience' for Christian worship is not the congregation, but the living God. The Christian thinker Søren Kierkegaard was deeply disturbed by many aspects of the 19th century Danish churches of his day. He argued that in Christian worship, "the actors are the whole congregation, who actively pray, praise, sing and listen; the prompters are the clergy and musicians, who help the congregation do their performance well, and the audience is God, before whom the congregation performs their worship."[4] Philips goes on to comment:

> If God is the one to whom worship belongs, then it is important that our worship be the sort that God would want. Congregations that do surveys to find out what sort of worship people want—without asking the prior question, "What does God want from our worship?"—are doing this backwards …
>
> When we gather for public worship on Sunday morning, or at any other time, our worship serves God through prayer and praise, shaping our lives for prayerful and faithful service of God in the world.

It is thus the living God—Father, Son and Spirit—who initiates, enables and receives our worship. The Spirit prompts us, as members of the body of Christ, to offer praise and adoration to the

---

[4] Cited in L Edward Philips, "Whose worship is it anyway?", in E Byron Anderson, ed., *Worship Matters: A United Methodist Guide to Ways of Worship* (Volume I. Nashville: Discipleship Resources, 1999) 80-81. I am grateful to Stephen Burns for this reference. *Kierkegaard's focus is on the preacher and listening, but applies more widely: see Purity of Heart is to will one thing* (1847; trans. Douglas Steere, New York: Harper and Brothers, 1948) 180ff.

Father. 'Performance' is thus a very useful way to understand this approach, especially when considering 'acts' of worship, 'liturgy'. Its strength is the light it sheds on how believers 'perform' in the presence of God, overdoing the importance of 'external' behaviour. Authentic performance sees the line blurred—but not eliminated — between actor and the character portrayed. Authentic performance of the Gospel sees us, as embodied creatures—but not the Creator—worship God 'in S/spirit and in T/truth' (John 4.24), integrating internal attitude and external activity.

But performance is not the only way in which Christian worship can be described and explored. Worship involves the ultimate mystery of life—who is it "in whom all things live and move and have their being" (Acts 17:28)? And what does it mean to engage with the living God—both love itself (1 John 4:10) and a "consuming fire" (Hebrews 12:29)? Susan White helpfully offers six main ways in which Christian traditions have approached worship: as service of God, mirror of heaven, affirmation of believers, communion with God and one another, proclamation of the Good News, and the arena of transcendence.[5] Each dimension can be a focal point for reflection on worship. This book sees these pearls as threaded on the string of performance—performance of the Gospel.

Arranging a performance

So what is involved in arranging a gospel performance?

The ***sponsor*** of all Christian worship, including liturgy, is the triune God. It is *God* who gathers us together as 'church' to love, know and obey the Lord Jesus Christ. Our meeting together is not merely a human decision, but one undertaken in response to the work of the Holy Spirit. The ***drama enacted*** is the gospel

---

5   Susan J. White, *Groundwork of Christian Worship* (Peterborough: Epworth, 1997) 2-16.

of God, the majestic good news of God's amazing love revealed in Christ. The *Book of Common Prayer* (1662), on the first page of the first service it contains, recalls 'why' Christians gather as the body of Christ:

> We assemble and meet together to render thanks for the great benefits that we have received at [God's] hands, to set forth his most worthy praise, to hear his most holy Word, and to ask those things which are requisite and necessary, as well for the body as the soul.

Thanks—praise—scripture—prayer. In short, the Christian Church meets together so that its members may have their living oriented and re-oriented to God, and God's purposes.

What **script** is involved in this divine drama? The fullest answer would be, the biblical story, as set out in the scriptures of the First and New Testaments.[6] But to get right through them, reading a chapter of both Testaments each morning and evening, takes several years! The Bible is a very long book. So from churches' earliest days, the scriptures' main thread has been spelled out through the choice of readings made, and by having the structure of services, and the words used in them, shaped by their content. From the First Fleet's arrival until the 1970s, Australian Anglicans

---

6   In this book, the Hebrew and Aramaic scriptures are denoted as the 'First Testament', reflecting their standing as the original written revelation of God, accepted as such by Jesus and the early churches. The term 'Old' runs the risk of seeing this Testament as secondary, sub-Christian or superseded. Yet for Christians to describe the gospels, letters and Revelation as the 'Second' Testament would be decidedly unhelpful: they are the 'New' Testament, dependent on the 'First' for their meaning. The use of such asymmetrical terms may look odd, but emphasises the necessity, distinctiveness and inter-relationship of both Testaments in Christian faith and life, and corresponds to Paul's use of 'first', 'new' and 'second' in relation to humankind in 1 Corinthians 15 and Romans 5.

performed the gospel using the *Book of Common Prayer* (1662—*BCP*). Its Prefaces emphasise the importance of hearing the scriptures, set in a biblically grounded liturgy, for forming Christian communities.

In 1977, *An Australian Prayer Book* (*AAPB*) was authorised for use alongside *BCP*, followed by *A Prayer Book for Australia* (*APBA*) in 1995. These—grounded in systematic reading of the scriptures—are now the 'script' most commonly used by Australian Anglicans. Similar ones are used by Uniting Church Australians—*Uniting in Worship I* and *II*. These books, and Roman Catholic rites in English, share the same system for reading the scriptures: the 'Three Year' (Roman Catholic) and (ecumenical Protestant) *Revised Common Lectionary*. The readings from the Bible used by these and other Australian churches are thus close to those heard, week-by-week, in other (western) Christian churches across the globe.

And what of the **actors**, especially those who play leading roles? Any performance depends to a large degree for its effectiveness upon them. Ordained ministers—notably a parish's rector/vicar and a diocese's bishop—bear responsibility for ensuring that the performance of Christian liturgy serves God's purposes. All those present in an act of Christian worship play an active part, but—except for singing—until the last 50 years or so, the upfront roles were performed by clergy. Given the more participatory ethos in western societies since the 1960s, the planning and performance of Sunday services is now typically shared across a range of people in a congregation. Changes in popular culture—from print to radio to television to video and now interactive media and the web—have seen sight predominate over sound, and lifted the standard of performance expected in any public event. So all involved in the performance of liturgy need to take on new performance skills, and work in teams: the 'one-man band' is sometimes needed, but not the best model. **Preparing a service of Christian worship today is** thus more like producing and directing a play than just choosing hymns and writing a sermon.

Performing the gospel: context and outcomes

The issues of the **context** and **setting** of a Christian service call for significant reflection. Church and society have been steadily moving apart across Australia in the half-century past. The setting in which the divine drama of the gospel is now performed is quite different from that of a couple of generations back. In November 1963, President John F. Kennedy and C.S. Lewis died on the same day, perhaps signalling the many changes about to break upon the western world.[7] How is the divine drama best structured and performed in our time, not least so that those unfamiliar with Christian faith are engaged, and come to belong to the community of Christ?

Are 'fresh expressions' of church needed today, particularly to enable people 'on the edge' of Christian life to explore faith and learn to participate in Christ's body? When this happens, the community involved will change; new Christians bring their insights and intuitions into its life—and that is likely to bring significant resistance.

> ### A note on 'fresh expressions'
> 'Fresh expressions' has come to cover a range of ideas in relation to worship. It is helpful to ask, 'fresh expression *of what?*' Fresh expressions *of the kingdom of God* can mean new forms of social concern, responses to emergency situations, welfare initiatives and the like—but may not necessarily see anyone be folded into God's people.

---

7   Martin Stringer, *A Sociological History of Christian Worship* (Cambridge: CUP, 2005) Chapter 7, 'The globalisation of Christian worship 1800-2000', offers an acute analysis, focussing on the rise of spiritual consumerism.

A 'fresh expression' *of church*, however, will be a community joined through baptism (or its re-affirmation), constituted by the ministry of the Word and sacraments, and be led by ministers accountable to the wider Church. How a 'fresh expression of church' performs these gospel realities is likely to be creative, and reflect the cultures of those who join—and its common life may even be difficult for long-term Christians to relate to. It may use a church building in new ways, or meet in other places or mainly online.

Most 'fresh expressions' lie somewhere between these two poles. They might best be described as 'fresh expressions *towards* church'. A group exploring spirituality, for example, may begin to pray, then reflect on the scriptures and enjoy arguing about their meaning. Accepting the 'partial' nature of such a group is important, though the possibility is there that it may never become 'church' and end up as a 'gospel-lite' spirituality club.

What then is the **response** looked for from Christian performance of the divine drama? After a concert or movie, the audience will often walk out feeling good, but quickly return to day-by-day life. Sometimes, however, what has been seen and heard will provoke discussion, and perhaps change attitudes and inspire action. This type of response is that looked for in the scriptures to acts of worship—indeed, those present are never just an audience, but part of the performance itself!

Each (northern hemisphere) spring, Israel of old, and Jews today, perform the Passover. Over the course of a special meal, the story of their rescue by God from slavery in Egypt, to become God's covenant people, is retold. For those who take part, this divine drama becomes *their* story, shaping their identity as members of

God's people. The story's script—drawn from Exodus 12–15—is read by the youngest person present, so that the oncoming generation is drawn in. Performing the Passover meal is thus a key way by which God's covenant with Israel is renewed year by year, and passes from one generation to the next.

The Christian tradition associates Passover (*pascha* in Greek) with Easter. (Its celebration of the death and resurrection of Christ is thus sometimes called the 'paschal mystery'.) Matthew, Mark and Luke describe Jesus' final meal with his friends as a *pascha*, while John has Jesus' death take place around the same time the paschal lambs and goats were slain. The roots of the service of holy communion, the eucharist or Lord's supper, are thus found in the Passover.[8] And the response envisaged is like that sought from Israel: that participants be formed as members of God's covenant people, now as 'the body of Christ' celebrating the 'new covenant' in Christ's blood. Our response is to lead out into Christian living: as Paul wrote to the Corinthians:

> Christ our Passover has been sacrificed for us: so let us celebrate the feast, not with the old leaven of corruption and wickedness, but with the unleavened bread of sincerity and truth. (1 Corinthians 5:7)

Thus, though the 'play' performed in a Christian service—whether eucharistic or not—has a gospel-shaped plot, the response looked for is *transformation* more than just *information*. Christian liturgy is more than just an entertainment, whether of highbrow

---

[8] This insight is the key to the 1971 'Agreement on Eucharistic Doctrine' by the *Anglican-Roman Catholic International Commission*, in Christopher Hill and Edward Yarnold sj (edd), *Anglicans and Roman Catholics: The Search for Unity* (London: SPCK/ CTS, 1994), pages 18-29. The text is available at www.prounione.urbe.it/dia-int/arcic/doc/e_arcic_eucharist.html

music, spine-tingling meditation, soul-stirring preaching or heart-warming singing. It is about our being 're-membered' in Christ, as through the Spirit we take our part in celebrating what God has done, and is doing still.

A note on 'members'

'Member' in older English referred to a limb or organ of the body (*corpus* in Latin)—an ear, eye, foot, heart, head etc.—as the King James Bible rendition of 1 Corinthians 12 shows. However, until recent centuries only a 'person' could act at law: a group could only have legal standing if classified as a person, a 'body corporate' or 'corporation'. Individuals who belong to the institution concerned are then its 'members'.

When speaking today of the 'members' of a congregation, it is this latter meaning that often predominates. The result is parishioners who treat church as a 'club' of people with a common religious interest, and clergy who see church as a corporation whose prime business is keeping its branches going so the local managers get paid.

Not so! In Christian use, 'member' refers to the distinctive part that each baptised person plays as organically linked to all the other members of the body of Christ. In this sense, I am not in the first place a member of St Georges' Trentham—I am first and foremost a member of *Christ*, expressing this (in part) through my participation in the life of that congregation.

Worship, and the questions that shape this book

Disagreements over 'worship' among Christians often arise from differences in things like musical tastes, cultural preferences or personality variations. But they may also reflect different beliefs about Jesus Christ, and the significance of his life, teaching and saving work. Divergent ideas about sin, grace, or even the good news itself can emerge. Ultimately, even different understandings of God may be at stake. So when we are on a hobbyhorse about something that happens in church, humility is the order of the day. On the other hand, being unwilling to name concerns about possible theological distortions is a sign of living out of fear rather than of trust in Christ.

Over the past 50 years musical choices have multiplied (aided by the web and data projector), the internal arrangement of buildings has continued to change, colour and sound and dance and symbols have proliferated, healing ministries and small home groups have enriched congregations, all this alongside churches that lack vision and seem content with bored apathy about the familiar. Given this kaleidoscope of practice, questions, issues and tensions inevitably arise. Some are of long standing, others more recent: the examples below are each developed in later chapters, as noted.

Liturgy and lifestyle: performing Christian worship (Chapter 1)

Exploring what worship involves is an obvious place to begin. But how we understand and practice performing the gospel is shaped by our individual personalities, social class, a community's ethos and political assumptions. 'Traditionalists' may see 'revival' services as cheap entertainment, for example, while 'charismatics' might view formal structures as impersonal and imprisoning the Spirit. Yet every Christian feels that their own (sub-) culture offers valid ways of sensing God's presence.

How does my Myers-Briggs or Enneagram score affect the way I relate to liturgy? And what assumptions are brought into church from the surrounding culture? Many congregations assume that 'good Christians vote Labor/Liberal/National Party/Green…'

without thinking about it. How do such political viewpoints affect what happens in worship—and vice versa?

Setting the scene: spaces for gospel performance (Chapter 2)

Human beings seem to need to regard some places as sacred: holy places are found in every culture, including Israel of old. What role do our instincts about place play in relation to church buildings—and can they lead us astray? Where a building is used for Christian worship, what ways of arranging the people and furniture best serve the performance of the gospel? Could this change for different occasions—and can a building dedicated to Christian worship be used for movies, a dance, barbeque or bingo?

Being 'upfront': performing and presiding (Chapter 3)

'Participation' means different things for different cultures and personalities, with corresponding different styles of leading. A *Book of Common Prayer* service may feel 'non-participatory' to people used to 'contemporary' services, for example, because almost all the words are said by the clergy. *BCP* regulars, however, see themselves to be actively participating though reverent listening to biblically saturated words and time-honoured actions. Conversely, a service in which a dozen or more people take leading roles can feel formless to a 'traditional' worshipper, while regular worshippers relate to this as a valid expression of Christian worship in a democratic society. How does the performance of liturgy, in particular how a service is led, relate to the social culture in which it takes place?

The words of gospel performance (Chapter 4)

Words are intrinsic to performance, and to performing the gospel in particular—but not the only element. Our age, in which radio has had to adapt to TV, and TV competes with the internet and computer games, is an increasingly visual and interactive one. What we say, hear and sing is affected by this changing context. How then do words 'work', especially where reality is 'seen' and 'experienced' more than 'heard'? What about potentially divisive words such as 'inclusive language', or war-words?

Performing the gospel 'according to the scriptures' (Chapter 5)

Do the scriptures dictate what happens in church, just offer some options for us to consider, or work in other ways? To what extent should the overall biblical 'story' shape a service? What principles guide the selection of scripture readings? Are biblical words and metaphors the only ones permitted in church? And how does the performance of God's word best take place through preaching?

The sound of music in performing the gospel (Chapter 6)

What part does 'mood music' play in worship? Does it manipulate people or serve God's purposes? How appropriate (or not) are various musical styles—folk, jazz, classical, country, plainsong, pop and rock—for use in a Christian service? How do the emotions stirred by music affect the way the words sung are internalised? What is the place of doctrine in the words of a hymn? How does what the song is felt to communicate change in different social contexts? Are God's people better served by professional musicians, robed choirs, singing groups or informal sing-alongs? How do musicians guard against their performance being seen as merely that, rather than serving the gospel? Should singers be seen upfront—whether robed choirs in a chancel, or a band with miked-up singers—or just heard?

Seeing is believing: liturgy on screen (Chapter 7)

Until television sets were found in most homes, communication culture combined hearing (radio) with reading (newspapers and magazines). Television added seeing as a major element—soon strengthened by the arrival of video players, then DVDs, the internet and interactive computer games. How far should this shift to a visual and highly experiential culture change the way we perform the gospel in liturgy? What does it mean to place temporary banners alongside stained glass windows? Should data projectors replace books—and display mainly words or images?

When we perform the gospel: times and seasons (Chapter 8)

The round of the seasons shapes life in temperate climes. This was the case for the feasts of Israel and our Christian inheritance: Passover in springtime, for example, shaping Easter celebrations in Europe and North America. The rhythms of the month and year have roots in the lunar and solar cycles, cycles that undergird nature-religions. But the seven-day week derives from the sabbath given to Israel rather than nature, and undergirds its distinctive agricultural-economic practice of the sabbath year and Jubilee (cf Leviticus 25). Our Christian time-cycles derive both from nature and the history of salvation. Thus the 'calendar' in the *Book of Common Prayer* is based not only on Christ's life, but also on northern hemisphere seasonal cycles. Australia lies in the southern hemisphere, and its civil year is shaped by public holidays, sporting events and 24-hour shopping: in what ways does this affect how Christians mark and are shaped by, the rhythms of time?

Common prayer? Planning to perform the gospel (Chapter 9)

Should regular Sunday services work towards 'deepening godly ruts' (the ministry of familiar forms) or 'empowering revival' (the spontaneity of newness)? Tradition—the process of 'handing over' something—is both critiqued and valued in the New Testament. It can be a 'torch' for passing on gospel (1 Corinthians 15:1-3) or a 'fossil' that imprisons or distorts God's truth (Mark 7:1-13). How does our performance of the gospel support 'common prayer' today, when common words are few? Common structures are emerging as a way forward, especially those that follow the shape of God's mission. What this can mean is explored using examples from *APBA*—with ideas for 'auditing' the way corporate worship takes place in your congregation in this 21st century context.

Conclusion

Weaving through all these questions is this key examination: What really matters about how we perform the gospel in church and beyond? Archbishop Roger Herft, at a workshop run by the Liturgy Commission of the Anglican Church of Australia, once stated:

> If the philosopher Descartes said, 'I think, therefore I am'; if the modern age says, 'I do, therefore I am'; if the commercial world says, 'I shop, therefore I am'; then the Christian says, 'I worship, therefore I am'.

That is what this book seeks to explore.

Chapter One
Liturgy and lifestyle: performing Christian worship

Overview

Part A   reflects on what 'worship' means, and addresses some confusing ideas about it—the 'theory' behind Part B.

Part B   explores the basic thesis of this book—that worship combines liturgy and lifestyle as interactive performing of the gospel.

Part C   is a little more specialist, outlining the Liturgical Movement. This scholarly movement did much of the 'back room' work that undergirds the changes in Christian liturgy over the past half-century. Many regular worshippers are unaware of its influence on their worship—but it is a story worth knowing, and lays foundations for later chapters.

Part D   poses questions about how worship works out in practice, especially in your local church.

Part A   So what is 'worship'?

To many, 'worship' is whatever people do when in 'religious' mode. It happens for an hour (or three) on Sunday mornings in a church building, where someone upfront, acting like an orchestra conductor, might be referred to as a 'worship leader'. Some speak of a 'worship time' during a service, meaning a period of intense focus upon God, usually involving singing or prayers tinged with emotion, and having a 'worshipful' tone.

Worship without a dimension of communal and personal experience can be barren—but making our experiences central is spiritually dangerous. We then tend to focus on our feelings; and leaders focus on feeling good about their speaking, singing or acting skills, rather than concentrating on performing the gospel. The outcome is spiritual consumerism—'church-hopping' for the best spiritual entertainment.

In reaction, other Christians emphasise that worship should be 'objective', a time when we engage together in time-honoured words and actions that recognise and express the 'worth-ship' of God. Taken to an extreme, however, this can end up in sub-Christian notions of going through ritual motions to gain divine favour.

Ideas like these are not untrue, but they are only part of the story. When they dominate our thinking they can be dangerous, distracting us from true worship—performing the gospel in and out of church.

Worship according to the scriptures

The Jewish and Christian scriptures describe 'worship' in a wide variety of ways, much wider and deeper than just 'religious' or 'cultic' activities (which are typically criticised sharply in the Bible, especially by the prophets and Jesus). Both First and New

Testaments present worship as *involving all we do in response to God's love*. As Paul summarises it in writing to the Roman church:

> Present your bodies as a living sacrifice, holy and acceptable to God, which is your reasonable worship. (Romans 12:1)

The performance of worship includes our bodies, and embraces our whole lifestyle as Christians—how we live out our faith in Christ year on year, both personally and as churches. Yes, worship is to take place on Sundays, but even more so in daily life: consider Isaiah 58 or Romans 12, for example. Andrew McGowan, concluding a scholarly overview of 'worship' in the New Testament, writes:

> 'Worship' henceforth means those practices that constitute Christian communal and ritual life, as reflected in the NT itself and thereafter ... 'Worship' in the sense employed here is about bodies and spaces and objects, as well as words.[1]

So when we meet together as 'church', we perform the core of Christian faith: we celebrate what God is, does and means for us, we feed on Christ through scripture and sacrament, and share the "fellowship of the Holy Spirit". But in doing so, we reflect on and are re-energised for our ongoing lifestyle of Christian worship. In short, **in church we perform the good news of God's saving truth** and so are formed into maturity in Christ (Ephesians 4:11), and become more skilled **to perform the gospel in daily living**.

In the scriptures, the words which the English term 'worship' usually translates are *abodah* (Hebrew), *latreia* and *diakonia* (Greek). Each carries the idea of authorised service or ministry on behalf of

---

[1] Andrew McGowan, *Ancient Christian Worship. Early Church Practices in Social, Historical and Theological Context* (Grand Rapids: Baker, 2014) 7-8.

others: in ordinary life they describe the skilled, thoughtful work that a person undertakes for others. So an ambassador 'serves' his or her nation by obediently representing it to others; a waiter 'serves' food and drink to guests on behalf of the host. This traditional meaning can be seen in the 1662 *Book of Common Prayer* wedding service, where the man says to the woman, as part of his marriage promise, "with my body I thee worship". The groom is not promising to 'worship' her as if she were God, but to 'serve' her in practical ways. In Israel of old, a priest 'served' God through offering tangible prayers and praises (i.e. sacrifices) on behalf of the whole people: Romans 9.4; 12.1; Philippians 3.3; Hebrews 9.1–6; I Peter 2.9–11 are typical ways in which New Testament writers took up these ideas.

In years gone by, signs outside a church building would often read 'Divine Service' followed by a time. This points up a nice double meaning. The phrase 'the worship of God' can be understood in two ways—the worship we offer God, and the ways in which God serves us. (In technical terms, these are the 'subjective' and 'objective' genitive ways of reading the phrase—the German *Gottesdienst* embraces both ideas.) Both senses are important: according to the scriptures, worship is grounded in God's 'divine service' to us, inspiring our response of 'service' to God (with all that entails for the whole of life).

And this is no half-hearted matter. In the scriptures, an *act* of worship is usually described as *hishtahawah* (Hebrew) or *proskuneo* (Greek). These carry a strongly physical sense—to lie flat on one's face before someone, to 'prostrate' oneself (see Exodus 3.6, Revelation 5:14 or Luke 4:8 for example). On God's part, 'divine service' entailed Christ's taking on our human form and laying down his life, even to death (see Philippians 2:5–11). On our part, such 'service' calls for a whole-hearted, Spirit-inspired response of reverent awe in God's presence, glad obedience to God's will, and treasured delight in God's word.

True, false and imperfect worship

True worship embraces the whole of our response to God's love—our attitudes, words, thoughts, behaviour, motives. In reality, our responses is never wholly true, since we are creatures and not the Creator, and live in a world distorted by sin and evil, and limited by death. As Christians, we offer worship in faith that God, who knows us inside out, sees us in Christ, and gladly accepts the true worship he offers on our behalf.

This does not excuse us from facing the inadequacies of our worship. In doing so, however, it is important to distinguish between *false* worship—serving ourselves rather than God, which is idolatry (see Exodus 20:3)—and *imperfect* worship, not serving God truly (consider 1 Corinthians 11:27-32).

We all worship imperfectly, but confusing this with false worship, especially when speaking of other Christians, leads to 'holier than thou' pride, and fosters division. And both categories apply to the whole of life, not just how we perform the gospel (or not) in church—consider 2 Corinthians 8 and Ephesians 5.5 for example.

To live falsely is to run the risk of denying the gospel; to live imperfectly is part of our human condition as finite mortals. Even so, we each live "by faith in the Son of God who loved me, and gave himself for me" (as Paul wrote in Galatians 2:20).

Part B Worship = liturgy + lifestyle

The proper term for describing what happens when we assemble as Christian people for worship is 'liturgy'. Some see this term as representing stuffy, controlled, boring and inflexible rites. But having this specific word 'liturgy' allows 'worship' to keep its wider biblical sense. The Greek word which 'liturgy' transliterates is *leitourgia*, the 'work [*ergon*] of the people [*laos*]'—or as we might render it, 'public service'.[2] Liturgy is of fundamental importance in worship, but does not exist for its own sake. Rather, its rhythms, rituals and familiar words lay 'godly ruts' in heart, mind, body and soul for our daily worship, following Christ as his disciples.

In short, 'worship' = 'liturgy' + 'lifestyle'. The gospel we perform in church shapes, celebrates and corrects the gospel we perform '24/7'. Frederic Buechner puts this in an interesting way:

> Phrases like Worship Service or Service of Worship are basically tautologies. To worship God means to serve him. Basically there are two ways to do this.
>
> One way is to do things for him that *God* needs to have done—run errands for him, carry messages for him, fight on his side, feed his lambs, and so on.
>
> The other way is to do things for him that *you* need to do—sing songs for him, create beautiful things for him, give things up for him, tell him what's on your mind and in your heart, in general

---

2   The range of the term can be seen in its New Testament usage: Luke 1:23 of Zechariah's service as a Jewish priest; Romans 13:6 of Roman government officials' work; Romans 15:27 and 2 Corinthians 9:12 of the collection for Jerusalem; Philippians 2:17 of Paul's self-offering, and 2:30 of Epaphroditus' caring for Paul; Titus 1:9 of offering service to God; Hebrews 1:14 of the ministry of angels, and Hebrews 9:21 of vessels used in Jewish worship.

rejoice and make a fool of yourself for him the ways lovers have always made fools of themselves for the one they love.³

So far 'worship' has been discussed from a 'Gods-eye' perspective, a *theo*-logical approach—performing the gospel of God. It is hard to think of a better Christian place to begin! But left to itself, this approach may not leave our human experience untouched—after all, worship involves our lifestyles. More 'descriptive' definitions of worship are thus both legitimate and necessary, expressing it in terms of what we humans so or experience.

Consider this suggestion, based on the lexical work of Nouw and Lida: "Worship is attitudes and actions expressing obedience and allegiance to what is worshipped."⁴ When people say things like "Chris worships the ground Lesley walks on," it is this wider understanding which is in view. Its particular strength is the assumption that all human beings engage in 'worship' of some kind—the question is whether or not the ground and object of our allegiance, and 'ultimate service', is the living God. Good things like sport, the arts, business, the nation, our family etc. easily become the central focus in our living, and thus become idols.

Some scholars seek to blend a more explicitly theological perspective with human experience in defining worship. So Evelyn Underhill describes it as "the response of the creature to the Eternal",⁵ while the Second Vatican Council in 1965 famously taught that worship involves "the sanctification of men in Christ,

---

3   Cited in William Willimon, *The Service of God: How Worship and Ethics are Related* (Nashville: Abingdon, 1983) 7.
4   Eugene A Nida and Johannes P. Louw, *Greek-English Lexicon of the New Testament based on Semantic Domains* (New York: UBS, 1996)
5   Evelyn Underhill, *Worship* (Scranton: Harper & Row, 1936) 3.

and the glorification of God".⁶ James White seeks to move beyond just words alone: Christian worship, he writes, is "speaking and touching in God's name"—a concept close to that of worship as performing the gospel.⁷

One useful aspect of a descriptive approach is that the tensions and balances encountered in reflecting on worship become more evident:

- True worship holds together both our *internal attitudes* and *external behaviour*. As Jesus told the Samaritan woman (John 4:23-24), we are called to worship God in spirit (i.e. in our Spirit-given attitudes) and in truth (i.e. in our actions). Again, in Christ's teaching on prayer he insisted that inward and outward performance cannot be separated (so Matthew 6:7-15).
- There is an inter-dependent relationship between *formal structures* and *informal or spontaneous elements* in liturgy. Without structures we easily end up doing what merely 'feels good'; without openness to adapt, worship can become rigid and mechanical. Paul's advice to the Corinthians is salutary: do (i.e. perform) all things decently and in order, but do not quench the Spirit (cf 1 Corinthians 14).
- Recognizing the inter-play between the *personal* and *communal/corporate* dimensions of liturgy is of vital importance. Even in a congregation of closely-related people from the same village there will be varied personalities and life experiences. So much the more is it the case where worshippers come from different social classes or ethnic

---

6   Second Vatican Council, *Constitution on the Sacred Liturgy* #10, available at www.vatican.va/archive/hist_councils/ii_vatican_council/documents/vat-ii_const_19631204_sacrosanctum-concilium_en.html

7   James F. White, *Introduction to Christian Worship* (Nashville: Abingdon, 1981) 22.

backgrounds in a city church. God calls people from "every tribe and race and language and nation", but helping this 'rainbow nation' perform the gospel together is no easy task!

A note on 'church' and 'worship' in the Anglican Diocese of Sydney

The teaching and practice of Moore College regarding church life, and worship in particular, holds considerable sway in the Anglican Diocese of Sydney.[8] Its Principal from 1959 to 1985, Dr Broughton Knox, steadily moved Moore from the conservative evangelical position of principals such as (later Archbishop) Marcus Loane, towards a 'Reformed' one. Knox argued that God's revelation is fundamentally propositional, i.e. is communicated through sentences whose meaning is not dependent on their context. Alongside this view, Donald Robinson (later to become Archbishop of Sydney), when he was Moore's Vice-Principal contended that, according to the New Testament, 'church' terminology is metaphorical, and centres around the meaning of *ekklesia* as 'assembly'. Properly speaking, he argued, the 'church of God' exists only in 'the heavenlies' (cf Hebrews 12:22–23), and is made visible only when believers 'assemble' for 'meeting'—a possible but unusual reading of Article XIX. Speaking of 'church' as wider than at local level, he contended, is thus questionable.

The combination of understanding 'church' in this way, alongside Knox's emphasis on propositional revelation—a combination Robinson rejected as archbishop—resulted in 'liturgy' being seen by their disciples as 'meetings' for 'Bible

---

8   A summary of the 'Knox/Robinson' position by the current Principal of Moore College, Mark Thompson, can be found at http://matthiasmedia.com/briefing/2011/12/knoxrobinson-for-today-extended/.

teaching' and 'fellowship'. In practice, these have a strongly 'horizontal' feel: 'cultic' expressions of worship in which the 'vertical' dominates are downplayed, whether 'revivalist', 'charismatic' or 'anglo-catholic'. Ordained ministry then focuses on authoritative instruction in the content of the scriptures ('Bible teaching'), a ministry from which women are excluded, while pastoral visiting and community presence receive low priority. Traditional Evangelical delight in reverent and devotional use of the gospel sacraments, while being suspicious of 'churchy' sacramentalism, gave way to radical questioning of the symbolic, in favour of verbal ministry. The outcome is teaching-focused 'meetings'—not 'services'—which generally lack liturgical shape or contents, ignore official lectionaries, make little if any reference to the Christian year, and whose ethos is felt by others to be dry, didactic and disorganised.

The strength of this view of 'church' is its dynamic quality: "to go to church" is read as a verb, "churching": 'church' is something to be *performed*. The emphasis on parishioners coming to know the scriptures and follow their teaching is most welcome. Further, it highlights the local congregation as where Christ meets with believers, offering a critique of wider structures overriding the local. The weaknesses, however, are significant: the outcome of services being viewed only as 'meetings' can be little sense of reverence, clergy controlling the interpretation of the scriptures, and diminished focus on corporate formation and engagement with wider society.

This 'meetings' view became a matter of concern for Archbishop Donald Robinson, and for his successor, Archbishop Harry Goodhew. The liturgy gap in many Sydney congregations saw the next Archbishop of Sydney, Peter Jensen, authorise *Sunday Services* in 2001, and *Common Prayer: Resources for gospel-shaped gatherings* (Anglican Press Australia, 2013).[9]

Worship and the Lord Jesus Christ

What difference, then, does confessing Jesus Christ as Lord—the earliest Christian 'creed' (1 Corinthians 15:1-3)—make to our understanding of Christian worship?

To start with, it is quite amazing that Jesus' first followers, faithful Jews, strict monotheists and strong opponents of idolatry of any sort, came to 'worship' him. Matthew's gospel is framed with this idea: the wise men from the East do so at his birth (Matthew 2.11), and the disciples do so at the end of Jesus' earthly life (Matthew 28.17). Early Christian communities began instinctively to express the 'worship of God' in and through the 'worship of Jesus Christ': Paul's ambiguous punctuation in Romans 9.5 shows how instinctive this sense was.

Further, just as the phrase 'the worship of God' carries 'objective' and 'subjective' meanings, so does 'the worship of Christ'. Jesus lived in the closest relationship with God, whom he boldly addresses and names as 'father', offering the fullest service to God which humans are called to perform. Christ's "obedience, even to death on a cross", as an early Christian hymn puts it (Philippians 2.8) saw him take on the consequences of our disobedience, thus making peace through the blood of the cross (Colossians 1:20). God raised him from death, opening the possibility of offering true worship to all believers, both in the new creation and here and now, through the

---

[9] Both books draw on David Peterson, *Engaging with God: A Biblical Theology of Worship* (IVP, 1992). David was a Consultant to the Liturgy Commission that drafted *APBA*. *The Briefing* is an influential Sydney website: the need for liturgical education is seen in the series of thoughtful articles in by editor, Tony Payne: http:// matthiasmedia.com/briefing/2009/10/so-what-does-the-gathering-look-like-part-1/ (and subsequent pieces).

Holy Spirit. So 'the worship of Christ' in the first place points up the 'service' which Jesus Christ rendered to us, showing us how God means us to live, and giving his life "as a ransom for many" (Mark 10.45, alluding to Isaiah 53). This calls from us an instinctive, Spirit-generated response, to live as disciples—that is, worshippers—of the Lord Jesus Christ.

Christian worship maps the whole Christian story: it derives from the perfect service of Christ to God on our behalf (from creation to new creation); is based on our being brothers and sisters 'in Christ', children of the same Father; and involves us in being members of the body of Christ, through the Holy Spirit. Christian worship is thus a *trinitarian* reality. It is lived out in obedience to the Father's will (John 6:37-40), is grounded in Christ's worship on our behalf (so Hebrews 13:10-16), and enabled by the Spirit's work in us (see Romans 8:1-26).

Understanding Christian worship like this has several profound consequences:

- Prayers of intercession and thanksgiving become instinctive activities "in the Spirit, through the Son, to the Father", rather than human religious efforts (false performance) to try and influence a distant deity (or deities) to take notice.
- Our worship lifestyle takes a 'trinitarian' shape—as seen in our personal character, care of others, social attitudes, graced behaviour, ecological action and the like. As children of our heavenly Father, in the power of the Spirit we obey and follow the Son, rather than trying to please life-denying Santa Clauses who insist that children "better watch out".
- We are Christ's through our being baptised into the threefold Name of God, not because of any human performance or experience. Our life in Christ is lived out in the 'communion' (*koinonia*) of the trinitarian life of the Father, Son and Spirit God—the *koinonia* of the body of Christ.

Part C   The Liturgical Movement: its story

The above issues are not just Australian or Anglican ones. Scholars in a cross-section of western churches have been exploring them in depth for many years, especially since World War II. Their work has come to be known as the 'Liturgical Movement', a ferment of activity exploring worship patterns across western churches. Unlike the two other major post-1945 Christian movements—ecumenical and charismatic—many Christians are unaware of the Liturgical Movement, though it has probably affected what they do on Sundays as much if not more than these two. Its greatest effect has been felt in the Roman Catholic Church, especially the change from using Latin to 'vernacular' languages in church, so the story begins there.

The Roman Catholic Liturgical Movement

This Movement's beginnings go back to 19th century Europe, where some Roman Catholic monastic communities began serious academic work on the history of liturgy, especially previously unexplored developments prior to the Reformation. By 1900, as debate raged about 'modernism' in the Roman Catholic Church, over 'fundamentalism' in US Protestantism, and around 'ritualism' in the Church of England, the work of these monks began to bear fruit. In 1903, Pope Pius IX encouraged "the active participation of the faithful" in Roman Catholic liturgy, and a 1909 conference in Belgium encouraged a more 'pastoral' approach to the way services were conducted. World War I wrought havoc in academic circles, but ground-breaking study continued at Maria Laach in Germany until 1939. When World War II broke out, its work was taken up at Collegeville, Minnesota, and continues there today.

The most practical outcome of these early stages of the movement was the issuing by Pope Pius XII in 1947 of the Encyclical, *Mediator*

Dei et Hominum—'The mediator between God and human beings'. Liturgy is central to church life, he wrote, rather than being just a clergy concern. He therefore introduced reforms designed to enable all the faithful to take part more fully in worship. The changes may seem minor by current standards—allowing Sunday services to start on Saturday evenings, relaxing rules about Friday fasting and so on—but signalled that change was possible, and under way.

The Second Vatican Council, of all bishops in communion with Rome, was (unexpectedly) called by Pope John XXIII, and its sessions took place from 1962-65.[10] Of many notable fruits, the one felt most strongly at the local level was *Sacrosanctum Concilium*—the 'Constitution on the Sacred Liturgy'.[11] Services were to be translated from Latin into local languages, and the scriptures made available to all. In Australia, the use of English removed the 'mystique' around Roman Catholic services, and—together with the renewed attention given to scripture—made possible some common sharing in worship across the Protestant-Catholic divide.

Another important change was encouraging worshippers to receive the bread (and optionally the wine) at each eucharist. For centuries, most Roman Catholics watched the priest's actions rather than receiving communion, perhaps engaging in personal devotions such as the Rosary alongside his prayers. More diverse musical styles and instruments were accepted, and many changes were made in pastoral services: so penance becomes 'the rite of reconciliation', while 'extreme unction' was widened to include

---

10 The First Vatican Council took place in 1871, but could not complete its work due to war breaking out. Vatican II can thus be seen as continuing the work of Vatican I, while transcending it to 'update' the Church to fulfil God's mission in the very different environments of 20th century societies.

11 Second Vatican Council, *Constitution on the Sacred Liturgy*, available at www.vatican.va/archive/hist_councils/ii_vatican_council/documents/vat-ii_const_19631204_sacrosanctum-concilium_en.html

healing ministry as well as the last rites. Church buildings were simplified: many statues were removed, seating arranged so all could see and hear, and the altar moved forward into a central space, with the priest facing the people across the table (the so-called 'westward' position).

The effect overall of these changes was dramatic. Large numbers of Roman Catholics came to delight in the scriptures, and a deeper sense of partnership between clergy, religious and lay people emerged. The effects soon spread to other churches, or gave permission for similar changes—"if the Romans can do it, so can we!" was a common attitude.

Vatican II also changed Roman Catholic official attitudes to other Christians: *Unitatis Redintegratio*, the Decree on Ecumenism, set out new goals for ecumenical relationships, leading to the opening up of theological dialogues. The *Anglican-Roman Catholic International Commission* (ARCIC) reached agreement in 1971 on the eucharist, for example, which influenced changes made in Anglican services. By the middle 1970s it could be difficult for other than scholars to spot the differences between typical Roman Catholic, Anglican, Lutheran and Uniting Church services. And over the same period, the charismatic movement spread across all these traditions and more.

The changes taking place in the Roman Catholic Church both paralleled and stimulated changes in the Protestant world, especially in North America. Bible translations multiplied: by 2000 over 25 versions were available in English, with the *New Revised Standard* and *Contemporary English Versions* prominent across the theological spectrum (the former being accepted by Rome). Among evangelical Protestants, the *New International Version* began to wean them off the 1611 *King James Bible*. Amongst Anglicans, Vatican II was a major factor in allowing many of the 'churchmanship' fights of mid-century to be left behind: from the

1960s, work proceeded apace across the Communion on revising the *Book of Common Prayer*.

Dom Gregory Dix, and the Church of South India

As in the Roman Catholic world, Anglican changes were preceded by scholarly work. The publication in 1945 of *The Shape of the Liturgy* by Dom Gregory Dix was very significant (it remains a readable and stimulating book). An Anglican monk, Dix was in contact with Roman Catholic scholars in Europe until the War prevented this, but he pressed on with his research, bringing an independent mind to analysing all the available evidence of early Christian practice. His conclusion was that—unlike much 20th century practice—Christian liturgy is something to be *done*, not just *said* (the 'protestant' emphasis) or *seen* (the 'catholic' tendency). After all, Jesus told the disciples, "*do* this for the remembrance of me". So, alongside the words used, Dix concluded, what *happens* in a service, and especially its *shape*, should match the pattern of God's saving work, if we are to be true to our origins.

Further, Dix argued that unhelpful confusion has resulted from the holy communion being viewed as imitating the **Last** Supper (which looked *forward* to the cross), rather than as a celebration of the **Lord's** Supper (which looks *backward* to the cross, and forward to the Lamb's wedding feast). The Last Supper, Dix pointed out, had a seven-fold shape: Christ took bread, gave thanks, broke the bread, and shared it; then 'after supper' he took the cup, gave thanks, and shared it. In the Lord's Supper, it is not the meal which matters, but its *meaning*: so the meal quickly became optional, and the seven actions folded into four: take (bread and wine), give thanks (for all God's work), break the bread, share the bread and wine—the so-called 'four-fold shape' of the Lord's Supper in the eucharist: the technical terms are offertory, canon, fraction, administration.

Dix's work found ready acceptance among scholars—but changing centuries-old rites was no easy task, and polemical memories were still alive. A way forward came from an unexpected source. In 1948, with India gaining its independence from Britain, the Church of South India (CSI) formed, embracing Anglicans, Presbyterians, Methodists and others. In this, all *future* clergy would be ordained by a bishop, but *existing* clergy would be accepted without re-ordination. In that same year the Lambeth Conference held its ten-yearly meeting: but a request to recognise this new regional church as part of the Anglican Communion was defeated. Though this decision caused pain, it allowed CSI to reconsider the *Book of Common Prayer* without the constrictions of belonging to the Anglican Communion. CSI church leaders decided to take on board many of Dix's ideas, and recover some ancient customs associated with early Christian worship in India.

So in 1950 the 'Church of South India Liturgy' was authorised (initially in English). This bore several distinctive features:

- A clear overall *structure* to the service was adopted: Preparation (possibly as a separate service), Word, Supper, Dismissal.
- Some non-BCP prayers from ancient sources were included: the invitation to communion comes from the NT era text, the *Didache*, for example.
- The peace (with an Indian handclasp) was revived.
- Dix's *'four fold shape'* theory forms the basis of the Lord's Supper.

CSI 1950 was the forerunner of changes that would sweep across the Anglican and Methodist traditions, and beyond.

The Liturgical Movement in the Anglican Communion

In 1955, the Church of England set up its first Liturgical Commission, followed by US Anglicans in 1960 and Australia in 1962: prayer-book revision was going global. Australian Anglicans were in the forefront of prayer book revision. In 1962, the national Church became independent from the Church of England, and became governed by the Australian General Synod. One of the Synod's first acts was to set up a Commission "to explore whether revision of BCP is needed". In 1966, this Commission's report came out as a small book—*Prayer Book Revision in Australia*. It not only answered the question with a firm 'yes', noting the need for both revision of existing services, and more flexible ones—and went on to included services of both types! Though strictly speaking this went beyond its terms of reference, its work was widely welcomed. Its 'A Modern Liturgy' sought to update BCP by using today's English, and integrating Morning Prayer, Litany and Holy Communion into a single rite (the shape set out by Thomas Cranmer). Significantly, the new service adopted Dix's 'four-fold shape' for the shape of the Lord's Supper. The outcome was a long service, but it set the agenda for the experiments that were to follow.[12]

It was in this context of internal Anglican discussion that Vatican II burst upon the world: the outcome was far-reaching changes now taken for granted across the western Christian world. On the words front, in 1968 an ecumenical group (now the *English Language Liturgical Consultation*, ELLC) formed to produce modern-language versions of common texts such as the Lord's

---

12   Responses came from congregations, colleges and scholars across the land, and, despite problems of communication, interest grew in what was happening among Anglicans overseas. Revised services were issued in 1969 and 1973. These led to 'Second Order Holy Communion' in *An Australian Anglican Prayer Book* (1977), lightly revised in *APBA* (1995), it has become the most commonly-used service among Australian Anglicans. Its structure is similar to those of the Roman Catholic, Uniting, Lutheran and other traditions' rites, employs a system of scripture reading shared across them, and is often accompanied by hymns from *Together in Song*, Australia's ecumenical hymnbook.

Prayer, Creeds and canticles. A year later, Rome issued the 'Three-year Lectionary', which was quickly taken up in other churches: Australian Anglicans did so in *AAPB* (1978).

Work also began on updating the Christian calendar, not least by Anglicans in the USA, whose civil calendar is not shaped by the church year. The outcome was greater emphasis on the distinctive place of Sunday, and two clear 'cycles' for the Christian year: Advent–Christmas–Epiphany, and Lent–Holy Week–Easter–Pentecost.

Conclusion

Church and society in the West have steadily pulled apart from the 1960s, not least in Australia. This shift in relationship affects many aspects of Christian worship, in both liturgy and life. It can be seen particularly in the way the beginning of Christian life is marked—baptism, confirmation and admission to communion. Though infants continued to make up the largest number of candidates, the 'norm' for baptism services has become the baptism of an adult. The *Roman Catholic Initiation of Adults* (RCIA) programme was based on the 'catechumenate' pattern of faith education found in the first few centuries of the Church, and soon followed in other Christian traditions.

Further, baptism has come to be seen as the foundation of Christian life and ministry, so that ordination is understood as 'within' rather than 'alongside' baptism. This gave space for people other than clergy to take leading roles in liturgy, feeding off the 'every-member ministry' movement of the 1970s. (Until then anyone other than 'the minister' doing almost everything in church was unthinkable, even in the most 'protestant' of congregations.) But it can also lead to thinking that 'lay ministry' is about what a few leaders do in liturgy, rather than focused on the lifestyle of all the baptised.

And the social context in which Australian lifestyles are lived has changed considerably, and quickly. The Pill became available from 1960, colour television arrived in 1977, the internet in 1991, the smart phone in 2000, the NBN started in 2012: these have brought shifts in gender roles, and increased use of colour, movement and symbols in liturgy. In daily life, however, these changes have seen Christian faith largely relegated to the margins, treated as a hobby or 'religious lifestyle preference'. These rapid social changes have put Christian worship—both as liturgy and lifestyle—into new and largely unfamiliar contexts.

Yet how we pray, especially when we gather for liturgical worship, continues to reflect and shape our worship as Christian lifestyle—in short, performing the gospel.

Part D   Reflecting on worship in your setting

Part A sketched a 'theology' of Christian worship, based around the concept of it 'performing the gospel' in both liturgy and life (Part B). Part C sought to explain how the 'shape' of modern liturgy developed since World War II, especially across the English-speaking world, particularly in the Anglican Communion.

But how do these ideas come together in the life of a local congregation? This Part offers questions designed to help you, and your congregation, reflect on the way it worships. There are some overlaps, and you are welcome to consider them in an order more relevant to your setting.

1. Think about the various things that go into putting in a play.
    Keeping these elements in mind, reflect on the most recent regular service of Christian worship in your local congregation.

In what ways did it 'perform the gospel'?
What aspects of the gospel were highlighted?
Did anything distract from the gospel?
(This is sometimes called a 'worship audit', a check-up on how a congregation 'does' its regular services, in order to affirm strengths, name weaknesses and improve.
Note: such an audit is best done by having someone from 'outside' to facilitate it.)

2. In this chapter it is argued that Christian worship is 'the service of God in Christ'. It can be understood in two ways (what scholars call the 'objective' and 'subjective' genitive). On the one hand, it can be read as God serving us in Christ—worship has its origins in what God does for us. On the other hand, it can be read as our response, in Christ, of service to God (which includes more than just on Sundays). Both are true. Worship begins with God, and leads into a life-wide response: 'Christian worship = liturgy + lifestyle'—a way of keeping 'Sunday', 'the weekend' and 'weekday living' together.
In what ways do you see this as helpful, or otherwise?
What dangers, if any, do you sense in such an approach?
How do you think it might work, or not, in practice?

3. 'Worship' is often seen as derived from 'worth-ship', affirming God's 'worth'.
In what ways do you find this helpful, or not?
How might it relate to, or detract from, seeing liturgy as 'performing the gospel'?
Seeing Christian lifestyles as 'performing the gospel'?

4. Consider the main social influences on the lives of you personally, and on that of your parish or

congregation—TV, the local pub or coffee-shop, social media like Facebook or Twitter, talk-back radio, and so on.

In what ways do they support/question/illuminate/contradict the performance of the Gospel, both in church and in the wider community?

5. Think about the typical Sunday service in which you take part.

    In what way/s, if any, do you see the influence of the Liturgical Movement?

    How is it affected by shifts in western culture, especially technology (e.g. a hearing loop, data projection)?

    How have changes in your local area been reflected, or not, in changes in church (e.g. a factory closing, new shopping centre, flood or bushfire, immigration)?

    How significant do you believe these changes are in illuminating or detracting from your congregation performing the gospel?

6. How does the way the gospel is performed in your congregation's regular services shape, or even distort, the lifestyles of worshippers and their communities?

    Conversely, what lifestyle issues impinge on Sunday services in your church?

    Some possible areas might be relationships, finances, caring for others, local politics, shopping, mutual support, justice issues, reconciliation, and advertising. In short, what might come out of a 'worship audit' of the ways liturgy and lifestyle interact in your setting?

Chapter Two
Setting the scene: spaces for gospel performance

Overview

Part A reflects on the ways that place and space are considered in the scriptures—sometimes blessing, sometimes curse.

Part B offers a quick skip through the history of church buildings and their design. You may be stuck with a building that seems to offer no possibilities for change or variation, but this Part hopefully offers some ideas—it can, in any case, help put your building in its historical and social context.

Part C is where we get down to the nitty-gritty of what is involved in setting the scene for performing the gospel 'in church': the various 'spaces' which shape the performance of the gospel in liturgy. If that is what matters for you, start there.

Part D is a 'church building audit' exercise. Please do it.

Every performance happens in a particular place, and this influences its outcome. An outside concert has different issues with sound and comfort from one held inside, for example. A church service in a familiar building will affect worshippers differently from one in a space newly experienced. And the locations in which we live our lives affect our lifestyle.

There is something special about memorable places. I have vivid memories of being at the Sydney Cricket Ground for the famous Wests–St George Rugby League Grand Final in the mud, ending with the embrace between Arthur Summons and Norm Provan that now adorns the NRL cup. On a very different level, I sometimes join in 'sacred harp' singing in an old weather-beaten church hall, a place that suits its strong earthy rhythms down to the ground. There is a place, a space, that seems 'right' for many performances.

And so it is with the people of God. A place where a martyr has surrendered their life for the gospel attracts people for prayer. Jerusalem and the Holy Land have held a fascination over the centuries: the Church of the Holy Sepulchre, with all its oddity and crazy mixture of traditions, 'does' something for me and for countless others. Special places for me include Cranmer's study at Lambeth Palace, Richard Baxter's statue at Kidderminster, the (now empty) Sydney site where Richard Johnston first led public worship in the new colony, the (now demolished) chapel at Ridley College where I taught for many years, the small church of St George's Trentham (with its dragon sign out the front).

The spiritual life of a congregation is shaped—for good and ill—through the building in which they meet regularly. Historic church buildings stand from generation to generation as eloquent witnesses to the presence of God in a community. A new building presents both interesting opportunities and significant challenges, since it will need to serve more than the current generation—and once it is in place, changes are not easily made.

The familiarity of a place where we sense what is going on around us without effort, absorbing the atmosphere unconsciously, has a major effect on worship. Most of us have a favourite spot in church—near a window given in memory of a friend, for example, or near the band, or just out of habit. The comfort and stimulation that familiar places evoke can also be dangerous. What happens when you find someone else sitting in 'your' pew or seat? Does it inhibit your praying, or are you glad that someone else can share your instinctive reactions to this familiar spot? Is the furniture so fixed that it images static formalism rather than dependable dynamism? Do things look so neat that it seems unlived in, or so scrappy that it seems we do not care about God?

Space, place and worship are inextricably related in the performance of the gospel. That is what this chapter is about.[1]

---

[1] A significant aspect of the Second Vatican Council's reforms to Roman Catholic liturgical practice was change to the arrangement of church buildings: see the *Constitution on the Sacred Liturgy*, especially Chapters I and VII. Much of what is said in this Chapter has its roots in the Council's work, which encouraged and 'gave permission' for other churches, including Anglicans ones, to respond creatively to changing relationships between church and society, not least in Australia.

Part A Sacred spaces in scripture: blessing and danger

According to the scriptures, God is always on the move, calling us to follow. The Tabernacle—a large, mobile 'tent of meeting'—was where Moses and the people of Israel met with God in their formative years (see Exodus 35). In it was kept the 'Ark of the Covenant', the powerful symbol of God's dynamic presence: the people learnt to their peril not to presume that when the Ark moved, so did the Lord (see 1 Samuel 4:1-11). David took this Ark—very carefully (2 Samuel 6:1-15)—into Jerusalem but was not permitted to build it a permanent home. As God spoke through the prophet Nathan:

> I have not lived in a house since the day I brought up the people of Israel from Egypt to this day, but I have been moving about in a tent and a tabernacle. (2 Samuel 7:6)

David's son Solomon built the magnificent Temple by his own decision (1 Kings 5:3-5; 6:1-14)—and after he had finished his own house (1 Kings 3:1-2). Despite its questionable origins, the Temple was where for generations Israel encountered God's presence (see Psalm 27:4; Psalm 48; Isaiah 6). It was accepted as "the place that the LORD your God will choose as a dwelling for his Name" (Deuteronomy 12:5-6, 11; 14:23-24). But when the people came to depend on the Temple rather than God, it was God who departed from it (Ezekiel 10:18-19; 11:22-24) and brought it down (Jeremiah 7:1-14).

Yet destruction is never God's final word. The desecrated Temple was rebuilt at the Lord's command, to serve the people who had returned from exile (Ezra 5:1-2; Haggai 1). Rebuilt again by King Herod, this third Temple formed the cradle of the earliest Christian community (Acts 3:1; 5:20, 42). It was around this time, too, that local meeting houses ('synagogues' in Greek) emerged in towns across the Roman Empire as places for Jewish learning, administration and communal worship. They took on some of the traditional roles of the household, as important places of gathering for prayer and teaching, focused around the Law and the Prophets, and special meals, most notably the Passover (see Exodus 12:1-5; Deuteronomy 6:7; Luke 22:7ff).

Jesus went to Herod's Temple often (e.g. see John 7.14) and likewise attended the synagogue, "as was his custom" (Luke 4.16): Luke places the commencement of his public life there. Jesus also foretold the final destruction of this Temple (Matthew 24:1-2): in raising up the body of Christ, God would establish a lasting Temple on earth, in which the Holy Spirit would dwell (John 2:19-21; 1 Corinthians 3:16-17; 6:19). The earliest Christian communities in Jerusalem consisted both of local Jews, and those who had come there for Israel's festivals (Acts 2:8-12). Many of these visitors remained there, living in 'communes' in which all shared their goods (Acts 2:44-46; 4:32-34), like the Essene communities in the city. Acts records that "They devoted themselves to the apostles' teaching and fellowship, to the breaking of bread and the prayers" (Acts 2.42)—a paradigm for what it means to perform the gospel as church.

Jesus' followers in Jerusalem continued to meet in the Temple until it was destroyed in AD70. But like Jeremiah and Ezekiel before him, the first Christian martyr, Stephen, proclaimed the danger of relying on particular places, rather than the God who made them. He emphasised that God's most important revelations to Israel took place *outside* the land—and paid for his witness with his life (Acts 7). Saul would take in this reading of Israel's story, however (see Acts 8.1), and, as Paul, use the network of synagogues around the Mediterranean as the entry-point to spread the gospel "as was his custom" (Acts 17:1—see 13:5,14; 14:1; 18:4,19 for example).

But whether due to opposition in these synagogues, or from opportunities arising through them, the movement soon spread to the households of well-to-do Greek and Roman citizens (Acts 16:40; 18:7; 19:9; 20:8).

Note: The early 'house-churches' (see Romans 16:5) were not 'nuclear-family' sized dwellings, but more like an Australian homestead, able to house several generations of the family, together with their servants and slaves.

In sum, according to the scriptures, the people of God have been blessed in being given particular places where they can encounter God, and celebrate God's mighty acts. But whenever such places were abused, or became more significant than the One they represented, they were desecrated and destroyed. The living Lord delights to be present with us mere mortals, as is shown decisively in the incarnation, and experienced through the coming of the Holy Spirit. But God is always on the move, drawing creatures towards the goal of new creation: to stand in God's way is perilous.

Part B   Worship spaces over time: a catena[2]

Beginnings

As Christian congregations grew, larger meeting-places were needed. Prior to around 325AD, when Constantine gave legal recognition to Christianity, however, belonging to a Christian community brought you under suspicion, shut you out of many occupations, and opened you to the charge of treason. Every time a church met, its members ran

---

2   A series of sketches showing many of the developments outlined here can be found in Peter G. Cobb, "The Setting of the Liturgy", in Cheslyn Jones, Geoffrey Wainwright and Edmund Yarnold sj (edd), *The Study of Liturgy* (London: SPCK, 1977) pages 481–487.

the risk of being exposed and brought before a magistrate. It was also Roman policy, to limit the possibilities of anti-imperial organising, only to permit associations for providing burial places. Given Christian belief in the resurrection, catacombs were used as meeting places, which others would shun, and they could be communally owned. Where it was feasible to do so, some congregations met in the open air, "assembling before daybreak on a fixed day and reciting by turns a form of words to Christ as a god".[3] As time passed, some Christian communities were able to adapt private dwellings to serve the church.

Whatever the meeting-place, church life was kept under wraps. People were checked as they entered, and the doors were shut once a service started: as Dix dryly put it, "people who are jointly risking at least penal servitude for life generally make certain that they know their associates".[4] The modern idea of holding services in public to which anyone might come was inconceivable. Further, explicit decoration in a meeting-place was unthinkable, so those that do remain are ambiguous. For example, a wall painting, which to a Christian spoke of Christ the good shepherd, looked like Orpheus to others. Stone coffins (sarcophagi), in which the bodies of higher-class Christians were placed to rot down, were often decorated with the story of Jonah, integrated with other biblical scenes, made to look like a Greek hero overcoming monsters of the deep.

In time, houses were adapted for Christian use: a classic example is the one at Dura Europos on the Euphrates River in the far east

---

3   Pliny, *Epistle* x.96. Sent by Emperor Trajan to regularise affairs in Bithynia around 112AD, Pliny included an account of Christian practice in his report, the earliest known source external to the churches.

4   Gregory Dix, *The Shape of the Liturgy* (A & C Black, 1945) 142. Dix draws a vivid picture of an early Christian assembly, set imaginatively in Roman London, and the consequences of its being discovered.

of the Empire, part of a town that was destroyed around 250AD.[5] One of its rooms seems to have been adapted for a baptistry, and another appears to be set up for eucharist. The wall paintings are ambiguous but, taken as a whole, there is little doubt that this is an early church building.

The Christian state

Christianity ceased to be illegal around 325AD—the precise date varied in different places, and depended on local officials' attitudes. Congregations grew rapidly: it would soon be impolitic not to be Christian, and from 381AD Christianity became the official imperial religion. Graydon argues that the change can be seen in the shift of symbolism from the fish to the cross, since there is no evidence of the cross used as a Christian symbol prior to Constantine, though after 325AD its use spread rapidly. In the early centuries, churches were disciplined communities of tested members living as 'fish' in the light of the resurrection, able to survive in an alien sea.[6] When Christianity became public, and then favoured, churches were flooded with 'ordinary' people, for whom the forgiveness of sins, and hence the cross, was central.

As regards meeting-places, catacombs and adapted houses were

---

5   Graydon F. Snyder, *Ante Pacem: Archaeological Evidence of Church Life Before Constantine* (Mercer University Press, 2003), 128ff. The house survived because it was built into the city wall, and was filled with rubble in order to defend the town more adequately, though unsuccessfully.

6   Jonah is the most common pre-Constantinian motif used in Christian art, around 75% of known examples. This choice may relate to Christ's reference to the 'sign of Jonah' in Matthew 12:39-40, but also corresponds to the early Christian message, which centred on Christ's victory over death, signified in baptism. The use of the 'fish' symbol not only has anagram roots (IXTHUS—*Iesus Christus Theou Huios Soter*—Jesus Christ, God's Son, Saviour) but suggests that Christians saw themselves as fish, able to survive and swim in an alien sea, following Christ in and through the deep, as typified in the experience of Jonah.

both impractical and unsuited for the official religion. Congregations moved into the local 'town hall' (*basilica*—'king's house'), and began to erect buildings on this model, often financed by the state, and decorated with unambiguous and triumphant Christian symbolism. Basilicas were one-room buildings with a large central space (without seating), a raised platform at the front (typically a semi-circular apse with seats for the 'seniors', i.e. presbyters) and an 'ambo' from which a gathering was presided over. A narthex (gathering place at the entrance) and aisles on each side allowed for informal meetings (e.g. between lawyers and clients). In Christian use, the basilica included a platform (altar space) with a lectern for the Bible and preaching, and a holy table for the eucharist. It was entered through a narthex, which could include the baptistry. In small towns and villages, church buildings could be quite small, but this 'one room plus focal point' shape became typical.[7]

The age of faith

In the early middle ages, monastic communities became the centre of many towns and villages, especially as civic government broke down prior to Charlemagne unifying Europe from 800AD as the Holy Roman Empire. Monks and nuns would meet each day in 'choir', that is, facing each other across the chancel (song room), set between the body of the church (nave) and sanctuary. The altar table, placed at the far end of the building, was typically set apart by a screen, especially after the Lateran Council of 1215, when the eucharist came to focus around the offering made by the priest. Liturgy remained in Latin, largely unknown to ordinary people, whose understanding of Christian faith was thus shaped by what they saw rather than what

---

7   A readable, well-illustrated overview of the development of parish churches in England is Kenneth White, *Shrines for the Saints. How Parish Churches evolved* (Bramcote: Grove Liturgy Series 3, 1975).

they heard: their own devotions (e.g. praying the Rosary) largely ran in parallel to the priest's actions. But the gospel continued to be performed, if interwoven with folk religion and even superstition. Church buildings were at the centre of village life, and the regular round of services, shaped by the church year and local festivals, undergirded what would later be seen as an 'age of faith'.

Reformation and Wren

With the Reformations of the sixteenth century, many continental churches had dominant pulpits built in them, to emphasise the priority of the ministry of the Word. Conversely, the Roman Catholic Counter-reformation saw baroque edifices rise to house the elaborate ceremonial of the High Mass. In England, cathedrals and many parish churches retained the three-roomed arrangement of the medieval period (nave/chancel/sanctuary) but added substantial pulpits at the front of the nave, from which Morning Prayer, Evening Prayer and Ante-Communion would be led, and preaching conducted. Participation in holy communion—rarely celebrated more than monthly—in these buildings required communicants to move, after the Prayer for the Church Militant, behind the pulpit to the 'communion room'.

After the 1666 Great Fire of London, and as England's population grew in the 19th century, new church buildings were needed. Early ones, influenced by Reformation ideals, followed the basilica design, one-room buildings in which hearing is to the fore. Notable examples are St James', Piccadilly and St Martin's in the Fields, London, designed by Christopher Wren, and many Episcopal churches in the USA. 'Dissenters'—Baptists, Quakers, Congregationalists, Presbyterians and others—were ejected from the Church of England in 1662: their chapels were built on similar lines to Wren's churches. And as prosperity grew, seating—an expensive item that few homes could afford—began to be introduced. Hand-built high 'box pews' initially housed the gentry, but as the Industrial Revolution took hold, pews as we know them spread, often funded by 'pew rents'.

The three-roomed building

The Anglo-Catholic revival, from the mid-19th century on, revived the mediaeval model in the Church of England. The three-room church design was successfully promoted by the Cambridge Camden Society (founded in 1845), whose publication *The Ecclesiologist* was influential in reintroducing Gothic architecture. A typical Camden Society building has a long nave, a chancel (housing a choir) with lectern and pulpit set on either side, and the holy table (altar) set against the 'east' wall, behind communion rails. As the Anglican Communion spread across the British Empire from the 1870s, this is what a 'proper' Anglican church building came to look like. In a few places 'riddell screens' were set on each side of the altar so that the priest had to stand in front of it, between the people and east wall, rather than on its 'north side' (as the *Book of Common Prayer* indicated). Heated debates and court cases took place over issues of architecture and furnishing such as this, continuing well into the 20th century. Only since the 1960s have tensions around these matters eased, though not entirely (see below).

The Australian experience

In the Australian colonies most church buildings were very basic—design issues hardly arose. And not everyone wanted them: the first church building in the New South Wales penal colony, chaplain Richard Johnston's wattle-and-daub hut in Sydney, was burnt down by convicts. More substantial buildings were erected with government support, and built on the Wren-basilica one-room model, focused around the congregation listening: St Matthew's, Windsor, NSW or St James' (old cathedral), West Melbourne are good examples.

As the population exploded in the wake of the gold rushes of the 1850s and 60s, new church buildings were needed. Where funds permitted more than a weatherboard room, designs typically followed the Camden Society's three-room plan, whatever the 'churchmanship' of the parish concerned: those designed by Louis Williams and William Butterfield in Victoria are high-quality examples. This pattern continued until the 1950s, as can be seen in some 'restorations' of church buildings: Christ Church, Hawthorn in Melbourne, for example, is an interesting example of a pre-Camden Society building later adapted to align with its principles.

On from the sixties

Several factors have seen this situation change significantly in the past half-century. At the sheer practical level, many church buildings needed major maintenance, which opened up opportunities for change. Theologically, the Liturgical Movement laid the groundwork for buildings being designed around the people rather than the clergy alone. Its fruit was seen in the changes made in the Roman Catholic Church following the Second Vatican Council (1963–65). Services being held in the language of the people (e.g. English) rather than Latin is a well-known change that was made, but another was moving the altar forward, so that priest and people face one another. This design quickly became standard practice in Anglican and other non-Roman Catholic churches: indeed, many mainstream Christians who have never experienced the older arrangement find it highly objectionable.

People-centred emphases like this were widely welcomed in the increasingly egalitarian culture of Australia. Church 'in the round' stands in contrast to the formal arrangement of the three-roomed building, with its separation of people and roles. The danger here can be that the group has no focal point beyond itself, and that the Gospel symbols (font, lectern, holy table) become secondary. This need not be the case: several Australian cathedrals have placed a platform at the central 'crossing', on which lectern and holy table are placed, surrounded by the people. Conversely, the rapid emergence of visual mass culture, initially through television and now via online media, has bypassed the 'radio culture' of much traditional liturgy. Large screens are commonplace in many church buildings, forming a new and dominant focal point, raising new issues about how the Gospel is performed when God's people meet for worship (see Chapter Seven).

Part C   Places and spaces to perform the gospel

Church buildings: 3D sacraments

Church buildings are shaped by the cultures and issues in which they are set up and used. They stand as "outward and visible signs"—rather tangible and three-dimensional ones—of the presence of God in a community. They are set aside to be places where people can encounter Christ through the gospel being performed in and around them.

Thinking of church buildings as "outward and visible signs" is how the Christian tradition speaks about sacraments. A sacrament is a tangible symbol given by God so that through it we may receive God's grace and know God's loving presence. As Article 25 puts it, Christ's sacraments are "certain sure witnesses, and effectual signs of grace, and God's good will towards us, by the which he doth work invisibly in us." Christians thus have the great privilege of engaging with God not only through their ears, but also in their bodily experience. But this can be misused. On the one hand, identifying the sign with what it signifies runs the risk of idolatry, worshipping a creature rather than the Creator (what might be called the 'catholic' danger). On the other, dividing the sign from what it signifies renders it useless, ineffectual (the 'protestant' danger).

These concepts are readily applicable to church buildings, as "outward and visible signs" of God's grace, and "a means whereby we receive the same". They thus have a sacramental character—an approach that not only values them, but also warns against their misuse. A church building points to God's living presence in a community, but there is always the risk that the sign, the building itself, becomes what really matters, the focus of worship. When this happens, like the Temple of old, it becomes a place of spiritual danger, and comes under God's word of judgment. When we focus on the spiritual heritage preserved in our church building, no matter how glorious, or allow a building to have a higher priority in our lives than the One to whom it is dedicated, our relationship with God is distorted, and the purpose for which the church exists is corrupted.

On the other hand, when the sacramental nature of a church building is devalued, neglected or ignored, it becomes a 'bare sign', with little if any link to the gospel it was raised to serve. Uncared-for grounds, out-of-date notice boards, dusty seats, cluttered floors and dirty toilets speak as much about what a building stands for as unfriendly welcomers, unprepared prayers, irrelevant songs, and preaching which ignores the scriptures. When this happens, the building can get in the way of the gospel being communicated, or worse, present a distorted version.

The places and spaces in which it is our privilege to perform the gospel have deeper and richer purposes. As years pass, they become imbued with the praises and prayers of the saints offered in them. They sustain precious moments and memories of encounter with God, through the preaching of the Gospel, administration of the sacraments and celebration of life's turning points—birth, marriage, illness, and death. They offer sanctuary to those in "trouble, sorrow, need, sickness, or any other adversity" (as the *Book of Common Prayer* puts it). They point beyond the immediate concerns of the community in which they are set, to the boundless love and eternal purposes of God.

How then, do we go about seeking to ensure God's purposes are set forward in the way we use the buildings God gives us? Whatever historical era(s) shaped a Christian church building, certain place and space constants remain, apart from liturgical fashion or architectural period:

- people space, for the assembly to participate;
- baptism space, for celebrating new life in Christ;
- word space, for proclaiming God's Word;
- table space, for offering thanks and receiving communion;
- music space, for playing and singing the Gospel;
- ministering space, for those who lead and preside;
- and, in more recent times, a gathering space, which is where this discussion begins.

Gathering space: for welcoming and naming

Christians come apart from their lifestyle worship to gather for liturgical worship—to perform the Gospel as God's people. We gather *together* as a Christian community, as a local expression of the body of Christ. From a human point of view this gathering is our action, but faith names it as our response to God's "call to worship" (as some traditions call the first part of a service). Gathering thus has two aspects: welcoming and naming.

'Gathering' happens not just as preparation for worship—it

marks *the transition from daily to gathered worship*. So welcoming is not just a job, it is a ministry: it enables 'regulars' to move into what is familiar, and helps visitors engage with what may be new to them: the welcome they receive as they enter will influence whether they return or not. A neat, culturally attractive and practical gathering space will support this ministry, whether it is a porch, foyer, narthex or just an area near the entrance. It will allow people to be greeted, and receive whatever books/service sheets are needed, rather than being an obstacle course to wade through. Welcomers should be aware of different people's approach to church: some will want to enter into quiet, others to engage in conversation, and a cuppa may be on hand. And gathering does not cease when the blessing is given: the dismissal marks the transition back to our daily worship. Using the gathering space for after-service activities or hospitality can further this process.

Gathering is also about *naming who we are*, and why we have come—it is part of performing the gospel, not just a preliminary. "We are the body of Christ", the priest declares in a communion service, and we respond "His Spirit is with us". So the 'we' involved is more than a collection of individuals doing together what each could do apart. We gather as a 'body corporate', in response to the Spirit's promptings; our 'members' are not merely people who have signed up to a club, but living organs of the body of Christ. The opening section of each Sunday service in *APBA* is thus called 'Gathering in God's Name', the Name into which we are baptised—we come together as if we were just emerging from the font, dripping wet.

In a 'traditional' church building, the font is the item of furniture first encountered; it marks the place where our entry into the people of God is performed. Baptism is how a person is sacramentally 'gathered in' to Christ: it enacts our 'crossing over' the flood of death and sin, into the promised land of new life in Christ and God's new creation. In some church buildings the font is filled with water, so that as people arrive they can trace their hands in it, or mark their forehead with the cross, as a reminder of their identity in Christ. If the font is located elsewhere, it is helpful for the gathering space to contain a symbol of who we are—individual Christians now gathered as a local embodiment of the Church of God.

How these two dimensions work together—welcoming, with its practical requirements, and naming, with its symbolic character—is an art. The gathering space will no doubt have a 'standard' arrangement, but it can vary depending on the time of year, type of service (e.g. for a baptism) and culture of the congregation. Done well, it will show how the gospel we perform symbolically in church is woven into the worship we offer in daily life. The gathering space is thus itself sacramental, an outward and visible demonstration of the grace of God, already doing the work of re-forming us into the likeness of Christ.

People space: for the assembly to particpate

A Christian congregation is not an audience. Church is not just a concert, in which we are spectators of a performance, but performs the faith in which all the baptised play their part. Those called to the ministry of the gospel will have the most public roles, notably presiding and preaching. Their ministry, however, is all of a piece with the participation of the congregation. Reading the scriptures, giving notices, leading in song, offering intercessions, taking up the collection—the same principle applies for all these. Sometimes 'participation' is understood as exercising a public ministry, while others are 'passive'. But, except in a congregation of a dozen or less, it is both impossible and undesirable for everyone present to speak. We gather as church to perform the gospel, and all are called to be part of the action: the issue is not *whether* all are involved, but *how*. What matters is that all take their part through active listening, singing and responding, engagement in 'common prayer', and participation in the sacraments.

The space in which a church (assembly) 'assembles' plays a large part in enabling people to join in proclaiming and responding to the gospel (or not). How people are placed in relation to the furniture, which symbolises the Gospel—font, lectern, pulpit and holy table—is of primary concern. As well as enabling effective seeing and hearing, the *relationship* of the people to these items says a good deal about what their participation means.

In a three-roomed church building, people take their place in the 'nave' (from the Latin for 'ship', based on thinking of church as 'ark of salvation'). Until the Industrial Revolution made seating affordable, the nave was an open space in which people could move around, and would stand or kneel during the service (those who needed support leant on the walls or 'sedillae', stones sticking out a little way from the walls). Today the nave often is filled with long pews designed for kneeling and sitting: ideal for listening, watching and meditating, but constricting other movement—even standing can be awkward. In traditional buildings the lectern, pulpit and holy table are set in the 'sanctuary' (from the Latin for 'holy place'), occupied by the clergy, servers and (in some places still) a robed choir. This, and similar 'upfront' arrangements, makes sense where the congregation is large, and is appropriate in cultures where structured relationships are significant, but they can be problematic in more egalitarian contexts.

Whatever their meeting-place, worshippers—clergy included—need to be able to listen actively, see easily, stand naturally, move readily, sit alertly, and kneel comfortably, so they can take their part in performing the gospel. Paying attention to how seating is arranged will meet many of these needs: but this depends on factors such as the age and shape of the building, how fixed the seating is, the size of the assembly and the culture(s) of its members. Differences in personality, life circumstances and musical tastes need to be taken into account so that all can engage in authentic performance of the gospel. Over the past half-century, popular culture has become focused more on relationships. Rows of straight pews might maximise the number of people who can fit in, but are perceived as getting in the way of fostering Christian community and communal worship. This situation could be improved, for example, by slanting the pews so people can see some other faces, rather than just the backs of heads. Good stewardship of space might mean removing some pews—rather than roping them off like a 'no-go' area—to create more space for other purposes, such as a nursery area, or more open gathering space.

And a congregation does more than listen, sit, see, kneel and stand. We need to be able to move in and out of our places to greet one another, to receive communion, to enter and leave the building, to gather at the font, and so on—in short, to perform by 'moving'. To foster this, in some places pews have given way to chairs, which are more comfortable, and (more significantly) allow for flexible arrangements. Different types of service can be served by different arrangements, each with its pros and cons. In a wedding, the bride may want the longest aisle possible, but those present being able to hear the couple's promises to one another matters more. In a funeral, how the coffin is placed in relationship to the font, family members and the wider congregation needs to be thought through, as appropriate to the deceased's relationship to each.

On Sundays, different arrangements can mark the seasons of the Christian year: thus a 'straight' one during Lent can encourage reflection, moving to a minimal setting for Holy Week: a dramatic change of seating arrangement can mark the celebratory tone of Easter Day. A 'choir' arrangement has the congregation facing one another—excellent for responsive singing, but difficult for people who need privacy. In multi-use buildings, flexibility means hard work in setting up for each week, though in my experience praying for the people who will fill the chairs as they are set out is a privilege. Circular seating is welcomed where egalitarian values are strong: this offers excellent sight and sound lines, and can evoke a sense of inclusive community. But it can also feel quite excluding for those uncomfortable in such a setting, or visitors—and if the lectern and holy table are placed outside the circle, the focus falls less on the gospel than on emptiness, or the group itself.

Listening space: for hearing and proclaiming God's Word

The public reading of the scriptures, and their proclamation in preaching, is the foundation of Christian worship. This 'ministry of the Word', through which God in Christ addresses us, forms the 'script' for the gospel performed in liturgy, and is the basis for our response in faith and living.

So the place where the church's copy of the Bible rests—the lectern—should have some dignity. The Bible itself is traditionally a substantial volume, both to indicate its significance, and so that the print is large enough to be read comfortably. The latter need can be met today by sheets with the readings in large type being placed on the lectern—both practical and allowing the symbolic function of the Bible to remain. Lifting up a piece of A4 and saying 'Hear the word of the Lord' does not quite convey its seriousness.

The pulpit (ambo) allows the preacher to be easily heard and seen. Some are so 'high and lifted up' that they set the preacher 'above' the people, overdoing his or her authority—'six feet above contradiction'. A well-placed, well-lit lectern may serve the purpose, but should reflect the centrality and fundamental importance of the ministry of the Word. It is essential that all can hear: many buildings do not need amplification, but a good sound system caters for the hearing impaired. Whatever the technology used, all engaged in the ministry of the Word need to be trained to project their voices, and use microphones well.

A note on microphones

Microphones have been around for decades, and are particularly relevant to the ministry of the Word. A fixed microphone works well for speaking from the lectern or pulpit, but is limiting for an acted-out children's talk, or where several voices do a dramatic scripture reading, or lead the prayers. Radio mikes ease this problem—but need to be turned off when the wearer is not speaking publically (e.g. during congregational singing, or while administering communion).

And whoever has the microphone is 'in the control seat'. Each person who uses one needs to understand how their ministry relates to that of others, so that their authority is seen in how they serve the assembly rather than dominating it.

Table space: for offering thanks and receiving communion

Just as the lectern and pulpit are central foci for the ministry of the Word, so the holy table[8] is central to the ministry of holy communion, the supper of the exalted Lord Jesus. Just as the lectern holds the

---

8   'Holy table' is used here since this is its consistent naming in Anglican formularies. It is often referred to as the 'altar', as the place where the Great Thanksgiving is offered. Given sensitivities about what 'sacrifice' means in the eucharist, however, 'altar' is unacceptable to many Anglicans and others. It is worth noting that, in the Eastern Orthodox tradition, the 'altar' is the space within which the holy table is set.

church Bible, so the table holds the vessels for bread and wine for the eucharist (Greek for 'thanksgiving'), and the presider's book.

Holy communion is a celebration in which the whole assembly joins, so the holy table is typically placed near the front in a central position. Gathering *around* the Lord's table is a primary symbol of the people of God, in the presence of the risen Lord Jesus, *together* performing the gospel of Christ's saving death, offering the 'sacrifice of thanksgiving' and joining in the Lord's supper. When set far away from the people, the nature of the eucharist as a *corporate* act of thanksgiving and sacramental meal is obscured. In three-room churches this can be difficult: in many places this is resolved by having a (second) 'forward' table. In some Australian cathedrals, Bendigo for example, it is placed on a platform at the transept crossing, with seating on all sides. On the other hand, using a small, temporary table can convey the message that the eucharist does not matter that much. Good design will communicate both the significance of the holy table, and allow for the presiding priest, other ministers and servers to be able to move around it as necessary.

Being practical about the distribution of the bread and wine is the other aspect of the table space. The *Book of Common Prayer* sets down that the thanksgiving prayer and receiving of communion be undertaken kneeling, a posture expressing humble gratitude for God's gift of Christ. In recent decades, standing has become common as the posture for both, expressing our joint participation in the "holy and royal priesthood" into which we are baptised, "to offer spiritual sacrifices acceptable to God through Jesus Christ" (1 Peter 2:5). Where many receive standing, communion rails may no longer be needed, at least not right across the table space, where they can be a physical and visual obstacle to the notion of 'gathering around' the Lord's table—yet making ongoing provision for communicants to kneel to receive is important. Again, communion should be distributed from the holy table at which the thanksgiving was offered: administering the bread and wine at rails near an unused east end holy table disturbs the unity between thanksgiving and communion. All these matters can raise practical dilemmas: imagination and discernment can resolve them—and there is a good deal to be said for some experimenting in any case.

Baptismal space: celebrating new life in Christ

In the past, baptism was commonly seen as a 'private' affair, a 'birth right' conducted on Sunday afternoons at a time to suit an infant's biological family; the font may have been placed in a quiet corner 'out of the way'. No age limits are placed on being baptised, since baptism is a sacrament of the gospel. But it is not a 'birth right' so much as a 'new birth rite', in which a person is symbolically drowned and buried with Christ, has the old life of sin and death washed away, receives the Holy Spirit, and so becomes "*the* child of God, a member of Christ, and an inheritor of the kingdom of heaven" (as the *BCP* Catechism teaches). Baptism thus involves the whole congregation: at each baptism we witness God's work in new Christians, pledge to support them in their faith journey, together confess the faith of Christ, and renew our own baptism promises.

Traditionally the font is placed in the gathering space, marking our entry to church. Whether the font is placed there or elsewhere during a service, is not nearly as important as having space around it to gather. Placing the font on a low platform, and lighting it well, will enhance its significance as the 'laver of regeneration', and allow not only candidates, ministers, godparents and sponsors to gather around, but enable all present to see what is happening, and make their responses with enthusiasm. Room is thus needed around the font for more than just two or three to gather. A small table in the baptismal space can hold the baptism certificates, candles, a towel and oil if these are used, with the (lit) Easter (paschal) candle (whether in the Easter season or not) nearby.

And the font itself is, of course, a water container—though many hold precious little. The rubrics of *BCP, AAPB* and *APBA* require that candidates normally be 'dipped' or have water 'poured over' them (never just sprinkled).[9] Places with a tiny font could consider getting a new one with a good-sized bowl for water, large enough for an infant to be 'dipped'—or go the whole way and install a font big enough for someone to lie down and be submersed. The traditional shape of a font is an octagon, a sign that we are baptised into the 'eighth day', God's new creation, in which we now live through the Holy Spirit. But whatever the place and shape of the font, and however water is applied, plenty should be used.[10] Baptism is a tangible sign of God at work, of the gospel of Christ crucified and risen being performed in the power of the Spirit—it is much more than just 'nice'.

Music space: playing and singing the gospel

A choir or singing group has the ministry of supporting the liturgical performance of the gospel. It is not there to 'perform' to

---

9   The technical terms are 'submersion' (when a person is dipped under the water, alluding to Romans 6:4), 'immersion' (when a person stands in water, which is poured over them) and 'affusion' (when water is poured over a person, alluding to Romans 5:5). Sprinkling ('aspersion') is not a mode of baptism, but is appropriate for occasions of re-commitment to Christ, such as is customary on Easter Day, or to dedicate something to God's service (e.g. a church building). Sprinkling can also be helpful for someone who, after an experience of renewal, seeks a rite of re-dedication that included water: this mode does not bring into question their stance as a once-baptised person.

For fuller discussion of these and related matters of baptismal preparation and practice, see Charles Sherlock, *A Pastoral Handbook for Anglicans* (Acorn, 2001) Chapter One.

10   *APBA* page 70, Note 3 states: "In the celebration of baptism the symbolism of water should be emphasised. Immersion or the pouring of a significant quantity of water shows this clearly. The pouring of the water both into the font and over each candidate should be done deliberately and with care."

an audience, as if church were a concert—whether classical, folk, jazz, rock, pop or whatever—to support the people's participation through listening and singing.

Traditionally, singers were placed at the rear of the congregation, often in a gallery. The 19th century re-emergence of three-roomed church buildings saw (robed) choirs placed in the 'chancel' (i.e. the place of song), between the people and the holy table, thus obscuring it and making it distant. When organs began to arrive in parish churches from around 1880, they were then often placed near the choir. In recent decades, the coming of amplified instruments and microphones has seen robed choirs and organ replaced by a band and singers, raising similar issues. When musicians are placed at the front, a false understanding of what 'performance' means in worship can be perpetuated. The congregation's focus can focus on the 'performers' rather than on the major symbols of the gospel, lectern and holy table. 'Word space' and 'table space' are then dominated rather than served by 'music space'.

These comments in no way undermine the vital ministries of music: in our contemporary sound-surround culture, they are enormously significant. Imagination and discernment are needed so that musicians and singers have useable space where they can play their part readily, and have access to good acoustics. The danger—whether it is robed choirs or mike-fronting singers—is that they may dominate or interfere with the performance of the gospel by other ministers and the congregation. And drum sets, instrument leads and keyboards on movable stands tend to make a mess. Negotiating around the issues involved are likely to be no easy matter. On the one hand, one person (e.g. an organist) can dictate the choice and place of music; on the other, enthusiastic amateurs may be keen to contribute, but not understand the issues involved in music ministry. Youngsters putting their toes in the water of learning to play and sing need to be encouraged; professionals are called to put their skills and experience in the service of the gospel ahead of career. Confidence in what each can offer, blended with humility, is the way of Christ.

Ministering space: presiding, leading and serving

The focal points in a church building are outward and visible signs of the gospel—font, lectern/pulpit and holy table. They should be arranged so that the people can see and engage with them. Those called to preside and enable worship have a key place 'in church', and their 'place' is to minister out of these foundational realities.

The person who presides needs a seat, placed so he or she can be heard and seen, and can see other leaders and the people. In a traditional Anglican church building, this seat faces 'sideways on' to the people, so that their focus is not on the minister, and that their view of the front is unimpeded.[11] This has the advantage of avoiding a 'personality cult', and suits 'Anglo-Saxon reserve', but in today's more relational culture people can feel that it is impersonal. So many church buildings today have the presider's seat facing the people, near the holy table and lectern. Further, when the priest stands to preside at the eucharist, today he or she faces the people, also standing, across the holy table. This means that whoever presides exercises their ministry from a highly visible place—and needs to come to terms with the effect of their body language on the congregation. Practicing in front of a mirror is not a bad idea—realising how others see you can be quite a surprise.

Those who read lessons, intercessions and assist in the administration of communion can sit in the congregation until the

---

11 This seat is distinct from the 'bishop's chair', usually left vacant and placed at the side of the sanctuary, as a sign of the bishop being the ultimate presider, normally delegated to the priest having the 'cure of souls'.

time comes for them to move to the word or table space. When they and other ministers are robed (e.g. servers) they need to be placed near to where they will minister, but not so as to detract from the congregation's focus on the symbols of the gospel. For services where a lot of movement is involved—a youth service, 'messy church', Palm Sunday processions—a rehearsal will take care of issues about who sits where, and how participants' movements are 'blocked out'. Indeed, every service is a performance, so a regular rehearsal as part of preparation is a good idea.

Weddings in particular need rehearsal, since the ministers of the marriage (the couple) and their 'servers' (bridesmaids and groomsmen) will rarely have taken part in being 'upfront' in a Christian service. It offers not only an opportunity to resolve practical issues and further relationships, but may also help those involved play their part, if unwittingly, in performing aspects of the gospel, as the union between Christ and the Church is symbolised in the 'solemnisation of holy matrimony'.

The ambience of gospel performance

A memorable performance is a piece of art. The overall impression made, the message left or reflection inspired is an amalgam of scene, script, performance and props, grounded in preparation and practice. There is not space here to discuss props, or the decoration of the various spaces discussed above. Colour, hangings and banners, flowers (or their absence), candles, stained glass, crosses/crucifixes, sculptures and so on—all affect the atmosphere of the spaces involved, and so contribute (or otherwise) to the ambience of a service. Yes, they can be used to manipulate people's emotions. But in many 'mainstream' churches this is less of a problem than giving people free rein to respond to the gospel in heart, soul and body.

Some elements of place are 'givens', unable to be changed, perhaps becoming so familiar that they cease to have effect. Focussing on one or two of these—pointing out the subject of a window in a sermon, for example—can help bring their ministry alive. Transient props or decor, on the other hand, need time, skill and money for their making and use—and it can be hard to let them go: more than one church has tatty, faded banners still hanging around. But it's worth noting how spending on such 'transient' things can be tight-fisted. To maintain a pipe organ costs several thousand dollars annually, so it probably costs around $20 or so to accompany each hymn. Spending $20 on a prop for a children's talk, for example, can be regarded as a 'waste of good money'. So the opportunity slips by for everyone to have candles for a 'carols by candlelight' Christmas service, or a one-off frontal for a baptism, or a pot of flowers to brighten a winter's day.

Whatever the layout and ambience of the building in which a church meets, and however it may have been renovated as liturgical fashions have changed, it was built and set aside to be a place where, in the power of the Spirit, the gospel of Christ will be performed week in and week out. Yes, the dangers of misuse need to be watched—church buildings exist for the worship of God in Christ, not as clubhouses for 'spiritual' types. They should be appreciated, honoured and used as 'three-dimensional sacraments', gifts of God's grace.

With all its faults and limitations, may your church building be loved as a precious place dedicated to the presence, love and word of God being made known and celebrated, not only among the people of God, but in society at large.

Part D A church building audit

This exercise can be undertaken individually, or by a small group (e.g. a liturgy planning committee). It would be courteous to let the rector/vicar/minister know it is being undertaken, since it is a primary 'work place' for them.

Making brief notes in response to each question will enable you to engage more fully with the final, summary question. You might like to write down your concluding answer and share it with the rector/vicar/minister, and then the Parish Council.

1. Walk into your church building and stand near the entrance.
   What things stand out as the most significant items visible?
   What do they appear to represent?
   How does their nature and placement relate to what you have read in this chapter?
2. Look around the area you have entered: to what extent does it invite you to come in?
   In what way does it work for gathering? What might hinder this ministry?
   If it is used for after-service activities, how do these work?
3. Sit down in several places, for example, at the sides, near the centre, right up the front.
   How does the arrangement of the furniture feel from these different positions?
   Which key symbols are close to some places, or else cannot be seen?
   If space is set-aside for musicians or singers, how does this work in relation to the various places in which you have taken a seat?

4. Go to the font. What do its placement, size and design say about what it means to be a Christian, to be 'born from above' into Christ?
5. Go to where the lectern and/or pulpit are set. Is a copy of the Bible there?
   What does their design and placement say about the ministry of the Word?
   How do these affect the performance of those who speak from there?
6. Go to the holy table. What do its design, placement and decoration say about the way the eucharist is celebrated?
7. Have a walk around to consider any art-works, stained-glass, candles, banners, crosses or crucifixes, plaques or texts on the walls, and the like.
   In what ways do you feel they relate to the worship offered in this building?
8. Return to take a seat in the middle of the building, and gather up your reflections.
   What do you most appreciate in this building? What, if anything, gets in the way?

Overall, how do you believe that the use of space, and the placement of things, assist or hinder the gospel to be performed in this place?

In our daily living, Christian worship is offered in all sorts of places. Some inspire the sense of God's presence—a welcoming hallway or kitchen, a park or community centre. Others are challenging: large shopping malls can feel like community 'temples' for the worship of consumerism. How might the 'church audit' be adapted to the places in which you seek to perform the gospel as your lifestyle in Christ?

Chapter Three
Being 'upfront': performing and presiding

Overview

Part A   concentrates on how the theology of ministry affects who should (and should not) be 'upfront'—the 'theory' behind Parts B and C.

Part B   bridging A and C, aims to help you work though wider issues about 'seeing, hearing and doing', especially as these are shaped by the cultures in which we live.

Part C   spells out the implications of Parts A and B, and focuses on 'how-to' ideas around leading in gospel performance.

Part D   is a 'performance audit'—please don't forget to do it.

At a concert or show people are typically divided into 'performers' and 'audience'. This division will be sharper when those 'upfront' need to be highly skilled—an orchestral concert or musical theatre, for example. Yet an audience is not just passive: its 'performance' in responding to what is seen and heard can make or break a stand-up comedy act or rock concert, for example.

When it comes to Christian worship, however, this distinction needs to be qualified. As emphasised in Chapter One, every Christian is called to perform the gospel, and the living God is the ultimate audience for our worship. Those 'upfront' in a service are not the only performers present, and the congregation is more than an 'audience', even an active one: Christian worship transcends the 'performers–audience' notion. Indeed, someone who does not want to be part of performing the gospel—for example, a family friend present at a baptism—will need to take care to avoid joining in.

That said, every service has those who will be 'upfront', whose responsibility it is to enable all present to participate as fully as they are willing and able. These leaders' ministry is a key factor in a congregation's healthy performance of the gospel in their daily lives. That is the focus of this chapter—in which significant issues of theology, culture and behaviour are involved.

A note on terminology

A variety of terms are used to describe the person who presides in Christian liturgy, some more helpful than others.

- 'President' is an obvious choice for someone who 'presides'—it is the term used in the Church of England's Common Worship (2000) books. But in Australia 'president' has both political and 'republican' associations, and feels awkward.
- 'Celebrant' at least has the benefit of sounding joyous! In the context of a wedding it makes some sense, but using it elsewhere only to refer to the one who presides is problematic, especially in speaking of a priest 'celebrating' the eucharist. Just as every Christian is called to perform the gospel, so each believer is called to celebrate God's love and justice, and especially so in the thanksgiving ('eucharistic') feast of Christ's atoning victory through suffering.

- 'Officiant' is the term used in government regulations for the person who presides as a wedding or funeral. It makes sense in terms of being 'official' and avoiding any 'religious' meaning, but is quite hopeless as a Christian term.
- 'Worship leader' has come into use more recently, and again seems obvious. But it goes along with the unhelpful idea that 'worship' is what happens in a religious event, or even just the 'worship' part of a service, rather than meaning our response to God across our living. And while 'leader' is not untrue, it suggests that others present follow their lead—possibly rather than God's call.
- So what is the best term? Scholars of liturgy suggest 'presider': this says what the presiding minister does, and avoids the problems of the other terms. Further, it is probably the earliest term used to describe the person who presides. Justin Martyr, writing in Rome around 150AD, uses it (*First Apology*, 67), and not only to refer to presiding 'in church', but in the wider ministries of the church to those in need.

Part A 'Decently and in order': a theological survey of public ministry

New Testament foundations

Most of what we know about the life of the first churches comes from their mistakes. The Corinthian Christians of apostolic times were notorious for doing things 'their way' with little regard for others, not least when it came to ecstatic expressions of faith. Paul did not squash their enthusiasm, but insisted that they focus on "a more excellent way", the way of love (1 Corinthians 12.31–14.1). He concludes his analysis by writing, "be eager to prophesy, and do not forbid speaking in tongues; but all things should be done **decently and in order**" (1 Corinthians 14:39-40). This last phrase has become a slogan for the conduct of a Christian service. But it can be overdone, not least in 'middle class' cultures where everything is 'nice', undisturbed by embarrassing in-breakings of the Spirit's work.

Indeed, the New Testament documents say little about how churches and the ministry of the gospel are organised—which frustrates those looking for a clear blueprint. Acts shows a gradual emergence of structures from the Jerusalem assembly, led by apostles and elders for whom Hebrew was the mother tongue, to Gentile congregations speaking Latin or Greek, in which prophets, presbyters and deacons ministered (see Acts 6.1-6; 11.19-30 for example). Acts portrays Paul as using the synagogue pattern of 'presbyters' (seniors, elders) for Christian churches in the Graeco-Roman world (Acts 14.23; 20.17). But the issue that dominates the first generation of leaders is whether Gentiles must be circumcised to become Christians: the need to resolve this shows authority structures emerging (Acts 15).

As the apostles aged, firmer structures are outlined. The apostles appointed deacons (sacred agents), presbyters (seniors) and bishops (overseers) in local congregations (see Acts 6.5-6; 14.23; 1 Timothy 3.1-13). No uniform pattern is found, yet a coherent ethos of Christian ministry is present, emphasising sound teaching and a lifestyle consistent with the gospel (see Acts 20.28ff; Titus 1.5-9). All were to exercise their *diakonia* (sacred ministry/divine service) as "ambassadors for Christ" (2 Corinthians 5.20), preaching the gospel, leading their communities and teaching the faith. Other *charismata* (gracings) are mentioned—evangelists, prophets, pastor-teachers, interpreters, widows, administrators, and so on (see Romans 12.6-8; 1 Corinthians 14; Ephesians 4.1-11; 1 Timothy 5.17-22). But how these relate to the above 'offices' is not wholly clear. What is emphasised continually is the importance of all ministries and charisms being directed towards enabling the gospel to be performed authentically: what happens 'in church' models and equips Christians to live out their callings in daily life.

Orders and ordination: early developments and centuries of change

This notion of gospel-enabling 'order' developed in the early churches into 'ordination', the recognition that some Christians are called to accept life-long public responsibility for the gospel: texts such as 1 Timothy 4.14 and Romans 11.29 were taken to teach this. Writing towards the end of the first century, Clement of Rome noted that the apostles "received their orders" (i.e. ministries—not just instructions) from the risen Christ, and went "preaching through countries and cities". In doing so, "they appointed their first-fruits, having first proved them by the Spirit, to be bishops and deacons of those who should afterwards believe" (1 Clement 42).

Alongside these ministries, early Christian communities continued the synagogue practice of being managed by presbyters. By approximately 175–180 AD—around the same time as the contents (canon) of the New Testament was being recognised—the 'threefold order' of bishop, deacons and presbyters is the pattern seen in all the churches we know of across the Mediterranean world. But how this worked out in different places does not correspond neatly to the various patterns of ordained ministries we know today.

What follows is a sweeping summary of the evidence, but it reflects what we do know of the first three centuries.[1] Each church (often

---

[1] A readable summary can be found in James Barnett, *The Diaconate: Full and Equal its Order* (New York: Seabury, 1981) chapter six. A brilliant pen picture of second-century Christian worship (set in a London suburb of the 1930s) which reflects both this 'ordering'—and its dangerous social setting—is Dom Gregory Dix, *The Shape of the Liturgy* (London: Dacre, 1945) 142–145.

made of several congregations) in a town or small region had one bishop, who presided and preached, assisted by deacons who led the congregation in worship, prepared people for baptism and looked after practical ministries (and commonly became bishops, not least because most deacons could read and write). Each congregation also had a small group of older Christians (presbyters, i.e. 'seniors', elders) who sat behind the bishop in church and acted as a 'sounding board' on major issues, yet seem to have had little if any liturgical role for some generations.[2] In short, the bishop's ministry was a personal one of presiding and preaching, enabled by deacons, while the presbyters formed a group of seniors with administrative and support responsibilities. Liturgy was led by the 'dialogue' of bishop and deacons: the one embodying God's initiative, the other the Spirit's enabling of the people—the *laos* of God, the royal priesthood (1 Peter 2:11)—to respond to God's call (see Part B p. 82).

This pattern went through drastic change from around 250AD as persecution changed from local, occasional pressure on believers to widespread, officially endorsed attacks on Christian leaders. The bishops' numbers were decimated, and their ministry of presiding locally was gradually delegated to a presbyter.[3] As churches expanded when persecution ended, the surviving bishops became the leaders of larger areas, coming together in 'synods' (from *syn* meaning 'together' and *hodos* 'on the way') to consider issues of concern across the churches. But perhaps the most significant change was that the presbyter acting as a bishop came to be called 'priest'. As Dix writes:

---

2   See Dix, 270ff, who describes the relation of presbyters with the bishop before the Council of Nicea (325) as that of an 'executive committee' to its 'chairman'.

3   The Council of Ancyra (314) forbade presbyters to preside, which probably means that some were doing so. The Council of Nicea (325) normalised the practice, however: see Barnett, 100.

It was a great loss when the idea of the corporate priesthood of the whole church in the eucharist was obscured by attaching the title of the eucharistic 'priest' especially to the celebrant-presbyter.[4]

'Priesthood' began to lose its biblical identification with the *laos* of God as a whole, and began to be understood in the Graeco-Roman sense of 'gatekeepers' who gave access to the world of the divine. In sum, the collegiate, administrative order of presbyters changed places with the personal and pastoral ministry of the bishop. In doing so, presiding at the eucharist took on a 'sacerdotal' understanding, and priests came to be seen as the central 'order'. In the process, the 'order' of deacons was reduced to a formality, with bishops taking on primarily administrative and conciliar duties.

Over the following centuries this 'ordering' became infused with sub-Christian, sometimes even un-Christian, practices of spiritual leadership—most notably, Graeco-Roman rather than biblical concepts of 'sacrifice' and 'priesthood'.[5] Official teaching may not have seen priests as 'turnstiles' through which people must pass to have access to God (or heaven). Yet for much of the Middle Ages this

---

[4] Dix, 270. Dix places considerable significance on the concept that "any particular eucharist is not the act of the local church only, even in its organic unity; it must be the act of the whole catholic Body of Christ, throughout the world and throughout the ages". Deacons and presbyters were appointed locally, whereas the bishop is "the only one member of a local church in pre-Nicene times who bears a commission from outside" and so is the only one authorised to preside and preach "with the universal consent of the whole catholic church". Dix's argument is important for setting ideas on ministry into context, yet the idea today of gaining "universal consent" among long-divided churches presents a major challenge to the mutual recognition of ministries.

[5] On this, see the Anglican-Roman Catholic International Commission, *The Final Report* (London: CTS / SPCK, 1981), 'Ministry', paragraph 13. For a fuller discussion of scriptural data around 'priest', 'High Priest', sacrifice and atonement, see Charles Sherlock, *Words and the Word. Case studies in using scripture today* (Melbourne: Morningstar, 2013) chapter seven.

concept dominated the popular mind, especially since the language of liturgy remained Latin when it had ceased to be the language of daily life. Further, corrupt practices developed such as the sale of church positions (simony), especially to family members (nepotism).

Protests against such evils (mixed in with other issues) grew steadily from around 1350 (think Wycliffe, Hus, Savanarola, Erasmus). But it was the selling of 'indulgences'—certificates claiming to forgive particular sins—to raise funds for rebuilding St Peter's in Rome which got under Martin Luther's theological skin. A variety of Reformations spread across Europe, each intertwined with national cultures and politics. Their leaders harshly criticised views of the eucharist, which they saw as undergirding practices like indulgences—the 'sacrifice of the mass'. Many refused to speak of clergy as 'priests', rejected the ministry of bishops (sometimes due to political circumstance), and reduced the deacon's ministry to a 'lay' one of practical administration.

The English Reformers were harshly critical of medieval abuse, but maintained the classic 'three-fold order' of bishop, priests and deacons, seeing these as embodying unfolding dimensions of responsibility for the gospel. In this context, it is significant that Archbishop Thomas Cranmer retained the term 'priest' in the *Book of Common Prayer*, rather than using 'presbyter' (as others Reformers and Richard Hooker did). It would seem that he did so out of a close reading of the First Testament, which sees a priest's primary task as "giving Torah"—interpreting the scriptures in ongoing pastoral contexts, often with a prophetic edge—rather than offering sacrifice.[6] Isaiah, Jeremiah and Ezekiel are alluded to in Cranmer's Ordinal as examples of what it means to be godly priests—"messengers, stewards and watchmen" of

---

6   This is why biblical scholars refer to much of Numbers and Leviticus as the 'Priestly Document', and the Graf-Wellhausen documentary hypothesis identified texts with a cultic interest as 'P'.

the Lord. The priests of Israel did supervise 'sacrifices', but these had little if anything to do with atonement (the distinctive ministry of the High Priest—see Leviticus 16). Rather, Israel's sacrificial system gave opportunities for God's people to offer 'three-dimensional prayers' of dedication, thanksgiving, humility and fellowship (see Leviticus 1–6). Each of these aspects is reflected in today's services of holy communion, without compromising the unique atoning work of Jesus Christ.

But the Reformers did not support an 'anything goes' attitude to ministry. They continued to maintain the classic position that presiding, preaching and leading public prayers belong to those called to ordained ministries. For the Church of England, Article XXIII (23), *Of Ministering in the Congregation*, states:

> It is not lawful for any man to take upon him the office of publick preaching, or ministering the Sacraments in the Congregation, before he be lawfully called, and sent to execute the same.

This stance raised few issues in the relatively 'hierarchical' societies of the past, in which each English person knew their 'place'. Further, while the three-fold 'order' of bishops, priests and deacons was retained in the Church of England, its 'reformation' focused on the ministry of priests, still presumed to be the central 'order' of ministry. Little if any reform was made to the complex 'growed like Topsy' patterns of English church life, whose structuring at local level remained largely unchanged: baptism or marriage records reveal few Reformation influences, for example. Structural reform took several centuries: until the 1830s Reform Acts, you had to be a member of the Church of England to go to university, join the Civil Service or be in Parliament, for example. It was *this* hierarchically-shaped Church of England that came to Australia on the First Fleet, and struggled to adapt the ordering of the 'mother country' to this new and very different land.

A note on terminology: 'lay', 'minister', 'member'

'Lay' is a difficult word when it comes to ministry. In everyday speech, it usually means 'unskilled', in contrast to one of the professions (typically law or medicine), but can also mean 'unpaid' rather than waged. In church use, however, it is generally used as the alternative to 'ordained'.[7] As such, 'lay ministry' is often (and unhelpfully) taken to refer to filling rosters 'in church', rather than calling all members of Christ (the *laos* of God, *including* the ordained) to live out their Christian vocations 'in the world'.

'Minister', especially when seen as the opposite of 'lay', also raises issues. In the New Testament, scholars argue that only those called and authorised to preach and teach (i.e. the 'ordained') are termed 'ministers'.[8] Such a conclusion rejects the fairly recent idea that each Christian is a 'minister', an idea (it is argued) that feeds into and out of the highly individualistic culture of modern western societies. Some church notice boards, for example, under the heading 'Ministers', say 'All members of the congregation'. This contrasts with the scriptural concept

---

[7] Despite the common use of the term 'lay' in recent decades, Anglican formularies rarely if ever employ it. It was the development from the 1850s of synods which include representatives of all the faithful which saw the term 'House of Laity' adopted (over against 'House of Clergy' and 'House of Bishops'). In 1992, the General Synod of the Anglican Church of Australia adopted a canon for 'Authorised Lay Ministry' (Canon 17), despite the urging of some that it be simply an 'Authorised Ministry' Canon.

[8] See for example John Collins, *Are All Christian Ministers?* (Melbourne: EJ Dwyer / Harper Collins, 1992). Grounded in a careful analysis of the New Testament evidence, his answer to the title question is 'no'.

of Christians-in-community being called *as a body* to 'ministry', in and for which each individual will make her or his distinctive contribution (so 1 Corinthians 12), as part of an interwoven cloth. The issue can be seen in another way by noting that while the Lutheran-originated idea of "the priesthood of all believers" is not inconsistent with the scriptures (though the phrase is nowhere found as such), "the priesthood of each believer" is not (especially when mixed up with sub-Christian notions of 'priest').

'Member'—how acceptable is this word for church use? A century ago in company law, a 'corporation' was defined as a group of 'members' who together acted as a single 'person'. (Note: 'corpus' is the Latin for body—so 'body corporate' is literally double-speak) As time passed, this use crossed over to clubs, so that today 'member' typically refers to someone joining a group of like-minded people. Thinking of being a 'church member' in such terms is highly problematic. It focuses on my individual choice to attend the congregation of my 'worship style' preference (rather than my response to God's call), and assumes that church is a gathering of the like-minded (rather than diverse people in communion with Christ). In contrast, Paul wrote, "For just as the body is one and has many members, and all the members of the body, though many, are one body, so it is with *Christ*"—**not** "with church" (1 Corinthians 12.12). 'Member' here has the old-fashioned sense of 'organ' or 'limb'—a body-part organically linked into, and inseparable from, the whole. As members of Christ we belong inseparably to one another, however difficult this may be, rather than to our religious club (until it does not meet my needs).

'Order' in today's Australia: every member ministry?

Since the middle of the 19th century, Australians have experienced democratic ideas sweep across politics, mass media flourish, Anglo-Irish dominance be complemented by multi-cultural lifestyles, gender relations shift and 'instant' electronic communication arrive. A growing outcome of these changes was 'lay ministry' coming to play a key part in many congregations' self-understanding. Paul's image of church as 'body of Christ'—the only metaphor without First Testament roots, incidentally—came to be applied to local congregations rather than to the church universal, supporting the idea of 'every-member ministry'. Its positive side, that each Christian has a God-given calling and responsibility to contribute to the well being of their congregation and the wider community, was much needed. Not a few churchgoers saw their priest/minister/pastor as paid to do the 'spiritual' work, lived in unhealthy dependence on him, and believed that 'father knows best' and/or that utterances from the pulpit were 'six foot above contradiction'. More deeply, as churches and western societies gradually pulled apart from the 1960s, the importance of "equipping the saints, for the work of ministry" (Ephesians 4:11–12) became more significant for healthy church life.[9]

---

[9] Until the late 19th century, deacons were almost all ordained priest after a year. The 'deaconess' order emerged in part as a response to the dark side of the Industrial Revolution, in part as women came to be accepted as able to engage in public life beyond the home. After World War II, partly in reaction to 'triumphalist' views of the church that identified Christian mission too closely with colonial attitudes, a revival of diaconal ministries came about in several Christian traditions, including parts of the Anglican Communion. This was typically understood as a 'serving' ministry of care, however, rather than around the New Testament's emphasis on *diakonia* as an 'ambassadorial' ministry of evangelism, equipping and social advocacy. Barnett's historically valuable book remains within the 'serving' paradigm; more recent studies focus around the work of John Collins, summarised in his *Deacons in the Church* (Leominster: Gracewing / Harrisburg: Morehouse, 2002) chapter 1. This latter approach is seen in The Church of England General Synod report, *For such a time as this. A renewed diaconate in the Church of England* (London: Church House, 2001), and the Ordinal for Deacons in *APBA*.

A consequence was that a typical Sunday service came to have more parts taken by other than ordained leaders. Today, from Roman Catholic to charismatic congregations, ministries previously undertaken by the ordained are commonly offered by others—scripture readings, intercessions and the administration of holy communion in particular. But not all ministries. In the Anglican Communion, discussion of the ordination of women led to debate about which words and actions were reserved for the one who presides at the eucharist (priests or bishop)—the 'ABC' of absolution, blessing and consecration.[10] This ultra-functional focus on 'who does/says what' fosters attitudes that detract from healthy church life, the practice of love in community—and gives space to 'lay presidency' ideas (most notably the Anglican Diocese of Sydney). An over-emphasis on 'democratic' ideas of participation can lead to resentment being felt towards clergy—or to those who seem to get on the roster too often. The key ministry of public reading from the scriptures can be done badly, while 'common prayer' can descend into 'gossip before God'.

As always, words matter—and intentions more. The motives behind speaking of 'every member ministry' and 'lay involvement' derive from fresh readings of the scriptures, in the light of cultural changes towards a more 'democratic' ethos in western societies. But these genuine responses also reflect the problematic side of modern times—rampant individualism, the undermining of legitimate authority and the retreat from seeing life from a worldview grounded in Christian faith. Today it is almost impossible not to think of "corporate worship being corporately led" (the slogan

---

10   Interestingly, at particular points in the *Book of Common Prayer* each of these three actions would seem to be able to be exercised by other than the ordained, notably Baptism (consecration of the water), the Visitation of the Sick (absolution of the penitent) and Solemnisation of Holy Matrimony (blessing of the couple). But making such 'picky points' does not address the deeper issues ...

used for student teams leading services in Ridley College chapel). But this means that those who are 'upfront' (ordained or not) need to have some understanding of the ministries in which they are involved, and have appropriate skilling to fulfil them creatively, "to the glory of God and the upbuilding of God's people" (the twin aims of Christian liturgy—sanctification and edification).

Part B Performing the gospel by presiding

Performing the gospel engages each Christian present in a service: the 'assembly' (*ekklesia*) is not just an audience, but a 'con-gregation', a 'flocking-together' (the root meaning of the Latin). Each Christian is called to participate actively in performing the gospel. But *how* each participates will depend on factors like their personality, ethnic identity, cultural tastes, education, relationships with others, mother tongue—and Christian maturity. No service can encompass everyone's individual preferences, so some 'give and take' is needed.

Perhaps this is why the distinctive New Testament image for church is 'body of Christ', in which each Christian is a living part, an organic member, though as different as ears, eyes, hands, teeth and our private parts. Further, this image shows us why a church service is not like a concert performance, which some might enjoy and others not. "If one member suffers, all suffer together with the body; if one member is honoured, all rejoice together with it," Paul teaches (1 Corinthians 12.26). So in Christian worship—whether in liturgy or life—we are not just isolated individuals who happen to be doing similar things in the same place (a collective), though sometimes we might sit like that. Nor are we just an audience watching others perform, though this is sometimes how services are run. Rather, we engage in *corporate* (body) activity, in which different 'members' offer distinctive contributions (see 1 Corinthians 14.26).

What does this mean for those called to take 'upfront' roles, especially presiding? A good place to start is with a reminder of the responsibilities involved. The Ordinal in *APBA* describes them like this:

> You are to encourage and build up the body of Christ, preaching the word of God, leading God's people in prayer, declaring God's forgiveness and blessing, and faithfully ministering the sacraments of God's grace with reverence and care.

This is a weighty calling, not least because the intention is that something might *happen* in Christian liturgy—that God's people encounter God, and be changed.[11]

The dialogue of initiative and response

Presiding, however, is not a one-(wo)man band ministry. It calls for other ministers, and happens within the body of Christ. Sunday services in *A Prayer Book for Australia* open with the heading 'Gathering in God's Name'. We do not gather because it is our idea—it is more than just the 'Gathering of the People' (see Chapter Nine, Part B). We are gathered by God, called into God's own presence 'dripping wet', as people baptised into the divine Name. Our 'democratic' culture fosters the idea that anyone can take an upfront role in performing the gospel in church. But a congregation is more than a shapeless mass of individuals who have chosen this Sunday morning to exercise their particular choice of religious franchise. Rather, as we say in the communion service, "We are

---

11 A classic text on presiding is Robert Hovda, *Strong, Loving and Wise. Presiding in Liturgy* (Collegeville MN: Liturgical Press, 1976), though oriented to fairly 'high culture' contexts.

the body of Christ"—and bodies have structures, sinews, heads and toes: a body is 'ordered'. The body of Christ has a head, the Lord Jesus, whose ministry is represented by those called to embody the gospel through ordination.

This (counter-cultural) stance has scriptural grounding—the term 'minister' (*diakonos*) is only used there in relation to believers authorised to take up such tasks. 'Ordered' ministry involves more than filling out a roster, as if anyone could be that week's ears, eyes, prophets, revealers or singers (see 1 Corinthians 14). It reflects a vision of the shape (economy) of God's people, led by Christ our head, through the Spirit. This is the ideal set out in the *Book of Common Prayer*, Ordinal and Articles, where the 'clergy'—the 'called-out ones'—bear responsibility to ensure that God's people are gathered, taught, fed and equipped for ministry. But this position does not see ordained ministry as a plain oneness: clergy are not all the same, even though in practice this is how they are viewed and act. Rather, each is called to one or more forms of the concentric, threefold ordering of Christian ministry, as deacon, and/or priest, and/or bishop. Taking this variety seriously avoids the dangers in treating clergy as an undifferentiated 'profession'.

So how does this variety work out? A twofold 'call and response' ethos lies at its heart, as we shall see. But the primary responsibility for ministry belongs to the bishop who presides over the 'local church' (the diocese). In performing the gospel, the presider represents God's initiative: speaking God's words of greeting, forgiveness, peace and blessing, and presiding over the ministries of scripture and supper.

A note on traditional ministry terminology

As noted earlier, this responsibility to preside on a Christian congregation came to be delegated to a local priest, as the bishop's delegate (vicar), given authority (as rector) for the 'cure of souls' in a particular locality (parish). This structure remained in place across the Christian West for a thousand or more years, including the Reformation and beyond. It is adapting, as the West becomes more a mission-field than a ministered society. But the principle that the bishop or priest delegate presides remains—as does the (mistaken) notion that presiding is primarily the ministry of the priest rather than bishop.

The term 'pastor' has come to be used for ordained ministers in some traditions, typically those that do not include bishops. 'Pastor' is the Greek term for 'shepherd', used in the New Testament of Christ (John 10.11; Hebrews 13.10; 1 Peter 2.25, 5.4; Revelation 7.17). It is not used for Christian leaders, but is employed once as a verb to describe the work of *episcopoi*, (Acts 20.28). In episcopal traditions it is usually applied to the bishop, but not other clergy.

Complementing the ministry of presiding is the calling of deacon(s), to enable our response to the gospel: leading us in confessing sin and faith, inspiring our prayers, gathering the offertory, preparing the Lord's table, and sending us to worship in daily life.

The *dialogue* of presiding/enabling (episcopal/diaconal) reflects the divine conversation and communion of Father, Spirit, Son. It embodies the *participatory* nature of leading, and points to a *responsive* ethos for performing the gospel (at any service, not just holy communion). On the one hand, the presider embodies God's initiative in gathering, addressing and coming to us. On the other hand, the deacon enables and focuses our response in prayer and offering. This does not mean that there has to be two clergy for a service to take place (which is a requirement in Eastern churches). Rather, it points up the theological as well as cultural validity of the variety of ordained ministries, and "corporate worship being corporately led".

This understanding of who should lead also provides an antidote to the danger of the 'one-(wo)man band' (high, charismatic, low or whatever). This temptation faces many clergy, especially when there is just one ordained minister in a congregation, and there seem to be few people suited to being 'upfront'. It is always easy to impose your ideas, or fail to use others' insights and skills. Dependent attitudes easily develop—after all, it is nice to have people 'need' you. There are situations, in small rural churches for example, where the minister has to do the preparing and take much of the service.

The classical threefold pattern of ordered ministry, understood as a form of 'dialogue' leading, points to a better way. Yet this traditional position, that presiding belongs to the bishop/priest, can lead to 'controlling' behaviour by clergy—and not a few Christians like being dependent, and enjoy a 'father/mother knows best' clergy style. But the 'people of God' is then reduced to being an audience for 'worship leaders' to work on, or mere spectators of clerical sport. Such 'clericalism' and dependence-seeking should play no part in Christian community life. In reaction against it, however, some clergy refuse to accept the responsibilities that come with being called to lead. Whether you like it or not, being 'upfront' means that ideas about God, church, Bible, life and so on will be placed on you by some—what scholars call 'transference'. Which leads into thinking about how personality affects ministry.

Presiding: service flow and feel

In my younger days I spent part a dozen or more summer holidays on beach mission teams. One daily activity was holding a children-friendly service on the beach on top of a large, gaily decorated pile of sand known as 'the pulpit'. There were two cardinal rules for anyone upfront. The first was this: NEVER wear sunglasses, no matter how glaring the sun. The point was not to encourage sight problems, but to let children see your eyes, your person. The second was easier on the eyes, but harder to keep: NEVER leave the pulpit empty. A child's attention span is short, and loss of continuity loosens their focus on what is going on. These two lessons burnt their way into my psyche.

Sometimes a service feels like a rabble. You don't really have a sense of where things are headed, and there is little 'flow'. A series of people appear upfront, in varying styles of dress, some speaking formally, others chatting on—you become irritated and disjointed. What is wrong? Possibly a number of things: but it is likely that (in beach mission terms) "the pulpit was left empty". The presiding was sloppy, non-existent, or had no sense of the flow of what was going on. The presider had abdicated responsibility, and the gathering had descended to become just another (ineffective) meeting. Another service may be beautifully ordered, every step, movement, verbal and symbolic nuance carefully planned, but lifeless, mechanical, rigid. Here it is likely that "the sunglasses were left on": the presider's personality was so hidden, perhaps out of respect for the objectivity of faith, that Christ was presented more like a moving statue than "truly human".

So presiding means more than 'leading'. To preside means enacting in a *personal* way the primacy of grace, that God takes the initiative towards us—we love God only because God first loved us (I John 4.10). Without the personal, purposeful love of God reaching out to enable it, our worship is mere activity. And without God's Word being spoken to us face to face, in a connected manner, our hearing, singing and speaking degenerate into a mere succession of theological terms or spiritual jargon. Effective presiding combines these things into a coherent whole. It effects the personal representation of Christ *to* us, and the enabling of response *by* us in a corporate way. We *feel* the gospel being performed.

Such a view tries to avoid two extremes: the "list of concert items" style of service, and the "master of ceremonies" approach to leading. The first lacks shape, continuity, flow: the "pulpit is empty"—the *organic* character of the body of Christ is forgotten. It is a danger into which more 'evangelical' ministers easily fall. The second extreme sees leading without feeling: the "sunglasses are left on"— the *communal* nature of the people of God has been suppressed. This is a trap for more 'catholic' clergy.

A note on terminology: in persona Christi, in loco Christi

A classical way of expressing the presider's call to represent God's initiative is the Latin expression *in persona Christi*— acting the part of Christ (*persona* means 'actor'). The truth represented here is that the presider plays a *representative* role: representing Christ to the people, and the people to God. You might question this doctrinally—it runs against our 'democratic' grain—but it recognises that we instinctively 'transfer' our ideas about God onto whoever leads a service (and vice versa). Which is scary!

This awesome responsibility is easily distorted into thinking that the minister somehow stands 'in the place' of Christ (*in loco Christi*), so that whatever they say or do is Christ's way. Luther railed against this corrupt idea when it emerged in the late Middle Ages, initially in relation to the 'sacrifice of the mass'. But the temptation to act *in loco Christi* continues—to give an example, for Protestant preachers to act like God in the pulpit.

In sum, Christian ministers are called to perform the gospel as Christ's *representatives* (*in persona Christi*), but not *substitutes* for Christ (*in loco Christi*).

Part C   Person and perfomance

Being upfront: what do you sound like?

What effect do you have on other people? Appreciating this matters a great deal when taking an upfront part in performing the gospel—whether in church or beyond. It means taking seriously your own personality, typical ways of behaving, your tastes in music, your cultural preferences, how your voice is heard. (Tools such as Myers-Briggs or the Enneagram are useful here—to learn about yourself, not to analyse others.)

Think how you walk from your seat to read from the Bible, for example. You might be thinking about pronouncing a difficult word correctly, wanting to avoid a 'parsonic' tone or speaking too fast. But the *way* you walk will already signal something about you, even though no one seems to notice (which is good). And how you walk will depend on the situation: a casual stroll to the lectern in a church packed for a funeral can cause offence, but will be right on the money for a youth service. Likewise, if when you speak you never look at those listening, it may be read as indifference or even arrogance. How you use your hands is important, too: presiders who look awkward when giving the peace, or raising hands for blessing, distract from the meaning of these actions. Looking embarrassed (or bossy) when handling the bread and wine at holy communion will communicate questioning (or over-confident) attitudes to this ministry of the gospel.

Our bodies 'speak' about us all the time, as every actor knows well. So, if you are called to take a public part in performing the gospel, be aware of your 'body language'. Ministers do so not only through 'public' means—baptising, reading the scriptures, preaching, interceding, presiding—but also through who they are as an embodied woman or man. My performance is affected deeply by how my body and voice communicates—the 'language' of my person, my 'sound'. The *musicality* as well as meaning of my words—my accent, natural pitch, timbre and rhythm—interacts with how they are received. The intercessions in *BCP*'s Holy Communion service thus pray for 'bishops and curates' that they "might by their *life* and doctrine [i.e. teaching] set forth God's holy and lively Word, and rightly and duly administer his holy sacraments."

The way I speak aloud is part of my personality—my accent reflects my upbringing, education, work context, favourite music and the like. When performing the gospel, the words need to be 'hearable'—whether reading the scriptures, leading in prayer, preaching, presiding or giving the notices. A variety of accents in a service speaks of God's delight in creative variety: but changing my natural way of speaking to a 'parsonic' tone sounds forced, 'churchy'. Making adjustments is sometimes necessary, however: the year I lived in the USA, unless I said words such as 'lace' like 'less', I was heard as saying 'lice'! I learnt to slow down, and stop running my Australian words into one another.

In sum, *we minister as embodied persons*. Taking this seriously matters even more today than in earlier ages. In our sound-surround, visually dominant culture, the gospel is judged even more by how it is performed. Yes, 'personality' can be overdone to the point where the minister gets in the way of the gospel. But performing in such an 'objective' way that the gospel comes across as an impersonal 'thing' is just as bad.

Being upfront: what do you look like?

One Sunday morning the family has a row over breakfast, and you say some things you regret. But you have a full day ahead, starting with an early service. You rush to church feeling particularly hypocritical because your sermon is on peace-making. You are caught between being a person and being the 'parson'. How do you cope?

A way in to this classic dilemma is dress. How I dress says a great deal about the way I understand myself, and my relationship to others. In daily life, knowing when casual or formal attire is appropriate matters. In working life, uniforms are often required: apart from possible practical need, they level out social and personal differences, give brand recognition, and can build a sense of team solidarity. When I put on my uniform, my personal traits remain, but become sublimated to my work-life identity. However bad my home-life might be, at work what matters is how I perform—which is very helpful when you are to lead a church service but feel anything but good about it.

In the Christian tradition, two major forms of clergy dress have emerged—for public wearing, and in church. Clergy public dress has changed over the generations, and no church law governs it, though some bishops may stipulate requirements in their diocese. In England, medieval cassocks gave way to 16–17th century 'collar tabs', then white floppy ties, and 'dog-collars' from the mid-19th century: in recent decades lapel crosses or a pendant cross have come into use. Clergy should be readily identifiable when visiting hospital, in civic emergencies, or simply to 'show the faith' around the community. But sometimes wearing a collar can strengthen the common idea that clergy are not 'normal' people, shutting them off from being taken seriously.

Anglican formularies and church law require clergy normally to be robed while engaging in public ministry. This is questioned today in some circles: it is argued (rightly) that clergy can 'hide' behind robes, or that distinctive dress puts up barriers to others—even to people seeking God. But even in Christian traditions where clergy are not required to dress distinctively, most adopt some style of 'uniform'. Among Anglicans, sharp debate has taken place about what robes are permissible, since some were taken to signify ideas about ministry contrary to the gospel. For Australian Anglicans, this issue has been set to rest by General Synod, whose 1992/1995 Canon states that it "does not attach any particular doctrinal significance to the diversity of vesture worn by its ministers."

So, here are a few considerations in favour of robes.

a) Robes indicate that ministers act as *representative* people: they set a 'distance' between you as a particular person, and as someone called to perform the gospel. And robes can help you keep going when feeling 'down', or when relationships are difficult.

b) Robes are a tangible sign that those called to perform the gospel do so in a tradition that stretches backwards (and forwards) from our day. Traditional designs derive from the court dress of earlier ages, but today's robes are cut in a 'timeless' style, which transcends particular fashions—the ecumenical 'cassalb' is a good example.

c) Weddings, baptisms and funerals will often have non-churchgoers present: at such occasions, robes allow them to identify who is the minister. When emotions run deep, s/he is then more readily able to be the 'still point' in a whirling sea, the 'God-person' whose performance of the gospel points to realities beyond the immediate present.

d) As a uniform, robes are a great 'leveller', removing differences of (sub)culture or class, economic circumstance or dress sense, and help build bridges across these.

e) Robes can bring a splash of colour and liveliness to a drab situation, mark the 'mood' of the occasion, and illuminate the church year.

Note: a good dressmaker or tailor will see to it that garments fit comfortably, 'hang' and wear well, and resist soiling.

The crucial issue is the quality of the ministry offered, more than the robes worn. But this is inevitably tied up with how you are seen: dress that is neat, clean and avoids undue show does not get in the way of the gospel.

Being upfront: person and office

I was once on a Princess cruise ship, on a deck normally used by the crew. Being a curious type, I could not resist reading a notice with the heading 'Passenger relationships'. The first of ten points read, "Remember, when you are with a passenger, you ARE Princess Cruises." What a great reminder of what it means to represent Christ when performing the gospel.

This is what the classical distinction between who I am as a 'person', and the part I play in performing the gospel in public—my 'office'—is all about. And it applies to more than just clergy. Think of welcomers: how you look, your body language, the words used as you greet people, the way you respond to questions (Where are the toilets? Can my child run about a bit?')—all these reflect something of your identity as a Christian. Think of the intercessions: 'common prayer' is about more than what matters to the person praying. A Sunday service is not a prayer meeting, where those present will know one another well, and can pray at length about personal concerns. Leading public prayer involves taking up an 'office' role. Whether or not it involves reading a script or praying *ex tempore*, it is most helpful when prepared thoughtfully, taking account of events beyond immediate congregational concerns, disciplined in length, and with eyes open to God's wide mission.

In sum, 'person' and 'office' are interwoven but distinct. How our personal identity comes across when performing the gospel says a good deal about what is being performed. The ways we move around, speak, dress, use our eyes and feet, shake hands—all these matter.

What does all this mean for performing the gospel in church? Be open to some training and feedback—being videoed can bring surprises. Be open to learning from how you and others see one another, and willing to reflect together on how who you are as a person interacts with how the gospel is performed among you.

Part D   A performance audit

This exercise can be undertaken individually, or by a small group (e.g. a liturgy planning committee). Since it concerns their ministry responsibilities, the rector/vicar/minister needs to know it is happening.

Making brief notes in response to each question will enable you to engage more fully with the final, summary question. The group might like to write down its concluding answer and share it with the rector/vicar/minister, and then the Parish Council.

1. Think back over the last 4–6 weeks of services in your congregation.
   Who took an 'upfront' role? How many people are we talking about?
   In what ways did they work together? What 'dialogue' took place among them?
2. Close your eyes, and think about the 'sound' of those 'upfront'.
   Could you hear what was spoken aloud?
   How natural was the tone of voice used?

What variety was there among the voices/accents heard? To what extent did this reflect the make-up of the congregation/wider community?

What silences took place? How helpful or embarrassing were they?

Is there anything you would suggest about improving the 'sound quality'?

3a. If you were the presider, how comfortable did you feel in moving and acting (especially in relation to the eucharist)?

What was most helpful about the way others 'upfront' ministered with you?

How do you receive feedback?

What would you like to change or work on?

3b. If you were not the presider, how comfortable were you about how the service was led?

What was most helpful? Was there a missed opportunity? Anything irritating?

How appropriate was each service's 'flow'? How 'rigid' was the performance?

In what way(s) can you make helpful feedback?

4. Close your eyes, and think about what you could *see* in a typical service.

What was noticeable in the body language used by those upfront, if anything?

How appropriate was it to the various contributions made?

What was most helpful about the service's visual aspects?

How effective were any colours, symbols, robes, banners—or deliberate absence?

On a scale of 1 to 7, how messy or neat was the space?
How far does your 'score' correspond to the lifestyles or culture of those present?
What (low cost) changes might enable the gospel to be performed more effectively?

5. Think about your congregation. Who typically takes parts in 'upfront' performance?
What affirmation of their ministries do you believe would encourage them?
What skills training might be of benefit?
Are there others (particularly from different cultural backgrounds) whom you believe could be called to 'upfront' ministry?
If so, what type of preparation would be appropriate for them, for other leaders—and for the congregation?

Overall, in what ways do you believe that how the gospel is performed 'upfront' in your congregation assists or hinders its ministry in personal and community daily life?

Chapter Four
The words of gospel performance

Overview

Part A   concentrates on the ways words work in worship—the 'theory' behind Parts B and C. And since God's nature is beyond words, how can we speak truly at all of divine things?

Part B   focuses on the language typically encountered 'in church', and reflects on some that has come to bother many today, notably gender terms and war-words.

Part C   gets you looking at how words work in worship.

In the musical *My Fair Lady,* Professor Henry Higgins makes a lady out of cockney Eliza Doolittle by teaching her to speak with a 'toffy' English accent. He succeeds, brilliantly—but Eliza receives no credit for her success 'playing the lady' at a high-class ball. She finally takes out her anger on her suitor Freddy, shouting that she's sick of words because it's all she hears all day long, and wondering if that's all 'you blighters' can do?

    Worship involves far more than words, but it is hard to worship without them. Without words there would be no script to be performed to the glory of God. Yet any attempt to speak of God touches on profound mystery, stretching the limits of human expression—which is partly why 'church' language is often not the way people speak in ordinary conversation. As well as seeking to help worshippers engage with eternal realities, the words used in a service will be spoken aloud, and require rhythms that will work when said together. Some Christians say that the words typically used in church are too complex; some look for the freedom to speak without using written texts; others argue that the language of liturgy should retain a sense of reverent dignity.[1]

The challenge is to find language that worshippers can use readily, but which stretches them to reach beyond the words employed. And language keeps changing—especially English, which is spoken in so many different places and ways. Social media means that new words spread rapidly, as does the way words are arranged (syntax) and the rules of order they follow (grammar). Fashions come and go: the hottest phrase to some is just jargon to others. In particular, three major cultural changes have come about in the past 50 years—the use of inclusive gendered language, sensitivity to war-words, and the growing gap between 'church' culture and that of the wider world. More on these later—but first a look at how words work generally.

Part A   Ways words work

There is something fascinating about words. We use words to speak of the wonders of the natural world, tell stories and jokes, order fish and chips or express our deepest feelings. As Paul writes about prayer, "The Spirit helps us in our weakness; for we do not know how to pray as we ought, but that very Spirit intercedes with sighs

---

[1] See further Juliette Day, 'Language', in Juliette Day & Benjamin Gordon-Taylor (edd), *The Study of Liturgy and Worship* (London: SPCK/Alcuin, 2013) 65-73.

too deep for words" (Romans 8:26). We use words to name things: but that only accounts for nouns. Words do more than just name our world—they help to form it. People may want to refer to humans generally as 'men', for example, because they don't want their world changed—or they can insist on using inclusive language because their world *has* changed.

And what of verbs, adverbs, adjectives, not to mention the way we put them together in sentences? We can tell when a sentence is *spoken* sarcastically—but how do we detect this when we *read* it? What is happening with words when someone makes a promise or a threat or a shout or a curse? Words not only form and inform, they can *do* things—what linguists call 'performative language'.[2] A shout expresses delight (great, awesome), surprise (wow, oh my goodness), agony (aargh); a threat makes you feel under pressure; a joke releases laughter; a command brings about action. Words represent meanings that transcend their face value content, and convey more than their literal sense—that is how poetry works. Sports commentators love to use rich metaphors to describe the action—'he just punted the red cherry a mile, right through the big sticks' will make no sense unless you follow Australian Rules football. The Christian gospel is performed for everyone, so the words used in a service need to be as accessible as possible.

The words used by Jesus

Prophets, psalmists, evangelists, visionaries, those who contributed to Israel's folk traditions and penned the wisdom writings and letters—all employ a wealth of imagery and literary techniques to communicate the word of the Lord. The doctrine of the incarnation teaches that the eternal Word of God, the self-expression of God's

---

2   See J.L. Austen, *How to do things with words* (second edition, OUP, 1975).

own being, took on our human nature in Jesus to express the inexpressible in our frail mortal flesh.

Yet—according to the New Testament—Jesus' characteristic way of speaking about God was indirect. When asked a question, Jesus typically responded with a question, deflecting uncommitted discussion of his identity, and tangling opponents in exegetical nets (see Mark 12.35–37, for example). He rarely used techniques like metaphor, simile or analogy, and the stories he told were in parable rather than in direct form (John 16.25 is interesting here). These drew on the life experience of his hearers, and were highly memorable—yet they hide as much as they reveal. Parables resist being summed up in a neat proposition: trying to explain a parable is like trying to explain a joke—the very attempt means that neither the teller nor the hearer 'gets it'. Enjoying a joke requires hearers to enter its world and its assumptions, only to find themselves laughing when the incongruence of their usual presumptions and experience is revealed. And it's just like that with parables.

That the Lord Jesus Christ, the Word of God incarnate, pronounced the words of God in parables has profound significance for Christian worship. His manner of speech both hid and revealed. So, while the words we use in liturgy need to be accessible, they must be more than 'plain', or their meaning will be earth-bound. The example of Jesus is important here: parables spare us from the cataclysm of hearing God's words directly. Yet for those who jump naively into the stories they tell, or for those who wrestle with their mysteries, and perhaps especially those who, like the twelve, remain puzzled but just stick around listening to Jesus—to such as these is disclosed something of the *mysterion*, the sacrament, of the kingdom of God disclosed in Christ's person and presence. This gives a clue as to how words work in Christian liturgy—and in *APBA* in particular.

Words and the Word:[3] 'sacraments of meaning'

Daily life is shot through with outward and visible signs of light-hearted and practical as well as deeper realities—acts of mercy, a loving kiss, signatures on cheques, greetings between friends, seals on contracts, football anthems, logos on business cards, and so on. Behind this is the reality that we live in a 'sacramental universe', one whose outward and visible nature points to inward and spiritual reality. Finite creatures cannot know directly our infinite Creator, who delights to communicate with us through material signs that signify divine realities, and enable us to receive them. In formal terms, this is the 'sacramental principle'. The Catechism in *APBA*, closely based on that in the *Book of Common Prayer*, describes a sacrament as "an outward and visible sign of an inward and spiritual grace, given to us by Christ himself, as a means by which we receive that grace, and a pledge to assure us of this" (page 817).

In Christian life, baptism and the holy communion have a special place, as 'sacraments of the gospel', signifying the death and resurrection of Christ, and communicating their benefits. Other sign-acts may be 'commonly called sacraments' (as Article XXV puts it), signifying consequences of the gospel: the laying on of hands as confirming a person's baptism; the reconciliation of a penitent as applying the truth of the gospel at the personal level; ordination as calling some to be 'walking sacraments' who "may both by their life and doctrine set forth God's true and lively Word"; married life as symbolising the union between Christ and his body; and anointing (unction) as a means of Christ's life-giving power being communicated in the face of death.

A helpful approach to words is to think of them as 'sacraments of meaning': outward signs of deeper realities. This is especially

---

3   See further Charles Sherlock, *Words and the Word*, chapter one.

so of the words of Jesus recorded in the scriptures, and indeed of the scriptures as a whole (see Chapter 5). As linguistic signs, words represent and communicate realities that transcend their immediate meaning—as is evidently the case in poetry. The idea is taken more widely in post-modern concern that words reflect the 'interest' of their authors: lest they impose totalitarian meanings on hearers, words must not be thought of as conveying any direct meaning. At worst, this 'ultra-protestant' reading reflects a lack of trust that any meaning can truly be shared between speaker–writer and hearer–reader. As Derrida's famous term *differance* expresses it, in every linguistic sign there is both an 'is' and an 'is not' in relation to what is signified. This alerts us to the presence of 'interest' whenever words are used: to what extent do we shape (consciously or otherwise) our words so as to shut off possibilities, pull the wool over hearers' ears, or simply manipulate them? This is a highly relevant issue when it comes to the words used in church.

Most people, however, assume that words communicate straightforwardly what they signify (recall Humpty Dumpty in *Alice in Wonderland*). Yet it is impossible to know 'the truth, the whole truth and nothing but the truth' in any statement. You may get what you think I am saying, but you cannot grasp entirely my nuances, associations and motivations. Even so, some continuity between utterance and hearing must be presumed in our common life, or we would never communicate with one another.

These contrasting viewpoints represent two contrasting errors. On the one hand, stressing too much the inadequacy of words to speak of God undermines the 'ministry of the Word': formally, this separates what is signified (meaning) from the sign (words) and empties a sacrament of value (the 'ultra-academic' danger). On the other hand, assuming that words ARE their meaning runs the risk of focusing on them rather than the Lord: formally, identifying the sacramental sign (words) with what it signifies (meaning) runs the risk of idolatry (the 'fundamentalist' danger). Sacraments—and sacramental words—'work' as a means of grace, not as automatically effective; through faith, not the certainty of sight; and in personal rather than impersonal ways.

Seeing words as the outward signs of what they represent, by which we can participate in what they signify, albeit partially, views them as 'sacraments of meaning'. Regarded in this way, the words used in worship can help bring to life the performance of the script. This approach respects post-modern suspicions about language being employed to define, dominate and exclude. Yet it affirms that words can describe, serve and include, and thus do their speaker-intended work of communication. They enable us to participate in reality, as 'pledges' of meaning that assure us we are not being puzzled by gibberish, but engaging in authentic, if always partial, communication. They are not 'neutral', and while they do much good, they can also bring great harm when abusive, used to bear false witness or deceive. Their performance affects our sense of identity as well as effecting communication—and especially so when we gather as church to engage with God.

Words: affective and effective

When performed in prayer or song, it is the way words work 'inside' our hearts and minds that really matters. Heart-familiar imagery gives voice to, and shapes, our subconscious attitudes, especially when divorced from the realities of daily living: they become 'spiritual'. So 'shepherd' imagery, while having little relation to most people's life experience today, is widely used in public to address God, especially at funerals (via Psalm 23). This 'primary' level of spiritual understanding engages and shapes the 'godly ruts' formed over the years by our participation in liturgy. This inchoate, unconscious level includes our emotional responses, aesthetic senses, folk-religious taboos, and will have elements of both light and dark, ignorance and purity.

The 'secondary' level is our conscious reflection on the gospel and Christian life.[4] This can happen when we are bothered about an accepted belief, or realise that we have little idea of what is meant in something said or sung. One level is not 'better' than another—both are just 'there'. The secondary level may not be as influential as the primary, but without it is easy to slip into mere formalism or superstition (the 'nominal' risk). On the other hand, if all that happens in church for me is at the 'secondary' level, then only my mind is engaged, and I am in danger of worship being 'wordy' rather than a means of grace, the language being a *sacramental* word (the 'academic' danger).

But the whole business is subtle: words that are fine in themselves can work against their surface meaning, producing a 'dissonance' between their 'primary' and 'secondary' references—think of what 'Onward Christian soldiers' conveys in different circumstances. Language can thus be 'socially dysfunctional'—what words *actually* communicate (intentional or otherwise) can conflict with their straightforward meaning. At the personal level, it is an instructive exercise to note the metaphors used by people when praying using their own words (*ex tempore*), particularly in settings where they feel 'at home' and can express themselves naturally. When only 'nice' images of God recur, the sheer danger of "falling into the hands of the living God" may be sublimated to middle-class comfortable values, even spiritual consumerism. Conversely, when 'overcome', 'put down', 'pin the devil to the wall, Lord' or even 'help us go for

---

4   Aidan Kavanagh, *Elements of Rite: A Handbook of Liturgical Style* (Pueblo, 1982) elucidates these categories, now standard in liturgical studies.

the jugular' images dominate, the signs are there that the heart is shaped by a militaristic mindset.

The images used in performing the gospel in church—in prayer, preaching, off the cuff comments, even the notices—say a lot about our actual understanding of God. They reveal our 'primary' theology, the 'godly ruts' formed over the years of life experience and spiritual practice. This contains elements of light, shade and darkness, ignorance and purity, alongside deep commitment and love of God, personal theological hobbyhorses, bits of folk-religion, and semi-superstitious notions. Most of us operate 'in church' (of whatever kind) at this 'primary' level, unless jarred by something extraneous—which is often necessary, the importance of the 'secondary' level.

The words used in public prayer and song are more than mere statements—they *do* things.[5] They are *effective* as well as *affective*. In fact, apart from the scripture readings and sermon, most of the words used in church are 'doing' words, expressing commitments and evoking emotions.[6] Think about the ways in which typical service elements work—greetings greet, offerings offer, blessings bless. Confessions enact repentance, absolutions pronounce God's forgiveness, 'Amen' joins us in praising and interceding, responses engage us in dialogue, dismissals send us out. And when they are done poorly, or even in ways that distort God's truth, these doing words can do great harm.

---

5   See further J. Lebon, *How to Understand the Liturgy* (SCM, 1986) chapters 11, 14, 15, 23.

6   Ideas for the public reading of the scriptures can be found in the next chapter.

Part B   Issues with words

The story of the tower of Babel depicts the confusion of human languages as one aspect of God's judgement on sinful human pride (Genesis 11:1-9). And this judgement can be seen at work amongst those who speak the same language. Most of us have been to meetings where enthusiasts for such things as a hobby, composer or sport do not realise how little others understand of their 'in' jargon. With words we can exclude or include others: the Babel curse still operates. Words can be used to make others feel fools, uncultured, or simply unwanted. Sadly, this sort of thing can and does happen among Christians. It ought not to be so: those in Christ have received the Holy Spirit, through whom the end of the Babel curse was seen on the day of Pentecost (Acts 2:1-11). Yet we await the time when it is fully abolished. In the meantime, James tells us, "the tongue is a fire": it can warm and burn, heal and hurt, bless and curse (James 3:1-10).

Gendered words in worship

A contemporary issue is gendered language. Until the late 20th century, 'man' and 'men' were used generically to refer to men and women alike: so in the *BCP* version of the Nicene Creed we confess "For us men and for our salvation [the Son] came down from heaven". But for a generation or more this has been problematic: most English speakers today hear 'men' as not including women. The point is made neatly in the comment, "When a man looks in the mirror he sees a human being; when a woman does so, she sees a woman." And when some Christians are offended by the words used in church, it is not good enough merely to say "that's their problem": whatever is another Christian's problem is to some extent mine. As Paul wrote, "If one member suffers, all suffer together; if one member is honoured, all rejoice together" (1 Corinthians 12:26). Modern liturgical books (including *APBA*) therefore employ words that include all Christians present: the ecumenical translation of the Creed, for example, reads "for us and for our salvation".[7]

But just saying 'people' all the time when we mean 'men and women' gets boring—and fails to 'make visible' that both sexes are there. It is better to name the variety of those present: so the *New Revised Standard Version* and other modern versions of the Bible speak of 'brothers and sisters' rather than 'brethren'. The official scripts of Anglican worship—the scriptures and current prayer books—have thus dealt with the issue of gendered words in relation to people.[8] Thus far, few today would contest this approach, though some see the issue as just one for women.

In English, however, it is difficult to express what is distinctive about being a male human being. By using 'man' and 'men' to refer both to 'males' and 'humans', what is distinctive about being male gets mixed up with what it means to be human. When English speakers say 'women', they know they are speaking of a particular gender. Yet if 'men' means both 'humans' and 'males', how do males know what is distinctive to being men? By seeking only to use male language when males are under discussion, we may gradually begin to separate being male from being human in our minds and hearts, and so give men words by which to speak of what is characteristic about them.

Further, 'man' is traditionally used to refer to the human race as a whole, as well as to an individual. One of the most famous instances comes in the Christmas hymn, *Hark the herald angels sing*—"pleased

---

[7] The translations in *APBA* of the Nicene Creed, and other texts common to all Christian traditions, follows the work of the *English Language Liturgical Consultation*, published in *Praying Together* (Norwich: Canterbury Press, 1988). See Notes 1 and 2 in *APBA*, pages 820-822.

[8] For examples in *APBA*, see Baptism #19; Holy Communion (First Order) #13, 17; Tuesday Evening Prayer #6.

as man with Man to dwell". The capital indicates that the corporate sense of 'man' is intended, affirming the truth that Christmas is about more than Christ the individual: the eternal Word took on our nature to identify with and bring healing to the human race as a whole. I know of no rewording which retains this truth easily—one Christmas a friend changed the line to "pleased as punch with us to dwell"! Yet when these corporate and personal meanings of 'man' are not clearly distinguished, doctrinal problems can arise around the incarnation and the doctrine of humanity.[9]

What of the way we speak of God, however? The scriptures use an astonishingly wide range of metaphors and images to describe God. Some are associated with particular people—"shield of Abram", "El-roi—God who sees" (Hagar), "El-shaddai—God almighty" (Isaac), "El-El-Israel—God, God of Israel" (Jacob/Israel). But most are masculine—lord, king, husband. Some gender neutral personal terms are found, such as shepherd, protector or sovereign, and a few feminine images: wisdom, nursing, mothering. And some non-personal terms occur: notably light, alongside rock and fortress, especially in the psalms, reflecting the physical setting of ancient Israel.

Most Christian traditions use only a sample of these images in liturgy, however, including the historic Anglican tradition. In *BCP*, royal metaphors for God predominate: this partly undergirded, and partly relativised, the social situation of Tudor and Stuart England. To pray to God as 'king of kings. lord of lords' was relevant to the times, but also made the point that earthly kings and lords are accountable to *the* King and Lord of Lords! In Australia, since 1953, the monarch has been Queen Elizabeth: so 'king' imagery is now just that, imagery, and carries generally negative connotations

---

[9] For further discussion, see Charles Sherlock, *The Doctrine of Humanity* (Leicester: IVP, 1996) 239-246.

outside church circles, largely due to its association with the abuse of power. It will be interesting to see how this imagery 'works' in Christian circles when a man comes to the throne, and 'king' returns to being a word in everyday use.

In *AAPB* (1977) and other books of that era, family metaphors are more frequent in speaking of God, especially 'Father': this corresponded to the felt need in the 1960s and 70s for a more intimate sense of God's presence, before sensitivity to gendered language had arisen widely. In *APBA* (1995), both royal and family metaphors are retained, alongside a much wider range of scriptural images. This can be seen most clearly in the way different prayers begin (collects and for Various Occasion), in seasonal material and the pastoral services. Close attention was paid to avoid putting male and power images together—the problem of 'patriarchy', the assumption that being male = using force. In particular, God is only once described as 'Father Almighty', in the (ecumenically agreed) Apostles' Creed: the Nicene Creed has a significant comma: "we believe in God the Father, the Almighty".[10] Which takes us to another problem area—military imagery.

War-words in worship

Many Christians are cautious about, or reject, the use of military imagery to express God's power in public worship.[11] Emotions are all too easily transferred from celebrating divine victory to feelings of pride at national might. The scriptures' war-words can be used, usually unintentionally, to reinforce social, national or even church-goers' attitudes in ways that contradict God's purposes. It is the very

---

10   The Hebrew term, El-shaddai, 'almighty', is about God being fruitful more than forceful ('all-mighty').

11   On this, and the wider issues involved around military language, see *Word and the Word* chapter five.

power of such language that is its strength, and calls us to guard against its misuse—yet military imagery is woven in to the scriptures. But this never includes a simple affirmation of the glory of war, or even of the unqualified might of the Lord. As Paul taught the Corinthians, "God's power is made perfect in weakness" (2 Corinthians 12:9) and the "word of the cross" is the "power of God" (1 Corinthians 1:18). Generations of Christians can join in celebrating the truth of the cross-shaped transforming power of God's love.

The war-words used in the Bible form earthy demonstrations of the cosmic reign of God, whose ultimate purpose is the establishment of peace. Ultimately this requires a new creation, a renewed 'heavens and earth', and this purpose calls all who follow Christ to live this out in the present age. Such an age, the scriptures claim, dawned in Jesus the Christ, the Prince of Peace, and has been the Christian hope ever since (see Leviticus 26.2; Isaiah 9.6-7; Zechariah 9.10; Matthew 5.9; Luke 1.79; 2 Thessalonians 3.16). There is thus a strong bias towards the imagery of peace in the scriptures, which comes through and transforms the imagery of war. Brian Wren points out that the first Christians were a persecuted minority, and pacifists. So for them to use battle imagery, as Revelation does, carried many less perils than it does for us. He asks, "Can we draw on the experience of World War Two, Korea, Vietnam, Iran's human waves, or the IRA's urban slayings, to describe the Christian life? And if so, how?"[12] Only the power of God can overcome evil, and free us mortals from death, sin and the demonic—a central facet of Christian faith.

How does this work out in Christian worship, both as lifestyle and liturgy? Sometimes contemporary sensitivity to war-words can

---

12 Brian Wren, "Onward Christian Rambos? The Case against Battle Symbolism in Hymns", *Journal of the Hymn Society of America*, 1987, 13-15, 14. We could now add "two Gulf Wars, Rwanda-Burundi, Al Qaeda, Iraq, Afghanistan, the Congo, Somalia, Syria ..."

get in the way of a peace-centred approach. Consider this example: Morning and Evening Prayer in the *Book of Common Prayer* (*BCP*) contain this prayer dialogue between minister and people:

V   Give peace in our time, O Lord,
R   **Because there is none other that fighteth for us, but only thou, O God.**

In *AAPB* and *APBA* First Order, this changed to:

V   Give peace in our time, O Lord,
R   **For you are our help and strength.**

The modern desire to avoid war-words here reduces the peace-making impact of the phrase. The traditional form has strong pacifist tendencies: if it is "none other" than God "that fighteth for us", why would we raise armies or consider waging war?

Another example comes from baptism. In *BCP*, the minister says these words when marking a newly-baptised infant with the sign of the cross:

> We receive this Child into the congregation of Christ's flock, and do sign him with the sign of the Cross, that hereafter he shall not be ashamed to confess the faith of Christ crucified, and manfully to fight under his banner, against sin, the world, and the devil; and to continue Christ's faithful soldier and servant unto his life's end.

The war imagery here is a statement of intention—"that hereafter *he* **shall** ...", and the verbs are all in the indicative (descriptive) case. The 'soldier' image is paired with a complementary one, 'servant', and the 'fight against' phrase is set alongside positive ways of being a

Christian—"confess" and "continue". These linguistic strategies reflect considerable care in using military language from the scriptures.

In *AAPB* (1977), however, the Baptism (Second Order) divides the words between the priest and people, to improve their participation. But the outcome was to give stronger emphasis to war-words.

> Minister: I sign you with the sign of the cross to show that you are to be true to Christ crucified and that you are not ashamed to confess your faith in him.
>
> People: **Fight bravely under his banner against sin, the world and the devil ...**

'Fight' is placed on its own, and put in the imperative: all present *command* the newly baptised to 'Fight bravely' (presumably to avoid 'manfully'). Such a change, while encouraging the congregation to 'own' the baptism, also means that a warlike approach to Christian life is instilled into people's memory, as baptism services recur.

When *APBA* (1995) was being prepared, several requests were made for 'fight' language to be removed altogether. The drafters chose not to do so, however, because the wording is scriptural, and familiar. They returned to the exact words of scripture ("fight the good fight", 1 Timothy 6.12) and followed *BCP*'s lead by blending 'fight' with the other images used for the Christian in the New Testament—disciple (learner), soldier and athlete—and returned these words to the minister. The outcome was that, after each candidate has been baptised and signed with the cross, the minister says:

> Live as a disciple of Christ,
> fight the good fight,
> finish the race
> keep the faith.

and the congregation responds:

**Confess Christ crucified,
proclaim his resurrection,
and look for his coming in glory.**

The congregation's response parallels the 'Christ has died/is risen/will come again' acclamations in the Thanksgiving prayers of holy communion. It is in this prayer that the most frequent use of war-words in modern services occurs:

Holy, holy, holy Lord, God of power and might...

— the ecumenical translation of the ancient *Ter Sanctus* (thrice holy) song. And it is said or sung as we stand, joining "with all the company of heaven" in a Great Thanksgiving prayer whose tone is unqualified praise. The rendition "God of power and might" makes it a blatant celebration of the unqualified power of God—yet few questions have been raised.

What then is its history? The phrase derives from the song Isaiah heard in the Temple: "Holy, holy, holy is the Lord of hosts (*tsaba'ôth*)" (Isaiah 6:3). 'Host' (*tsaba*) in the singular means 'army', but while the plural 'hosts' has a military background, it is mainly used for the 'hosts of heaven', carrying a sense of awe (e.g. Deuteronomy 4:19; 17:3; 1 Kings 22:19; 2 Chronicles 33:3-5; Acts 7:42—and note Luke 2:13). 'Lord of hosts' would become a stock phrase in later Old Testament books, but occurs first on the lips of David, as he challenges Goliath: "I come to you in the name of the Lord of hosts, the God of the armies of Israel" (1 Samuel 17:45). The Ark, moved by David into Jerusalem, is then called "the Ark of God which is called by the name of the Lord of hosts"

(2 Samuel 6:2), and becomes a key part of the Temple, where Isaiah heard the *Ter Sanctus*.[13]

The first translation of the *Ter Sanctus* into English is in the *Book of Common Prayer*: "Holy, holy, holy, Lord God of hosts" and many musical settings use this rendition (which is retained in *APBA* First Order). It carries a sense of reverent mystery about God's might, shown in Christ's paradoxical victory over death by dying, the focus of the eucharist. Further, the words are said or sung while all are kneeling, and is followed by the 'prayer of humble access'. This all conveys an attitude of reverent humility, and the great privilege we have in being able to join in the song with "all the company of heaven".[14]

Perhaps this has been too much detail about fine points—but hopefully the discussion shows the importance of being careful about the words we speak, pray and sing, both in church and in our daily lives. We can become so afraid of saying the wrong thing that we remain silent about God, even in church. Then it's time to recall Luther's dictum, that if we have to sin, then sin boldly—and yet believe more boldly.

Part C   Looking at how words work in worship

1. From your Bible and/or prayer book (e.g. *APBA*) find words and phrases used as a greeting, curse, exhortation, promise, act of praise, and act of penitence.

---

[13] The Greek Old Testament occasionally renders 'Lord of *tsaba'ôth*' as 'Lord Allmighty' (cf Revelation 4:8), but generally leaves its meaning open by transliterating the Hebrew: 'Lord of Sabaoth'. The Te Deum in BCP Morning Prayer has "Lord God of Sabaoth", reflecting the Greek translation.

[14] Although the change was not made due to concerns about military language, the new Roman Catholic translation has adopted this wording: the initial (1968) Roman Catholic Mass in English used "God of power and might".

How do they work when read silently? When read aloud? When sung?
2. Have several people read quietly over Mark 16:1-8 for a few minutes.

   Then have three different voices read it aloud, taking the perspective of:
   - one of the women mentioned;
   - Pontius Pilate;
   - a male chauvinist.

   What difference (if any) did these different *performances* of the passage make to the way it was *heard*?
3. What do you find makes an effective leader (or otherwise) of a Christian service, in terms of how they use words?

   Does a person's accent affect their ability to take a leading part? Are any parts of the service notable for people using different accents (e.g. Notices)? Why might this be so?
4. What are the advantages and disadvantages of silence in worship? Would your answer be different for a small group setting or a Sunday service?

   Where would silences be best used in the service you experience regularly?

   Think about silences left before the confession of sins, or after a reading or sermon. What is the most helpful length for each occasion? (It can take time for some to stop shuffling and realise that the leader hasn't lost the place.)
5. Write down as many words as you can that are commonly used to refer to God.

   Share your lists.

   Which names best express the nature of God to you? Why?

What are their limitations? Can any be taken literally? Do they mean different things to different people?

6. Read together Psalm 136:1–9 (*APBA* pages 367–8)
   Read it again, saying 'God' or 'God's' for 'he/his': "for God's mercy endures forever"
   Read it again, using 'you/your' for 'he/his': "for your mercy endures forever"
   Read it again, replacing the masculine pronouns for God with feminine ones: "O give thanks to the Lord for she is good, for her mercy endures forever."
   Which way of reading did you prefer? Did you feel any was difficult? Why?
   Which was the easiest exchange of terms to make?

Conclusion

Language is a mysterious and marvellous form of human communication. The words we use in liturgy and living articulate our faith, shape our understanding, and express the way we imagine reality—especially when spoken informally rather than from a prepared text, or when we are angry. Our 'primary' language is then on show, revealing some of the secrets of our hearts as well as the formed thoughts of our minds.

The words of *APBA* pay close attention to what is true, not only in doctrinal terms, but also in seeking to take account of their effect on our affections. The challenge to all who plan and lead liturgy is to sense which words best enable the worship of God for everyone present, and to avoid words that do harm. Gender language is a current example of the first challenge, war-words of the second. Sexist, violent, racist and insulting language poses similar challenges in our everyday words.

Chapter Five
Performing the gospel 'according to the scriptures'

Overview

Part A   begins at the beginning, exploring why scripture reading matters in performing the gospel.

Part B   focuses on why 'traditional' practice for reading the scriptures is what it is, then expands on this to explore helpful practices in more contemporary style.

Part C   covers the 'what' and 'why' of the three-year system of Sunday scripture readings—but even if you do not follow this, its rationale is well worth considering.

Part D   offers ideas for doing some local research into performing the scriptures.

Readings from the scriptures have been central to every act of corporate Christian worship from the earliest days. As a Jewish man, Jesus heard the 'Law, Prophets and Writings' (the First Testament) read systematically in the synagogue, and knew them well. His scriptural interpretations drew strong responses from 'ordinary' people (e.g. Luke 4.14ff) and his disciples (e.g. Matthew 13, Mark 4) and led him into hot debate with scholars of his day (e.g. Mark 12.13-37).

As well as continuing to hear readings from the First Testament, early Christian communities listened to God's 'good news' as taught and lived by Jesus. The letters written by Paul, Peter and other apostolic figures to particular churches were not only heard there, but also circulated and read in other churches (see Colossians 4.16, 2 Peter 3.15-16). In the decades following Jesus' earthly ministry, the Gospels we know—Mark, Luke, Matthew, John—were gathered together, as were the apostolic letters. But this was well before the advent of printing, modern transport and communication: different churches around the Mediterranean had slightly different collections. When some groups began to question which writings were appropriate to be read in church—and thus be accepted as 'scripture'—the need arose to clarify the writings that could be set, alongside the Testament they already knew, as the 'New Testament'. By around 180AD there was widespread agreement, but small variations continued until Christian faith was no longer persecuted, but recognised.

Whatever the formal state of the 'canonical' (i.e. fixed) list of writings acknowledged as Christian scripture, their witness to the gospel has formed the 'script' for its performance across the centuries, and across countless languages and cultures. The faith in Christ we confess is 'according to the scriptures', as Paul wrote (1 Corinthians 15.3, 4) and the Creeds affirm. And this 'canon' governs our worship, "not only with our lips, but with our lives".

Part A Performing the scriptures: what matters?

The script-ures of the divine drama

If someone said, "In this fridge is all you need for a great feed," you'd rush to open it. The way Article VI begins, "Holy scripture containeth all things necessary to salvation," should create a similar expectation: that we will be quick to open the Bible to find in its pages the resources for true life. The scriptures of the First and New Testaments express in writing what the Christian faith knows of God's life-changing self-revelation. Penned over a dozen or more centuries, they are the script of the divine drama that revolves around Jesus Christ, the Word of God in living human flesh.

This Bible, though typically bound today in one volume, is not a single, tightly edited manuscript that has been checked carefully by a modern publishing firm. Rather, it brings together several collections of writings, gathered over a millennium or more.

- The Law (*Torah* in Hebrew): the first five books, outlining God's creative and re-creative work in the people of God, especially Israel under Moses.
- The Prophets (*N^ebi'im* in Hebrew): Former (1 Samuel to 2 Kings), telling of Israel's experience of prophetic guidance and discipline until they were sent into exile; and Latter, recording the oracles of the writing prophets to Israel—four 'major' (Isaiah, Jeremiah, Ezekiel and Daniel) and twelve 'minor'.
- The Writings (*Kethubim* in Hebrew): the Psalms, wisdom writing (notably Job), five 'festival' books, and the liturgy-focused story of Israel before and after exile (1 Chronicles to Nehemiah).
- The Gospels: Matthew, Mark and Luke (called 'synoptic' gospels because of their similar structure and many parallel

sections), and John. Each speaks in a distinctive way of the origins, ministry, passion and resurrection of Christ.
- The Letters ('epistles' in older English), most written by Paul for early Christian communities around the Mediterranean, together with others attributed to Peter, James, John and Jude, plus the letter to the Hebrews.
- The Revelation to John the Divine: dream-like visions of Christ's full glory and God's ultimate purposes.

This wide-sweeping script is like a cloth woven from a variety of threads using a range of stitches, across which distinctive patterns engage and converse. Given the extent and diversity of their contents, the unity of this script is more like that of a multi-faceted jewel than of a uniform block of ice. Their integrity and harmony lies in their multi-faceted witness to the nature and purposes of the one God, whom they name as Father, Son and Holy Spirit. They give us access to what we know of God, and God's ways, but offer more than just information. In hearing, reading and reflecting on the scriptures the people of God find themselves becoming more like Christ, and guided as to what that transformation means for their living and lifestyle. As Archbishop Thomas Cranmer memorably put it, the scriptures are the 'food of the soul'. A proper diet needs a mix of foods for wholesome development, so in the preface to the first *Book of Common Prayer*, Cranmer insisted that all parts of scripture were to be used in church (see 'Concerning the Service of the Church').

The scriptures: food of the soul

In the pre-Reformation Church of England, the scripture readings were meagre, and—in part due to the high costs of producing books—Bibles were rare. The epistle and gospel in the eucharist was repeated each year, and while other daily services (mostly used by nuns and monks) covered the whole psalter, only brief sentences were read. When the *Book of Common Prayer* was drawn up from 1548, the holy communion readings were left largely unchanged.¹ Those for daily Morning and Evening Prayer, however, in each year covered the New Testament twice (except for a few chapters of Revelation), the First Testament once (omitting genealogies and cultic regulations) and the Psalms twelve times (i.e. monthly). This 'lectionary' (i.e. Bible-reading scheme) was probably the first to attempt to cover the whole book—though only made possible due to the arrival of printing. That it was placed at the beginning of each edition of *BCP* shows the importance given to it.

Such an 'immersion' approach reveals a profoundly catholic consciousness of the *whole* story of the divine drama of God's dealings. Only when some overview is grasped can the parts of scripture be appreciated properly, even if many passages were 'too high' for the 'simple'. Cranmer saw that as no excuse for not using 'difficult' texts, however: "He that is so weak that he is not able to brook strong meat, yet he may suck the sweet and tender milk, and defer the rest until he wax stronger" as the Homily on Scripture puts it.² This emphasis on sensing the 'whole' of the divine drama is like being in a cathedral, where you have a sense of an over-arching 'framework' for performing the gospel.

But too much emphasis on the 'whole' can lead us into overly simplistic ideas. Current debates often focus on issues about which the scriptures say little directly. Paying attention to what each passage says—and does *not* say—is crucial here. In the case of the

---

1 Until the law changed in 1871, Sunday morning service in the Church of England consisted of Morning Prayer, Litany and Ante-Communion, with Communion continuing if at least three people had given notice to the local priest that they intended to communicate. Overall, this meant that worshippers heard one First and three New Testament readings, and recited several psalms.
2 Note on full details and web availability of Homily

gospels, comparing how each portrays what Jesus did or said can help us gain a sense of the distinctive emphasis of each. For example, accounts of Jesus' temptation are given in Matthew (4.1-11), Mark (1.12-13) and Luke (4.1-12). Mark is very brief, but notes that Jesus was 'with the wild animals'; Matthew and Luke are similar, but give the temptations—bread, kingdoms, Temple—in different orders: Matthew's is bread, Temple, kingdoms; Luke's is bread, kingdoms, Temple. Harmonising these two accounts is impossible, and may distract from using them as 'food of the soul': what matters about the order of Jesus' temptations for the gospel message? But using Matthew and Luke's differences to tease out their distinctive approaches to presenting Jesus can be a fruitful resource for reflecting on the gospel drama. Close attention to the details—a 'detective' approach—complements understanding each part in the light of the 'whole', the 'cathedral' outlook. This is also why at least two readings—and usually at least one from each Testament—are used in every traditional service. In their 'conversation' with each other, we hear in 'stereo' rather than 'mono' (see more below).

Understanding the scriptures as spiritual food points to their sacramental nature (see Chapter 4). Their words are the 'outward and visible form' of the divine drama set out in the Word of God, given to *transform* as well as *inform*. As the Homily on Scripture continues:

> The words of holy scripture be called words of everlasting life; for they be God's instruments, ordained for the same purpose. They have power to turn [convert] through God's promise, and they be effectual through God's assistance, and (being received in a faithful heart) they have ever an heavenly spiritual working in them.

So, in the holy communion service of the *Book of Common Prayer*, intercessions are made for:

...this congregation here present; that with meek heart and due reverence they may hear and receive thy holy Word; truly serving thee in holiness and righteousness all the days of their life.

In short, the scriptures 'work' as the script that not only *informs* us of God's work, but *draws us into* the divine drama. This 'ministry of the Word', which entails the interaction of 'cathedral' and 'detective approaches, equips us for godly living: the immersion of the people of God in the scriptures is about more than imbibing correct teaching, though that matters. It is rather, as the Homily continues, that the people of God "might be stirred up to godliness", "profit more and more in the knowledge of God" and take on "wholesome doctrine", teaching that built up healthy lives as well as informed minds.

As drink is pleasant to them that be dry, and meat to them that be hungry; so is the reading, hearing, searching and studying of holy scripture, to them that desirous to know God, themselves, and to do God's will.

According to Anglican formularies, then, the scriptures show us God (Father, Son and Spirit, not some dry philosophical deity), our own true nature (sinful people, yet created to share God's goodness) and how we should 'frame our manners' to do God's will. In sum, the scriptures are the key element of liturgy, in order to shape our lifestyle.

Part B   Performing the scriptures in church

Performing 'script'-ure

In any performance the script plays a central part—and *how* it is performed has a great deal to do with its effectiveness. In particular, those who act out a script need to know their parts, be able to articulate them, and be willing to work on them in rehearsal.

Reading the scriptures aloud is one of the most significant 'parts' in performing the gospel. In the early churches, the skilled ministry of *lector* (reader) was taken with great seriousness, heightened by the fact that not many could read. In our age, when literacy is widespread, it is tempting to think that anyone can be asked to do a reading. Yet whoever fills this part typically has more words to say than anyone else, besides the preacher. If the scriptures are the food of the soul, then their being performed matters greatly: this is why traditionally only those licensed by the bishop acted as *lector*. Today imposing this strictly is unlikely to be helpful in local congregation (though 'Safe Church' rules are beginning to make it necessary). The concept remains, however, that readers should be people recognised as called to exercise this ministry. Criteria will include the person being able to read well, but other factors also need to be considered. For example, I have known an illiterate worshipper to learn a reading off by heart, and recite—no, perform—it from memory. Willingness to prepare and rehearse is a good sign of someone having a sense of dependence on the Spirit to guide and equip them for this ministry.

Many factors affect how the scriptures are performed, especially our **accent**. 'Parsonic' tones are still around, even from younger people. Some turn on a more 'American' accent when speaking in church, especially the terms 'God' ('Gaarrd'), 'Lord' (Loooord') and 'word' ('whirrred'). One friend told me about their experience in a diocesan worship committee: "I was the only one who didn't speak with a plum in my mouth." A change of accent between daily life and public worship separates person and role/office, indicating a lack of integrity in ministry—liturgy is in danger of being divorced from lifestyle. On the other hand, I once heard an Australian accent criticised as 'un-Anglican', and I remember with shame a man whose English was excellent, but was asked to take English lessons because he spoke with an Indian accent.

Whatever our accent, class, education, gender or experience, **clear articulation** is essential. Just filling rosters to encourage 'participation' without regard to calling is a grave mistake—practical, pastoral and theological. We can learn here from the Jewish custom of the bar/bath-mitzvah, in which the young man or woman is trained to be able to lead the congregation in reading. New readers can start with group work, where a weak or nervous voice is helped by others, and team ministry is fostered.

Teamwork is also a great way to perform a passage that tells a story—**'dramatic/dialogue reading'**. When different voices read the various parts, it can come alive for listeners.[3] In many churches the long reading of the passion narrative on Palm Sunday and Good Friday is undertaken like this—but just handing out sheets before the service is not good enough. Dramatic reading needs rehearsal; especially where brief phrases like 'and he said' are omitted from the narrator's part. Using more than one voice can also be helpful where a reading involves an unfolding argument, such as a prophetic oracle or

---

3   *The Dramatic Bible* has every passage arranged for reading by more than one voice. It offers useful ideas, but not all will find its approach helpful, and there is no variation in translation. The availability (e.g. on www.biblegateway.com) of electronic versions in a wide (too wide?) range of English translations allows working on a script, and making copies for each participant, a straightforward matter. Deciding who says what is less simple, however, and requires skilled discernment.

a doctrinal passage from Paul: its steps can be allocated to alternating voices. Again, rehearsal is essential so that readers know how their reading—pitch, pace, tone, volume, body language—interact with what they are reading.

The **places** where the scriptures are performed also need to be considered. Traditionally, a large copy of the Bible is placed in a prominent place in church, reflecting its significance as the Word of God written. Most readings then take place from this 'lectern' (i.e. reading stand), situated so that all can hear. Sometimes movement is involved: in the *Book of Common Prayer* holy communion service, for example, the Epistle was read from one side of the holy table, the Gospel from the other, and the book moved across between the readings. In Eastern Orthodox churches, the gospel book is processed into the body of the church before being read, symbolising the incarnation of the Word. Today the gospel reading sometimes takes place in the midst of the people, as they stand facing the reader, together attending to the words and deeds of the Lord Jesus. Such a 'gospel procession' makes performing the gospel visible in worship focused around ministry of the Word. This can be fussy, with performance being highlighted rather than the script performed. Yet paying little, if any, attention to how the scriptures are placed, read and heard is a missed opportunity to assist the people of God to hear and respond to the Word of God.

Scripture readings: number and order

The pattern by which a church regularly reads the scriptures says a good deal about how they view their status and nature. It is one thing to accept that "all scripture is inspired by God and useful for instruction" (2 Timothy 3.16), another to demonstrate this in the choice and arrangement of readings. It is clearly impossible to read everything, and different patterns are appropriate for Sundays and weekdays, not least because of length: if two chapters were read each Sunday, it would take two decades to read the whole Bible, though both Testaments can be comfortably read on a daily basis over two years.

What then is at stake in the choice of readings for use in church? How many readings should there be in a typical Sunday service? And does their order matter? From its beginnings, Christian practice has been to have two or more readings in corporate worship, drawn from different parts of the scriptures. This can be seen in the *Book of Common Prayer* and its successors, including *APBA*, where there are two readings (plus psalms) in each Sunday service; in the holy communion the gospel reading, heard standing up, is the climactic one. In this way the scriptures are heard in 'stereo', as it were—one passage feeds into and out of another, encouraging a 'bifocal' perspective. This 'conversation' between readings from different biblical books draws listeners into a dynamic hearing of God's Word written. As with Christian prayer, this 'conversation' reflects the dynamic, triune nature of the living God: in the written Word, inspired and illuminated by the Spirit, the living Word reveals the Father to us. Reducing the conversation to a monologue runs the danger of 'flattening' our understanding of the scriptures—and distorting our understanding of the God revealed in them.

To what extent does such practice matter today? In what circumstances might or ought it be changed—and why? Some find the modern ecumenical system of up to four readings for a main Sunday service to be an indigestible, overly rich diet. Practicalities such as time-pressure, the shift from 'hearing' to 'seeing' cultures, or embarrassment about what some readings say, can mean that readings are cut short, 'filleted', or even slashed to the verse or two on which the sermon is based.

"Having just one reading lets me get across one simple message," some might say. Apart from underestimating the congregation, who are rarely 'simple', this looks for the Bible to be heard in 'mono'. The passage has most likely been chosen by the preacher, and its 'reading' is likely to be framed by what s/he wants to say, rather than being heard in its own right. For a lecture, Bible study or evangelistic meeting—and possibly a 'fresh expression' of church—this approach can make sense. But for a regular Christian service, aiming to feed the people of God with a balanced spiritual diet, it narrows the congregation's exposure to the breadth of God's ways. There are occasions when two readings will be enough—when many children are present, or a baptism service, for example. But the 'stereophonic' principle still applies.

What then matters about the order of readings? The traditional order in 'services of the Word' is to move from First to New Testament reading (surrounded by psalms and other songs). In classical holy communion services, a reading from the letters precedes one from the gospels.[4] Modern liturgical revision, as seen in *AAPB* and *APBA*, combines these services with this order of readings: First Testament (Acts in Easter), psalm, letter, and gospel. Having a New Testament reading before one from the First Testament undercuts the relationship between these Testaments. As these names imply, the divine drama is read from God's foundational work in Israel 'forward' to the New Testament, so that we might understand its fulfilment in Christ.

In holy communion, the gospel reading traditionally comes last—does this order matter? It could be argued that, since the gospels precede other books in the New Testament, this order could be reversed. In the biblical drama, the gospels' witness to the teaching

---

4   As noted in a previous chapter, Church of England practice until the late 19th century was to have Morning Prayer, Litany and Holy Communion as one service, with four readings plus psalms all up, and the sermon leading into the Lord's Supper.

and example of Jesus Christ is central—in theological terms, the living Word is the key to the written Word. In translating the scriptures, or introducing someone to Christian faith, starting with one of the gospels is obvious, since they tell the central story of the scriptures, the life and work of Christ. Which is one reason for their being placed to open the New Testament, so that *readers* encounter them first. On the other hand, in the eucharist *hearing* from the gospels comes as the climax of the 'Ministry of the Word', because they form—and perform—the focal point and climax of the divine drama. So the traditional order, while not compulsory, makes sense when the readings are understood as *performing* the gospel—being agents of transformation more than just information. Christian education is vital, especially in a mission context—and many long-term Christians are not at home in the scriptures. In corporate worship, however, the readings are not there primarily to inform hearers, so much as to form and transform the people of God into becoming more Christ-like.[5]

'Stand up. Stand up for Jesus.'

What then of the long-standing custom—mandated in the *Book of Common Prayer*—that the congregation stands to hear the gospel reading? We stay sitting when a New Testament reading at a service of the Word is from the gospels: why then stand to hear it read in a eucharistic setting?

Some object to standing, on the grounds that it lends greater importance to the gospels than other parts of the scriptures. And

---

[5] When the sermon in holy communion is preached from a reading other than from the gospels, some suggest that this reading come last, so the sermon can follow it. But it is rather odd to stand for the gospel and then for another reading! Better to have the sermon next to the reading expounded, leaving the gospel reading to be last: it can then come as a response to the Word preached.

yes, it does. All scripture is inspired and useful, but (as noted above) the gospels *are* more important than other scriptures because of their witness to Christ. That is why we introduce enquirers to them first, and give them priority in translation. Others see standing as discouraging people following along using a Bible or pew sheet. When a reading from the prophets or a letter takes the form of an argument rather than a story, this can be helpful. But when the emphasis is on *listening*, not least to the words and deeds of Jesus Christ, reading along can get in the way. Standing has the practical value of encouraging us, when in church, to *hear* God's word—the situation for which the scriptures were written—rather than *study* them. Indeed, until printing, universal education and technology, which saw Bibles cheap enough for each family to own one (i.e. mid-19th century), listening was the only way the scriptures could be encountered by most people.

The tradition of standing to listen to the words of the Word thus makes good spiritual sense. Also, standing to listen to the words and deeds of Christ in the context of the sacrament of the eucharist pushes us beyond *my* to *our* listening. It indicates the tangible response we are called to make to Christ *as a body*—not just my personal assent of mind and heart, but also our public, corporate commitment to hear and follow Christ *together* as we prepare to gather at the Lord's table. Further, in the context of holy communion, standing indicates the *sacramental* character of the Word read (see Chapter 4). The table of the Word thus converses rather than competes with the table of the Lord. Personal learning and reflection on the scriptures is a necessary part of Christian growth. But there is deep benefit in the corporate movement represented by standing for the climactic gospel reading, in which we hear Christ together in the 'audible

Word', as we move together to encounter Christ in the gospel enacted, the 'visible Word'.

In sum, hearing the scriptures in stereo, following the movement from First to New Testament, and entering into the sacrament of the living Word, both audible and visible; these traditional practices in performing the gospel enable the people of God to receive the Word of God personally with mind and heart, and corporately as members together of Christ's body.

Part C The pattern of performing the scriptures

Who should say what is read in church? Can this be left to locals, or does the wider church have a part to play—and if so, how wide? The *Book of Common Prayer* opens with tables of scripture readings to be used daily, covering pretty much the whole Bible, a pattern that continues across the Anglican Communion (see more below). There are several advantages in congregations hearing the same passages as other churches Sunday by Sunday. Practically, it makes it easier to provide resources for preaching and education. Ecumenically, worshippers can have the sense of listening to the scriptures along with the wider people of God. Spiritually, having a system that requires us to engage with a full range of the scriptures runs a better chance of us being exposed to the 'whole counsel of God': locals are likely to choose readings from a narrow range, thus restricting the spiritual diet of a congregation. On the other hand, there will be times when the 'set' readings are not appropriate, or the spiritual needs of a church are better met by them being varied. Also, most English-speaking Christians today can read, and can afford to own a copy of the Bible: so individuals can follow a scheme of daily Bible reading and reflection that complements what they hear on Sundays.

The pattern of reading the scriptures as the script performed in Christian liturgy is what undergirds a 'lectionary'—a Bible-reading system. In modern times, Christians typically take part in corporate worship weekly (mostly on Sundays), and engage in personal prayer and reflection on other days. With this in mind, two lectionaries were provided for Morning and Evening Prayer in the Church of England from 1871, one for Sundays and major festivals, the other for weekdays. But until the 1970s, those who attended only holy communion rarely heard passages from the First Testament, apart from the Ten Commandments, and only a small selection from the New.

The Second Vatican Council (1962–65) saw revived emphasis in the Roman Catholic Church on the faithful knowing the scriptures. For daily services, a systematic set of readings was established for the eucharist, over two years, covering much of the New Testament and some of the First. For Sundays and major festivals, a three-year pattern of readings was developed, known as the 'Three-year Lectionary'. This focuses on the gospels of Matthew, Mark and Luke in Years A, B and C respectively; a systematic reading of the other New Testament books; and a First Testament reading and psalm chosen to match the gospel reading. This 'Three-year Lectionary' gained widespread acceptance in many non-Roman Catholic churches, including the Anglican Communion. *AAPB* (1977) took it up, with minor changes, for Sundays and festivals, together with a revised form of the 1871 daily lectionary for daily Morning and Evening Prayer.

The Revised Common Lectionary

The Three-year Lectionary, while widely appreciated, received a number of criticisms.

- The First Testament is read only in the light of the gospels, and briefly. In North America, the ecumenical 'Common Lectionary' saw the Hebrew scriptures read in their own right in 'ordinary' time, while still being linked with the gospels in the Advent, Christmas, Lent and Easter seasons.
- The continuous reading of New Testament books is not carried through fully, and some books are covered in a fragmented way, notably John's gospel.
- The details of names and places are often omitted: texts written for particular situations can appear to teach 'abstract' truths rather than contextual wisdom.
- Women's participation in the biblical story is minimised, and passages traditionally heard as carrying anti-Semitic or racist overtones are not used sensitively.

Over the past half-century, considerable work has gone into thinking about how public reading of the scriptures is best done today. Churches' experience of the 'Three-year Lectionary' and *Common Lectionary*, and the criticisms noted above, provided significant input into lectionary production on an ecumenical basis. The result was *The Revised Common Lectionary* (Canterbury Press, 1992) for use on Sundays and some major feasts.[6] Most New Testament readings remained unchanged from the *Common Lectionary*, but adjustments were made to bring about greater continuity. Semi-continuous readings from the First Testament are included for the Sundays after Pentecost, as well as the gospel-based ones of the Three-year Lectionary (in parentheses). In Australia, *RCL* (ecumenical) or Three-year (Roman Catholic) Lectionary are used

---

6   The Consultation on Common Texts, *The Revised Common Lectionary* (Norwich: The Canterbury Press, 1992). It includes the history and principles of RCL, as well as tables of readings and full Indices. A wealth of web resources is available—the Wikipedia article on RCL is excellent.

by Anglican, Churches of Christ, Lutheran, Roman Catholic, Uniting and many Baptist and other congregations.

The overall pattern of Sunday readings in *APBA* over the three years look like this:

	First Reading	Gospel	New Testament Letters
Year A	Genesis, Exodus (*Torah/Law*)	Matthew John	Romans, 1 Corinthians 1–4, 1 Peter, 1 Thessalonians
Year B	1 Samuel–1 Kings 8 (*Former Prophets*) Job, Proverbs, Ruth (*Writings*)	Mark John	1 Corinthians 5–9, 2 Corinthians 4–8,12; 1 John, Ephesians, James, Hebrews 1–9
Year C	1 Kings 19–21 Jeremiah, 'minor' prophets (*Latter Prophets*)	Luke	1 Corinthians 12–15, Galatians, Hebrews 10–13, Colossians, Philemon, 1 & 2 Timothy, 2 Thessalonians

Psalms: Whatever set of Sunday readings is used, the psalm is chosen to foster the response of the congregation to the first reading. Some claim that only a limited number of 'nice' psalms are chosen for Sundays. In the *RCL/APBA* lectionary, however, which covers 156 Sundays over three years, selections from 117 different psalms are used, including laments, praise, royal, personal and penitential psalms. Musical settings of all the psalms in *RCL* are included in *Together in Song: the Australian Hymn Book II*.

Part D Performing the scriptures: doing some local research

1. To explore these issues further, obtain a copy of *The Revised Common Lectionary* (Canterbury Press, 1992) or look it up on the internet.
   Note today's date, turn to the places in *RCL* for the Sunday in the week following, and consider the choices offered.
   How does each reading in each of Years A, B and C relate to those of the previous and following weeks?
   How does each relate to the 'supplementary' set?
2. Look up the psalm for next Sunday, and read it aloud.
   In what way(s), or not, might it form a response to the first reading with which it is associated?
3. Turn to a Sunday after Pentecost, and look up the bracketed first reading.
   How do you think it relates to the gospel reading?
   Look at the *sequence* of first readings over any three Sundays after Pentecost in the same Year. How do the semi-continuous or gospel-related (bracketed) readings 'work' in practice?
4. How might your congregation work out a preaching series based on one of the cycles of readings? What changes might be needed to the set of passages considered?
5. What possibilities exist for arranging for the readings to be performed in some way as drama or dialogue?
6. In what way(s) might *RCL* (or a similar) system assist you in daily reading?

One interesting task is to use its indexes to work out which passages are *not* read.

Why do you think they have not been included?

Conclusion

Script of the divine drama, food of the soul, sacrament of the living Word, being approached with a 'cathedral' or 'detective' mentality—these and similar concepts are what lie behind worship 'according to the scriptures'. Precise adherence to the lectionary, skilled and varied performance, comprehensive personal reflection—all can be helpful. What ultimately matters, however, is our engagement with divine drama, centred on the living Word, the Lord Jesus, to whom the Word of God written bears witness. And for this no one reading scheme is adequate. Yet without some pattern of reading, itself discerned 'according to the scriptures', God's people are likely to be fed thin gruel, an unbalanced or inadequate diet—at worst, to become malnourished. To cite Thomas Cranmer again,

> Let us reverently hear and read holy scriptures, which is the food of the soul. Let us diligently search for the well of life in the books of the Old and New Testaments, and not run to the stinking puddles of men's traditions, devised by men's imaginations.

Chapter Six
The sound of music in performing the gospel

Overview

Part A   Music has come to have a dominant place in modern societies. The landscape of sound is explored as some necessary background to reflecting on music in gospel performance.

Part B   focuses on the issues around the sound of music in church. There is a lot to discuss, not least the supposed 'music wars' of recent decades.

Part C   is where the specifics of choosing and using music in liturgical worship are considered.

Part D   offers ideas for putting the sound of music into practice, and some resources to take you further.

This chapter owes a great deal to Fay Magee, whose ministry, friendship, musical knowledge, research and (especially) drafting and comments undergird it.

Part A The musical landscape of gospel performance

What is the sound of music in performing the gospel?
Some may have sublime heights in mind, the 'music of the spheres' of which the ancient Greeks spoke, the sounds behind the story of God's healing of the whole cosmos. In centuries past, and still today in some places, the emotive power of music was distrusted, and 'objective' styles preferred:[1] popular music has found an accepted place in church only in the past 250 years. For many Christians today, however, life-changing experiences that came through hearing or performing music will come to mind. Music associated with the gospel revolves around the world of song: tunes of familiar songs evoke a sense of being close to God, or give us heart-felt assurance of some gospel truth.[2] As regards the music used in church, some focus on its emotional impact; others look to the theological 'correctness' of the words sung with it. We instinctively prefer (or hate) specific musical styles—Gregorian, classical, pop, 'Moody & Sankey', rap, rock, folk and so on.

When 'performing the gospel' comes into view today, music contributes a vital element—but is 'performing music' in the same category? Consider the stage musical (Oklahoma, Carousel, Hair, Cats etc.): its basic framework is a story acted out with music and lots of dancing. These continue to captivate audiences, particularly

---

1 So Augustine of Hippo, *Confessions*: "I waver between the danger that lies in gratifying the senses and the benefits which, as I know from experience, can accrue from singing ... Yet when I find the singing itself more moving than the truth which it conveys, I confess that this is a grievous sin, and at those times I would prefer not to hear the singer." (Book 10 chapter 33)

2 The term 'hymn' referred traditionally to the text of congregational song; 'song' is used here to refer to all texts sung in liturgy. See Kenneth R Hull, "Text, Music, and Meaning in Congregational Song," *The Hymn* 53/1 (January 2002), 14–27. https://babel.hathitrust.org/cgi/pt?id=mdp.39015054346070;view=1up;seq=7

as technology has increased expectations of a grand spectacle. But what part do music and movement play in performing the gospel? How does music both contribute to and reflect on 'the action' in this performance? And are the 'performers' or the gospel to the fore?

Worship—in life and liturgy alike—engages us with God's perspective on life, and the God-given nature of the created order we enjoy. Music is part of this larger worldview: it is best considered, not just as something we 'make' or 'do', but as part of a "sonic order" reflecting the *physicality* of creation, engaging us by its appeal to bodily involvement or response.[3] Moreover, music is embedded in our days and in our lives, associated with particular seasons and evoking deep memories: through music we participate in time in a distinctive way. So a musical performance is not a 'thing' or 'object', but an *experience*, part of the embedded and embodied life of the people of God. It is not something 'outside' us, but touches the "sonic order" in which we live. Our musical experience is shaped by the multitude of influences from the various (sub-)cultures in which we find ourselves playing a role.

Recognising that music is an experience, embodied in time, is vital when it comes to considering its place in performing the gospel in liturgy, Sunday by Sunday and more. But it can be a complex business. Frank Burch Brown speaks of "finding a compass" in the middle of a "sea of options".[4] And it is not a 'culture-free' zone: as John Witvliet writes,

> So many of our culturally shaped assumptions ... go unchallenged and unrefined by the church. Our artistic experience in worship

---

[3] Jeremy S Begbie, *Resounding Truth: Christian Wisdom in the World of Music* (Grand Rapids, Michigan: Baker Academic, 2007), 47, 217.

[4] Frank Burch Brown, *Inclusive yet Discerning: Navigating Worship Artfully* (Grand Rapids: Eerdmans, 2009), 3.

is then shaped more by the norms and values of other cultural institutions than by the norms and values intrinsic to worship.[5]

So, when looking to perform the gospel in current contexts, it is necessary to be open to evaluating music, and other creative arts, using a range of gospel-grounded criteria. It is important to be willing to go beyond our own 'comfort zones' to allow effective and regular critique—possibly uncomfortable—to be made of our own practice.

Music and today's cultures

It may seem strange to 21st century experience that church music was for many centuries at the forefront of new styles and practices—think Gregorian chant, Thomas Tallis, JS Bach, the Wesleys, Sankey, Sydney Carter. In contrast, Quentin Faulkner argues, these days it "only follows trends established by the surrounding culture," trends that are many and varied.[6] The way we think about music is affected by cultural influences, which have gradually developed across recent centuries. Major 'events' such as the Reformation, Enlightenment, industrial revolution, spread of global empires, world wars, harnessing of electricity, emergence of radio, TV, mass media and the fast-moving technology revolution—all have changed the ways we view the world, how we think about meaning in our lives, and the way music 'happens' in society. The cultural contexts in which we gather for worship, hear the scriptures and sing our songs, are continually changing. The ways we experience music 'outside' church directly influence the music we bring into liturgy, and how we think about that music. So what place does

---

5   John D Witvliet, "Series Preface" in Frank Burch Brown, ix.

6   Quentin Faulkner, *Wiser Than Despair — the Evolution of Ideas in the Relationship of Music and the Christian Church* (Westport, Connecticut: Greenwood Press, 1996), 192.

music have 'in church'? And how does it shape our experience of the gospel being performed there?

Two major assumptions today about the arts, and particularly music, are a) that we expect to be entertained and b) that music is about expressing ourselves, and specifically our emotions. This framework of music as entertainment underpins so much of our culture: "entertainment is the metaphor for all discourse—and off the screen the same metaphor prevails," as Neil Postman puts it. Again, music is 'used' to suit or maybe change our mood, which is why it is has become integral to television and movies: it "helps to tell the audience what emotions are called forth".[7]

These two significant issues—entertainment and emotion—need to be kept in mind when thinking about music in liturgy. It is "so easy to confuse depth of emotion with intensity of immediate feeling," as Don Saliers comments.[8] What music is for, and how it works in performing the gospel, needs to be considered in our cultural contexts. A liturgical lens offers the opportunity for music, and particularly song, to have great significance, but in deeper ways than a simplistic "what I think people like" approach.

Listening alone, singing together

This chapter focuses on congregational song, since this is how music is mainly experienced in church. By this is meant any sung repertoire intended as the action of the whole community present, whether it be a psalm, a setting of part of the eucharist, a short song, a plainsong setting such as "Come, Holy Ghost, our souls inspire", or the latest upbeat praise hit. Yet in general, Elizabeth Smith claims,

---

7 Neil Postman, *Amusing Ourselves to Death — Public Discourse in the Age of Show Business* (London: Methuen, 1986), 95, 90.
8 Don E Saliers, "The Integrity of Sung Prayer," *Worship* 55 / 4 (1981) 293.

"Australians do not sing in public":[9] compare the way English soccer crowds sing together. Brian Wren goes so far as to state "our culture undermines it".[10] The increasingly individualised experience of music for many people, especially those of younger generations, is a major factor behind this 'down under' reality. On the other hand, it is now recognised that there are health benefits of communal singing, and there are hopeful trends emerging in community music-making.

The widespread use of 'personal listening devices' (think iPods, MP3/4) means that each person's music collection, no matter how esoteric, revolves around her or his preferred styles of music from current or eras past. The advanced state of music recording, reproduction and marketing enables us to obtain the musical 'objects' of our personal choice from a wide range of possibilities. Further, these factors contribute to the way in which music is seen as a factor in individual and group identity. This personalising of music is one of the most significant cultural influences to recognise when planning congregational singing: it means that many worshippers expect that 'their music' will be important in corporate worship. The 'worship wars' that emerged in the 1980s were partly fuelled by this thinking. Taste or preferences can become the arbiter of value: "what I like must be good".[11]

Today the widest range ever of musical and text styles is available through the internet: there has never been a time in Christian history with such a wealth of new composition. A typical hymnbook

---

9   Elizabeth Smith, "Crafting and Singing Hymns in Australia," in Stephen Burns and Anita Monro (edd), *Christian Worship in Australia: Inculturating the Liturgical Tradition* (Strathfield: St Paul's, 2009), 185. Observe how major events now typically engage a noted solo singer rather than a choir to perform the National Anthem.

10 Brian Wren, *Praying Twice: The Music and Words of Congregational Song* (Louisville: Westminster / John Knox, 2000), 53.

11 Calvin M Johansson, *Music & Ministry: a biblical counterpoint*, 2nd ed. (Peabody, MA: Hendrickson, 1998), x.

includes several hundred songs—but sites like (the excellent) *Hymnary.com* offer tens of thousands. Yet paradoxically, many congregations are familiar with a quite restricted range of material, whether from the latest offerings from a particular source (Hillsong is a significant Australian example) or in a particular genre. The 'canon' of fifty or so hymns well known across the English-speaking Christian world has shrunk, or been replaced by a variety of 'canons' depending on where a congregation situates itself.

Another significant influence has been the development of marketing concepts to boost church attendance in the face of falling numbers. Much effort has gone into analysing generation-based tastes, leading to extreme claims such as, "almost everyone has a personal preference regarding the musical style and hymn-type used in worship. For each person, worship is better *when the music is right*."[12] The development of 'niche church communities' can be encouraged by using specific styles of music—but how these stay 'in communion' with others is difficult when the musical style adopted comes to define the congregation, and others feel excluded.[13]

But it is not all doom and gloom. The flowering of new lyrics and music over the past half-century means a wealth of resources are available for congregational song. Clergy, musicians and liturgical leaders are all involved in discerning the significance of the music used as part of 'performing the gospel' through music—not just 'performing the music'. Each leader brings their own skills and viewpoints, but the need is to focus on gospel-effective outcomes, taking account of cultural influences. This could form the basis for ongoing conversations.

---

12 David Bales and Herb Miller, "We Are Singing the Right Hymns…Aren't We?," *Church Effectiveness Nuggets: Volume 32* (2007): http://bishopperryinstitute.org.au/uploads/ChurchEffectivenessNuggets-Volume32.pdf.

13 For fuller discussion, see Pete Ward, *Selling Worship — How what we sing has changed the Church* (Milton Keynes: Paternoster, 2005).

PART B Music, words and musicians: how do they work together?

Tunes and texts

Liturgy involves more than words—and so does singing, which entails more than words set to music. However, assessing the words sung in church is often done without reference to the music to which they are sung. Lyrics, which exist as texts, are typically considered to be of primary importance, whatever the range of musical styles. This can be seen in the way songs are often listed by topic or theme, assessed by their content as text rather than for the style or mood of their musical setting. But the emotional impact of a song's words is all of a piece with the music associated with them. The idea of assessing both words and music *together* is occasionally found in significant works on the subject, yet there is little general awareness of the distinctive criteria involved. We live today in a 'sound-surround' culture, in which most people identify a song by its sound more than its words. This seeming dichotomy between words and tunes causes unnecessary arguments about church music. So let's have a deeper look at this, starting with the origins of 'hymns' as we know them today.

The publication of *Hymns Ancient and Modern* (1861) was a watershed for church music. Prior to around 1750, congregational song in English-speaking churches centred on metrical versions of the psalms: popular ones were those by Sternold and Hopkins, and Nate and Brady, which can be found bound up with the *Book of Common Prayer*. Until the work of Isaac Watts, then Charles and John Wesley, few songs with non-biblical texts were accepted as suitable for use in church, besides the small number of hymns attributed to saints such as Fortunatus or Bernard of Clairvaux. The *Methodist Hymnal*, arising from the Evangelical revival, pioneered the acceptance of new words and tunes for congregational song, but 'A&M' meant that hymns as we know them entered 'mainstream' church culture. Hymn collections ever since have largely seen the attachment of particular tunes to familiar texts. Over the intervening time, the identity of a 'hymn' has become fixed on a particular tune: a leader will quickly be told "that's not the right tune" when a change is made. So the term 'hymn' has taken on a more inclusive usage, as referring to the song as a whole, lyric and music together.

This combination of words and music contributes meaning in terms of the effect on singers' hearts and minds. Even so, the "Western Church has historically given primacy to words over other forms of expression."[14] This focus has over-ridden consideration of how music (and other non-verbal arts) shape and contribute to the actual meaning experienced when a hymn is sung in church. This is not to say that theologically the words of a song do not matter—but music as sound has a profound place in the contemporary western world. This is where it is imperative to consider music as being embedded in time, a 'time-art'. Poetry or words belong to what Susanne Langer terms 'virtual memory', so that a sense of the familiar past is happening when we engage in congregational song. We bring these two dimensions together effortlessly as we sing: as she writes,[15]

> Words and music come together in song, music swallows words … song is not a compromise between poetry and music … song is music.

This does not result in the words being meaningless, but (as David Cole puts it) "it does suggest that in the overall experiencing

---

14   David Cole, "Hymns and Meaning," *St Mark's Review* (Autumn 1991), 15.
15   Susanne K Langer, *Feeling and Form* (New York: Charles Scribner's Sons, 1953), 152.

of song, the meaning of the music becomes dominant". Further, "music certainly brings added depth and meaning to the words, but it can bring a multitude of additional meanings, precisely because it is music and not words".[16] This is reflected in the strong opinions that exist about the musical styles appropriate (or not) for use in Christian worship, and reflects Brian Wren's claim about the "ambiguous power" of music.[17]

So, recalling how words operate as "sacraments of meaning" (see Chapter Four), consider the claim that "music as sheer moulded sound has the potential to bear sacramental meaning."[18] This implies that the meaning of a song can only be found in the experience of singing it—which points up the significant ways in which performing music engages with performing the gospel in liturgy, and the significance of different 'song styles'.

Song styles: naming the music

Terms such as 'traditional', 'contemporary', 'praise and worship', 'classic', 'contemporary worship music', are typically used in ways that promote congregational song more as a 'product' than an activity. These terms are also ambiguous, so can have diverse meanings for different people in different settings. Moreover, the polarisation implied in speaking of 'contemporary' and 'traditional', or of a 'secular–sacred' dichotomy, are not ways of thinking about music or song as such, but rather apply to the way their sound is used. Such 'binary' thinking can shut down useful dialogue, and see congregations locked into an expectation of the endlessly familiar (of whatever type) in a world rich with musical possibilities.

---

16 Cole, 17.
17 Wren, 66.
18 Albert L Blackwell, *The Sacred in Music* (Louisville: Westminster John Knox Press, 1999), 16.

At this point two misconceptions about music styles in church need to be cleared up. One is the assumption that 'traditional' hymns are old (well, at least before the person claiming they are was born), and that their tunes come from a 'classical music' scene. They are thus viewed as belonging to an elite culture, or one that is irrelevant to contemporary people. Yes, some tunes to 'traditional' hymns have been composed by 'classical composers' (Handel, Purcell, Vaughan Williams, for example). More significant is the quality of the music, whenever composed or from whatever source: folk songs have been often taken up, for example. Skilled Christian musicians want to support good congregational song.

Another misconception is that 'traditional' writers of hymn lyrics such as Luther and Wesley used any old song from the popular culture of the day, even drinking songs. The music they chose, however, was not simply because it was popular, but because it was appropriate, and enabled congregations to participate in singing. Martin Luther was noteworthy for encouraging the wider use of congregational song, including setting part of the liturgy to music. Responding to the idea that he used drinking songs, Jonathan Aigner comments:

> When it came to music, he wrote his own tunes based on existing chants and religious tunes, and folk melodies. They were chosen, not necessarily because they were already well-known tunes, but because they were accessible. That was the key. They were singable. In practical terms, they were not melodically or rhythmically difficult, didn't stretch the average vocal range, and set the text with dignity, beauty, and artistry. It wasn't that he was trying to engage secular culture, it was that he wanted people to be able to participate. [19]

---

[19] Jonathan Alger, "Which of our favorite hymns are rewritten 'bar' songs?" http://www.patheos.com/blogs/ponderanew/2015/11/02/which-of-our-favorite-hymns-are-rewritten-bar-songs/

Aigner goes on to cite Luther's preface to the 1524 Wittenberg Hymnal:[20]

> These songs were arranged in four parts to give the young—who should at any rate be trained in music and other fine arts—something to wean them away from love ballads and carnal songs and to teach them something of value in their place, thus combining the good with the pleasing, as is proper for youth.

Dean McIntyre, having examined closely the Wesleys' use of 'secular' music, comes to similar conclusions:

> ... in every case where they made use of secular music for their hymns, it was always of the very highest caliber, never a little ditty, jingle, or disposable contemporary pop tune of the day that would be cast aside as soon as the next one was penned.[21]

Terms that define different styles by their musical elements or origins are a better way to go. When choosing music suited to performing the gospel, the criteria used needs to transcend and get beyond preferred styles, with their attached assumptions. A good case can thus be made for encouraging the thoughtful inclusion of varying musical styles in each service.

Michael Hawn outlines seven helpful categories of congregational song since Vatican II (1962–65), based on evolving historical and cultural streams:

---

20 "Preface to the 1524 Wittenberg Hymnal" in Vol. 53: *Luther's works, Liturgy and Hymns* J. J.Pelikan, H. C. Oswald & H. T. Lehmann, Ed. (Fortress Press: Philadelphia, 1999, c1965), 315.

21 Dean McIntyre, 'Debunking the Wesley tavern song myth' https://www.umcdiscipleship.org/resources/debunking-the-wesley-tavern-song-myth, point 4.

1. Roman Catholic liturgical renewal hymnody
2. Protestant contemporary classical hymnody
3. African-American gospel and spiritual songs
4. Revival/gospel songs
5. Folk song influences
6. Pentecostal songs
7. Global and ecumenical song forms.[22]

Each of these categories is represented in recent collections such as *Together in Song: The Australian Hymn Book II*.[23] Here are some examples, with Australian contributors named:

1. Do not be afraid, I am with you (16 Christopher Willcock)
2. Where wide sky rolls down (188 Elizabeth Smith)
   When his time was over (357 Robin Mann)
3. Let us break bread together with the Lord! (511)
   The blind man sat by the road and he cried (579)

---

22 C. Michael Hawn, "Streams of Song: An Overview of Congregational Song in the Twenty-First Century," *The Hymn* 61/1 (Winter 2010), 18–19. https://babel.hathitrust.org/cgi/pt?id=mdp.39015080918306;view=1up;seq=1

23 *Together in Song: the Australian Hymn Book II* (East Melbourne: Harper Collins Religious, 1999).

This book was drawn up by representatives from the Anglican Church, Churches of Christ, Lutheran Church, Presbyterian Church, Roman Catholic Church and Uniting Church. It includes a "blend of hymns, psalms, songs and responses" from 48 countries, of which almost as many are from the 20th century as from earlier ages. *Together in Song* is available in Harmony, Melody and Large Print editions. The Harmony edition includes full tunes and excellent indices (tunes, metres, composers, authors, scripture passages (19 pages), subjects (56 3-column pages), church year (8 pages), children, dance, first lines); the Melody edition includes the tune line and words and first lines index; the Large Print words only. All the book's music and words in the public domain are available from: http://smallchurchmusic.weebly.com/together-in-song-au-1999.html

4. Great is your faithfulness (154)
   Just as I am (584)
5. Create in us a clean heart, O God (712 Digby Hannah)
   This day God gives me (642 James Quinn)
6. Lord I come to you (658)
   Shout to the Lord (738 Darlene Zschech)
7. The great love of God (164)
   Kneels at the feet of his friends (640 arranged by Lawrence Bartlett)

This seven-part schema provides a good reference point for reflecting on the diversity of contemporary congregational song. The weekly song repertoire of many congregations ranges over several categories, and these days within any congregation there are likely to be people who come from varied musical cultures and church backgrounds. Each of Hawn's categories is suited to particular places, occasions and functions in worship, some of which are more appropriate than others: for example, 'Just as I am' is more appropriate during communion than 'Shout to the Lord'; 'When his time was over' works well in Holy Week, though 'Where wide sky rolls down' might not. Identifying the categories that are typically used in a congregation can offer strategies for songs that employ music from the variety of traditions in our Christian heritage, rather than being restricted to just one. It is important to identify music that promotes the performance of the gospel rather than be just focused on musical style or origin. A rich repertoire is available.

In terms of music style, three broad categories can be identified: unaccompanied chant, the chorale-hymn, and folk-rock styles. For examples in life generally, think of chants at football matches and demonstrations (Wadda we want? ...); or "God save the Queen" and

"Waltzing Matilda" as examples in general life. Here the focus is on the *harmonic structure* of the song repertoire. This approach encourages examination of how the style of music 'works' on our emotions and understanding, and how it serves as congregational song. [24] It is the harmonies and chord sequences that largely propel our experience of music through time: these underpin other musical elements such as melody and the 'inbuilt' rhythm of the harmonies involved. Setting aside unaccompanied melody such as Gregorian chant, the other two categories offer a helpful understanding of how music works in congregational settings. They also indicate some of the issues about what instrumentation is best suited to accompany singing—see Part C below.

Two examples illustrate these differences. The melody "Nun dankett alle Gott" has been used for four centuries with the text, "Now thank we all our God" (*Together in Song* 106). The music is harmonised into four-parts for standard soprano/alto/tenor/bass singing, with frequent chord changes. Now consider the folk melody "Sally Gardens", which accompanies the modern words by John Bell and Graham Maule, "Inspired by love and anger" (*Together in Song* 674). The harmonies change less frequently.

---

24 See Fay Magee, "Examining Contemporary Congregational Song—Beyond Sung Theology" (University of Divinity, 2012): http://repository.divinity.edu.au/id/eprint/1240

Both tunes are easy to sing, but the 'chorale' type has more complex harmonies than the 'folk' one, in which the melody is to the fore, over a simpler harmonic structure. The emotional affect of these harmonic structures is different, so that the way each tune relates to the words it accompanies is different. How these structures work to create musical meaning can vary, but can assist in assessing how text is carried by the music. All congregational songs can be analysed in this way—theological criteria that apply then include questions such as:

- To what extent does this melody work appropriately with these words?
- Is the affective weight given to the text by the harmonic and melodic structures suitable—that is, does the musical accompaniment support singers' engagement with its meaning, while not manipulating feelings?
- Is the music and its rhythms too bland for the text, or do they overwhelm it?

The two practical categories of congregational song proposed include a great variety of types of melodies and settings. The examples above illustrate two of the possibilities. The folk-rock style can include examples from various historical sources, for example those in the Wild Goose repertoire from the Iona Community and John Bell. Contemporary composers such as Robin Mann (Australian), Thomas Troeger (US) and Stuart Townend (English) often produce songs in this style. Many gospel songs have their origins in the Victorian 'music hall' tradition of Moody & Sankey, or country music: what is often called 'contemporary worship music' extends this to upbeat soft rock from the pop world. The strong emotions evoked in these styles are significant in the personal lives of many Christians, but reliance on emotion is an inadequate criterion for them to dominate a service.

In sum, both music and text matter in church—and their combination results in more than we can imagine or predict. As David Cole notes, hymnody can "take worshippers beyond the physical moment of a liturgical action to another sphere of experience and understanding".[25] Try speaking a song text, and then singing it, and you will agree.

Song-words: how do they matter?

What then of the words? Brian Wren contends that "a good congregational song lyric is devout, just, frugal, beautiful, communal, purposeful, and musical."[26] Quite a demanding list of criteria. However, many hymns written over 50 years ago that meet the criteria use 'thee/thy' and 'hath/doth' spelling and grammar, or do not reflect modern sensitivity to language that excludes. The committee that prepared *Together in Song* sought to address these concerns, while recognising that "some of the great hymns would sound hollow if they were modernised": an example is 'Guide me, O thou great Redeemer' (569). On the other hand, "Where it was possible to modernise the language, this has been done with great care and respect for the original."[27] 'Great is your faithfulness' (154) is a good example.

---

25 Cole, 17.
26 Wren, 189.
27 *Together in Song*, Foreword, vii.

Gail Ramshaw offers eight questions to consider when evaluating a text: [28]

- *To whom is the hymn addressed?* (it might be ourselves rather than God)
- *How is the Bible used?* (it might be quoted so out of context as to be misleading)
- *What is the theological content?* (it might be so outdated so as now to be false)
- *How does the hymn employ metaphor?* (word images help us explore layers of meaning)
- *How inclusive is the text?* (it might exclude sinners, or women—or both)
- *What is the implied description of the human being?* (too 'I'? too easy or hard on us?)
- *Who wrote the hymn text* ('give three points to a hymn written by a great saint for a renowned situation ... none to one written by yourself or your best friend')
- *What is the liturgical fit?* (Christmas carols on Good Friday?)

Ramshaw's second question raises the issues around singing words from the Bible—on the surface this seems unarguable with. There is a tendency in some contemporary repertoire to credit a song's biblical base by using scriptural words and phrases, as if that validates the text and the song. But care needs to be taken that the context in which the words appear in the scriptures *and* the context in which they are sung are not in tension with one another. Two particular areas are language about 'love' and 'war'. Love is central to the Christian understanding of God. But in the highly sexualised cultures in which we live, word–music combinations that arouse feelings rather than perform the gospel are decidedly unhelpful.

---

28 Gail Ramshaw, "Words Worth Singing," *The Hymn 46/2 (April 1995) 16-19.* https://babel.hathitrust.org/cgi/pt?id=mdp.39015033625891;view=1up;seq=97

Singing 'his banner over me is love' is to my mind hard to justify, even though the text comes from Song of Songs 2:4—and there are many similar examples. But it is also a question of who sings them, and when and where. 'Lord I come to you' (*Together in Song* 685), with its powerful chorus, 'in the power of your love', is a case in point: chosen for a late-night event at a youth camp is not wise, but in a Sunday service it can be most appropriate. Similar concerns apply to war-words, though most congregations today are sensitive about this: 'Onward Christian soldiers' has gone out of fashion due to its associations with false nationalism, even though it is worded with care—'marching *as to* war'.[29]

A well-constructed text will often use images and insights that reveal a resonance with and embedded sense of scripture rather than direct quotations. This is one reason why a good number of Charles Wesley's hymns survive—more than 40 in *Together in Song*. Many newer songs do likewise, and also use straightforward sentence structures, though in contemporary rather than 'thee/thy' language. When each line contains an idea that links to the next and beyond, this allows the music to function in singable 'sound bites', while progressing the meaning.

In sum, music and text work together in a variety of ways. The music can dominate the lyrics, though it is their doctrinal correctness that is often the concern. The above analysis, however, shows that there are several dimensions to a song's meaning as it is actually being performed in congregational song: considering the way music and lyrics work *together* is what matters in seeking to ensure that the *gospel* is performed authentically.

---

29 See Charles Sherlock, "Fight the Good Fight: Military Language in Public Liturgy", *Australian Journal of Liturgy* 2/2 (1989) 74–91.

Musicians and microphones: what is their place?

Performance is a central concept for musicians, whether instrumentalists or singers. In a concert setting they perform for the audience. In church this is sometimes the case—when a choir or singing group performs an 'anthem' for example. Most typically, however, the place of musicians in liturgy is playing and singing to further the performance of the gospel. The most common aspect of this is accompaniment, a skill that requires them to give a lead, yet remain 'in the background' so that it is the singing of the entire congregation that is to the fore. (Much the same can be said for a pianist who accompanies a violin or wind soloist.)

So where are musicians, particularly instrumentalists, best placed in a church building? Until the rapid spurt of church building from the 1860s on, choirs sang from galleries at the rear, while the organ or fiddle was there or at the side: musicians were to be heard but not seen. These new churches, however, typically placed the choir between congregation and sanctuary, both to enhance the visual drama and to highlight the spiritual hierarchy of people, (robed) choir and clergy. Alongside this, general prosperity and growing musical literacy meant that each church building was expected to have a harmonium or organ, and one or more people to play it. Since the 1960s, many churches have been re-arranged towards a more 'inclusive' ethos, with seating that offers a stronger sense of community, and lectern and holy table placed within the assembly and its leaders. Further, the range of musical skills has widened: suburban congregations may have one or more instrumental groups of keyboard, flute, guitar, violin and so on, while small rural churches might sing to music downloaded from the internet (see Resources section), or sing unaccompanied.

How musicians and singers are placed in such settings affects not only their performing, but how the gospel is performed. It has become quite common to have a band and singers (at microphones) at the front of the congregation. While this is good in a concert setting, it significantly alters several aspects of the focus of Christian worship.[30] Does the congregation become an 'audience'? Is the band performing for the 'audience', or leading the congregation in engaging with the gospel? Is the visual focus more on the musicians than on the lectern, pulpit or holy table—the items of furniture associated with performing the gospel? Returning to a form of the traditional placement, with musicians and singers to the side or rear, or spread among the congregation, has much to commend it.

A related issue is the now widespread use of microphones. It is worth remembering that even cathedrals functioned without them for centuries: has good voice projection become a lost art? Most church buildings today are not so large that amplification is necessary for a well-placed singing group. The congregation's singing is encouraged when people do not sit apart from one another, and can see others: even slightly curved or angled seating works to naturally amplify the vocal sound. Where amplification is used, it is important that it not drown the congregation's own voice, but enable them to participate actively.

A major reason for amplification being introduced is the use of amplified instruments—organ, harmonium or piano are loud enough of themselves, and enable harmonies, not just the melody, to be played (typically in four parts). Instruments like the flute, trumpet or violin can be loud enough, but only provide the tune, while guitars generally provide chord harmony and rhythm—which is why the combination of these complementary sounds in a band or ensemble works well.

The main challenge as regards sound level and sight lines is

---

30   The issues around sight lines, in particular the use of data projectors, are taken up in the next chapter.

usually a drum kit: once one appears in the mix, other instruments need to be amplified to balance the volume. Further, a drum kit is fixed in place, and imposes strict, accented rhythms when accompanying singing. And many drummers have not learnt to play with sensitivity to the space in which worship is taking place. This makes it unsuitable for quieter songs, or those with less defined rhythm (think 'Abide with me' or 'How great thou art'). When amplification is needed, the band can be placed anywhere in relation to the congregation, since the sound will come from speakers that can be placed to suit. Acoustic instruments can be supported by smaller, flexibly placed and more diverse percussion instruments, which are less dominant than a drum kit—maracas, tambourine, bells, castanets, kettle or conga drums for example. These can create an interesting layering of timbre without drowning out singing, and can be played by those with little musical training, but a good sense of rhythm—children can be involved in this way (along with reliably-performing adults).

PART C Selecting music

No doubt you are looking for ways to refresh and extend the musical dimensions of your congregation's life. Such a project is not simply a matter of looking for new material or novelty. Rather, it is one of affirming the possibilities for greater depth in experience and understanding, taking seriously the role of music in performing the gospel. It is also an opportunity to explore, listen to and/or participate in unfamiliar material—which need not just be 'new' in terms of recent. Most congregations are pretty settled in their singing patterns: even with several hymnbooks and internet sources in use, the range of songs sung over a year rarely exceeds 100. A long-term audit of songs in current use can show up 'gaps' in theme, style or 'feel': once done, keeping a record from week to week facilitates having a review once or twice a year (see Part D1).

The songs of scripture

Singing psalms and other scriptural songs ('canticles') is an age-old practice in Jewish and Christian worship. It goes back to the time of Miriam and Moses (Exodus 15 and Deuteronomy 32), of David (2 Samuel 22–23, Psalms 3–9 and many more) and numerous unnamed choirs (Psalms 42–29 for example). In the Middle Ages, nuns and monks sang the whole Psalter at least once a month—a practice Archbishop Thomas Cranmer continued in the *Book of Common Prayer*. In parts of the Reformed/Presbyterian tradition, psalms converted into metrical verse were the only songs permitted to be sung, a practice that continues in some places today.

Until the 1960s, Anglican congregations encountered the psalms in Morning and Evening Prayer, but not in Holy Communion. The liturgical changes of the 1960s saw a psalm restored to the eucharist in the Roman Catholic, Anglican, Uniting and other traditions, though more often said rather than sung. The translation used in *APBA*, *The Liturgical Psalter*, takes the practice of reading 'in choir' into account: leader and people, or each side of the congregation, say the first half of each verse (to the colon) with the others responding, or by alternate verses.[31] Indeed, this is how the original Hebrew is set out, so that all present both proclaim and hear the psalm. In the 1800s the practice of 'Anglican chant' began, each verse being sung to ten notes, six to the colon and four for the remainder, in 'speech rhythm' so that the words' meaning is brought out. Once learnt, this method of singing the psalms is satisfying, but it has been less followed in recent decades, though contemporary composers (such as Christopher Wilcock) have explored new ways of achieving a similar result.

Several English language metrical versions of the psalms have been issued since the Reformation—as noted earlier, some were bound together with the *Book of Common Prayer* to form the earliest 'hymnbooks'. Quite a few metrical psalms remain in hymnbooks— Psalm 100, for example, is probably best known as 'All people that on earth do dwell', sung to the tune 'Old Hundredth'. The twentieth century has seen more musically adventurous compositions, notably the 'Grail' psalms: these typically provide a refrain for the congregation, while a cantor sings the verses, usually rewritten in poetic form. Modern hymnbooks provide a wide range of psalm settings: in *Together in Song*, the first 97 songs are psalm settings

---

31   *The Liturgical Psalter* derives from the psalter included in BCP, attributed to Miles Coverdale. The BCP translation preceded that of the King James Bible: the small differences between them can be a cause of occasional confusion. Likewise, *The Liturgical Psalter* has slight differences to the *New Revised Standard* and *New International* versions, which are designed for study and public reading rather than congregational use.

Note 9 in the Preface to *APBA* (page x) allows for other versions of the psalms to be used.

in a range of musical styles, covering all the psalm portions of the *Revised Common Lectionary*.

Song selection

Selecting the songs for a service is a significant ministry: well chosen songs make a positive contribution to performing the gospel. Several matters come into consideration:
- the community that gathers,
- the song resources available,
- what instrumentalists are available to accompany singing, and/or what singers can lead the congregation, particularly if singing unaccompanied, and
- how both effective and affective outcomes can be achieved.

The main principle for selecting songs is: *follow the shape, focus and action of the service.* As regards *shape*, the Sunday services in *APBA* and similar books follow a pattern grounded in the mission of God: gather, listen, pray, do (typically holy communion) and be sent out.[32] The service's *focus* arises from the scriptures read, and the season in the Christian year; its *action* includes how the service 'flows' towards and from its climactic 'doing' moments. But taking in all these aspects can be rather daunting. Where do you start?

A good place is hymnbook indexes—most provide ones that can help identify hymns appropriate for a service. *Together in Song* is outstanding in this respect: its Harmony Edition includes extensive indices on both music (composers, tunes, metres) and words (scripture passages, subjects, the church year): the 'subject' category includes sub-headings for the various stages of a service. (Even if your congregation does not use this book, owning a copy for its indexes is worth it, as many hymns appear in other collections.)

---

32 Chapter Nine explores this concept of common prayer being supported today by 'common structures'.

So a first step is to compile a list of possible songs, even if you are not familiar with them: a new one every month or so will refresh the repertoire. It is likely that you will have a dozen or so written down: now the task is to think about which really 'click' and fit an obvious place in the service (e.g. to commence or conclude the service, or before or after a scripture reading to which it relates).

Which takes us to a further issue: song placement. The scope for including music and singing at different points in a service is wide. Beyond any 'rules', Note 6 in the Preface to *APBA* says that songs "may be sung otherwise than where provision is made for them". It goes on to say that in their selection, "careful attention should be given both to the appropriateness of the words to the themes of the service and also the relation of the hymn chosen to its position within the service".

All services begin and end. Opening song(s) should focus our hearts on God in whose Name we are gathered—just choosing well-known ones to get the congregation's voices warmed up in a singalong is not good enough. Likewise, closing song(s) should enable the people to leave with a sense of being sent out to continue God's mission in the worship of daily living. Songs linked with key actions of the service—framing scripture readings (ideally including a sung psalm), welcoming the Gospel, supporting the preaching and prayers, during the collection, accompanying preparation for holy communion.[33] Distributing communion takes time, and involves the congregation moving to receive: this is an ideal time for reflective music (sung or instrumental) to be offered;

---

33 Various notes regarding music selection and placement are made in *APBA*. Morning & Evening Prayer (Second Order) #3 reads, "A time of praise follows, including suitable hymns, songs and prayers" (page 36). Holy Communion (Third Order) "may begin with songs or hymns of praise and thanksgiving" (page 168). The Funeral Service notes that a "hymn, anthem or canticle may be said or sung, or music may be played" (page 712).

it is also a good time for short unaccompanied songs. When the service includes baptism, healing, ordination, a wedding, songs that celebrate God's grace in these ministries will be included.

When and how many songs to sing is a matter for local custom, but often follows a fixed pattern. There is value in reviewing such patterns from time to time. As well, the seasons of the church year give opportunities for change, and most congregations welcome intelligent experimentation. Short chants can provide a more reflective mood than songs, and be used flexibly. For example, "He became poor" (*Together in Song* 721) can work well as a repeated chant to open Advent services, or as a reflective response to Christmas readings. Likewise, the Taizé chant "O Lord, hear my prayer" (*Together in Song* 741) can be used as a congregational response to spoken prayers, or during a time of quiet reflection.

So, now you have your dozen or so possible songs for the service. Two or three typically choose and place themselves, leaving a couple more to be chosen. Here criteria beyond just the lyrics come into view: sometimes the length will exclude a song for this occasion. More significant is taking into account the musical styles of the songs chosen, checking that a reasonable variety of styles is included in the service overall. A final check concerns transitions in the service: when a song accompanies movement (e.g. a procession, taking up the collection, moving to the font, preparing the holy table), is it suitable, singable and long enough? And of course the skills of accompanists need to be considered—where the tunes may be new, it is essential that musicians are given a least a week's notice. Ideally, leaders and musicians work together in selecting songs, and for a month or season at a time, though ultimate responsibility rests with clergy.

Communion settings

Modern holy communion services use updated words for parts traditionally sung—'Glory be to God on high', 'Lord have mercy', the Lord's Prayer, 'Holy, holy holy' and so on. As far as possible, the texts of these in *APBA* follow the ecumenically agreed wording of *Praying Together* (see Note 1, p. 820). Composers have been active in writing new music for these new words, across the English-speaking global church, including several Australians (e.g. Lawrence Bartlett, Geoffrey Cox, Michael Dudman, Philip Matthias, Beverley Phillips, Christopher Willcock). As it does with psalms in Section I, *Together in Song* provides a range of communion settings in Section XV.

Many congregations will have a standard set of tunes, but special occasions warrant extra effort, a practice time a few weeks in advance helps. A season may be illuminated by using something different: the 'Kyrie eleison' (*Together in Song* 736) from the Ukrainian Orthodox community, for example, is easily learnt and builds up into wonderful six-part harmony. When a setting seems tired, learning a new one can be a staged process, a new section being gradually introduced over several weeks.

Accompanying congregational singing

A growing number of congregations struggle with the practicalities of providing suitable accompaniment for songs. Singing round the piano at home has been largely replaced by personal listening devices, while fewer people seem to be learning keyboard playing. Some congregations are able to provide a significant pool of instrumentalists as well as organists—flute, penny whistle, guitar, bass and hand percussion such as bells (see p. 158 on drums). When a band/instrumental ensemble is available, a variety of accompaniments can be used, as suited to the song and the musicians' abilities—and a verse or two sung unaccompanied does not go astray, and allows people to enjoy the sounds of their own combined voices. Using the variety available in a music group can also assist in taking the focus away from specific 'styles' of music, or just one style that always uses the same combination of instruments, and provide richer and deeper experiences of how music works in liturgy. Note: clergy need to appreciate the time commitment involved in having a musical ensemble, which calls for players to rehearse regularly.

Some congregations, however, especially outside major centres, lack musicians. The growth of community music-making has seen growing confidence in unaccompanied singing, and some congregations find this rewarding. A practical way forward for many situations is using recordings from the internet: the smallchurchmusic and *Hymnary* sites offer excellent resources, and once a tune has been downloaded it can be called up easily. The *Australian Hymnbook Company* has produced CDs of accompaniments out of copyright. (See Resources section.)

Selecting songs from YouTube, or recordings made by skilled performers, is another possibility, but it can be harder to sing alongside a choir, sometimes the words differ, and the pitch may be challenging.

Another critical musical issue for choosing music is pitch range—how high or low some notes are. It needs to be set in a range suitable for communal singing: unless they are trained singers, few people are comfortable with more than 8–10 notes span. Songs from older books, or those primarily written for solo or choir performance, typically have the range higher or wider than most people can manage: a case in point is Londonderry Air ('Danny Boy'), which is used for some songs. Newer collections choose musical keys that take into account pitch range practicalities, and also that most congregations sing in unison rather than parts: *Together in Song*, for example, keeps the top note of most songs to the D an octave above middle C. It is sometimes worth transposing the accompaniment to a more suitable key, but this calls for skilled musicians or a modern electronic keyboard.

What to do when the words are spot on, but the tune is unknown, or beyond your musician's capabilities? Here is where the wonderful 'Metrical Index' comes into its own. This lists tunes by the number of syllables in each line: so the metre of 'Our God, our help in ages last / our help for times to come / be now our guide through troubles past / our help for years to come' is 8.6.8.6—so-called 'Common Metre' because many tunes use this structure. In theory, any 8.6.8.6 tune can be used to accompany these words—but not all will fit, depending on where the stress is placed in the words. Where the metrical index in your book shows only one or two examples of the tune you are considering, you are probably out of luck—so learn the new tune.

Music for the congregation

To this point, performing the gospel through music has been largely considered from the viewpoint of what the congregation does—sing together, perhaps supported by a singing group or choir. Music directed towards the people, whether singing or instrumental, plays a complementary role. Morning and Evening Prayer in the *Book of Common Prayer* includes a note: "In Quires and Places where they sing, here followeth the Anthem." Not only at this point, but anywhere helpful, a choir or singing group can offer the ministry of song to the congregation—the 'anthem'—from a wider range than what is possible for all to sing.

Similarly, instrumental music played *for* the congregation has a vital place in liturgy. People do not always appreciate how music played before or after a service assists their participation in worship.

In some traditions it is customary for the sermon or prayers to be followed by a period of music for reflection. Again, music often accompanies movement—processions, offertory, the administration of communion, and can contribute greatly to the ethos of a service such as a wedding or funeral, in which there may be little singing. The selection of appropriate music played for the congregation calls for musician(s) with knowledge of both the instruments involved, and what is appropriate at different times in a service. If musicians are not available, playing recorded music can be helpful, for example, to contribute to a quiet reflective time before the service commences, or during the administration of communion. But 'live' music is preferable: instrumentalists have much scope to explore the use of the non-verbal art form of musical sound in worship.

Part D   Putting the sound of music into practice

This Part offers some ideas for exploring and deepening the sound of music in performing the gospel in your congregation(s). The order of ideas is not significant—just please engage in two or three of them.

1. Taking an audit of your song repertoire

Why not undertake an audit of the songs and settings known and used in your congregation? It will be quickest to find records of the previous months, perhaps from pew sheets or records kept by clergy or musicians. Six months will probably provide a reasonable indication of the range of repertoire and the frequency of use, but a full year is ideal.

A spreadsheet can be set up to show not only the first line and date(s) used, but categories such as musical style, season/theological theme: Hawn's seven streams could be useful in setting this up. Where possible, indicate at which point in the service a song is used, and from where it was sourced. If a song is used often, there may be good reason—but ask 'why?' or maybe look for another song for the same theme.

When this work is done, work through the book used in your congregation, noting what well-known songs have never been used—and what interesting ones might be learnt.

2. Exploring your congregation's music

It is a rare congregation in which no one has any musical interest or skills. To judge what range of musical styles is favoured by regular worshippers, a survey could be conducted to determine what music they listen to *during the week*. Likewise, it could find out what participation they may have in professional or community music-making. Some with a reasonable level of music literacy might like to join a singing group or explore playing in a music group.

At a social occasion (e.g. church pot luck dinner) a selection of parishioners could present a piece of music significant to them. This can be important for affirming what each person brings, and presenting an idea of their broader musical world.

3. Introducing new congregational repertoire

Some congregations can be a little wary about learning new material, so it is important to do it well. From a musical point of view, hearing a new tune unaccompanied (i.e. by itself, without singing) is most effective, along with (where possible) learning the words by ear. This requires a confident but not necessarily 'talented' singer leading, but it is a worthwhile role to develop. Most communities have people who are good at helping others improve their singing: inviting such a person to come to the parish and run workshops, or perhaps organise a Hymn Festival, perhaps with other congregations in your area, is a possibility. If the congregation does not include a singing group or choir, try getting a few enthusiastic people together to learn a new song in advance. Listening to a recording can be helpful to give people the 'feel' of its rhythm, tune and words.

Learning a new short song or chorus can help build confidence. If a new song has long verses, say with eight lines, learning two lines at a time works well, with the next pair added until the whole verse is covered. If possible, repeat new songs regularly over several weeks. By then you might be ready for another one.

4. Experimenting with resources

Select a few well-known songs for which different tunes can be used (metrical indexes can help you find possibilities). Gather some friends for a singalong through your list. Discuss how the different tunes affect the way you each perceive or react to the text, and to the whole experience of the song. Do different tunes place certain parts of the text in more prominence? Does the text have a focal point, and is this matched by the music?

An interesting example is Elizabeth Smith's text, "Holy Spirit, go before us" (*Together in Song* 420): compare singing this to 'Maria's Tune' and 'Blaenwern'. Another interesting comparison is setting "Take my life, and let it be" to the new tune 'Charlton' which results in three verses rather than six: other familiar tunes for these words are 'Nottingham' and 'Savannah' (*Together in Song* 599(i) and (ii) = 219(i)). Listen to these tunes on the *Together in Song* CD2, and consider new ones you could introduce (see Resources section).

5. Reflecting on the power of music

With a small group make a selection of songs, ideally including some psalm settings. Take some time to read the texts aloud, and then sing them to a suitable tune(s). For example, there are several well-known settings of Psalm 23 in common use. A recording of a choir singing each song could provide useful comparison.

Give time to allow each person to reflect on what they observe and learn from the experience. Share your reflections and observations, and how these might deepen your understanding and appreciation of some of the texts and settings.

Pastoral theologian Marva Dawn wrote *How shall we worship?—Biblical guidelines for the worship wars* (Tyndale House, 2003). This small book—an evening's good read—takes its framework from Psalm 96. The last section is entitled, "How does worship form us by the future to live in the present?" The book would make for a good small group discussion perhaps over three to four sessions. Questions are provided for each section.

Conclusion

Music in worship is often a contentious area, where trends and tastes will ebb and flow, empires rise and fall. The challenge for those entrusted to choose, lead and perform music is to be so immersed in the flow of a service as to sense the best ways and means for the gospel to be performed.

There are so many rich angles from which to explore the ways in which music can contribute to this ministry. Along and together with the words used in liturgy, music shapes us, and forms (or deforms) our insights into the wisdom and ways of God.

Resources for music ministry
Song selection

The UK-based *Royal School of Church Music* provides four issues per year of *Sunday by Sunday—the RSCM guide for all who plan and lead worship*. Belonging to the RSCM will ensure it is delivered to you in sufficient time in Australia for advance planning. It follows the three-year lectionary readings, and a wide range of songs is represented; 16 sources cover a variety of musical styles, plus categories for psalms, short songs, world music and instrumental music.

www.rscmaustralia.org.au

Milgate, Wesley, and Wood, D'Arcy. *A Companion to Together in Song: Australian Hymn Book II.* (Sydney: *The Australian Hymn Book Company*, 2006).

This resource began as Wesley Milgate's companion to the *Australian Hymn Book* (1977), updated for *Together in Song* (1999) by D'Arcy Wood. Each of the over 700 songs has notes about its origin, author and composer.

Congregational song support

- Four CDs of keyboard accompaniments for songs in *Together in Song*, recorded for congregational use, are available from *The Australian Hymn Book Company*. As well, learning new hymns can be assisted by recordings of choirs singing songs from *Together in Song*: a double CD of 66 songs is available, and another CD with 34 songs first published in *Sing Alleluia*. www.togetherinsong.org/Products/tabid/80/Default.aspx
- The *Hymnary.org* is a collaborative North American site that allows the words and tunes of a huge variety of songs to be sourced: it notes that *Shout to the Lord*, for example, is available in 16 hymnals. A topic or theme can be used to develop a list of suitable songs for services, and flexible scores and arrangements are available (as PDFs). www.hymnary.org
- The smallchurchmusic site was developed in Australia by a Baptist pastor in a rural area. This provides accompaniments on pipe organ, keyboard and small band for a wide range of songs in the public domain, while a related site gives access to

copyright materials for a small fee. A wealth of information for musicians and other church leaders is included, plus links to Hymnary.org and to the English site 'Jubilate', which provides "free access to hundreds of contemporary hymns and arrangements by a group of the UK's leading Christian composers and writers." http://smallchurchmusic.weebly.com www.jubilate.co.uk/
- The 'CCLI' site is another source of (purchasable) song materials, and offers a way to record the usage of copyright works. http://au.ccli.com

Chapter Seven
Seeing is believing?
Liturgy on screen

Overview

Part A   explores the social and cultural context of using projection screens in church. Might this be a betrayal of the Christian tradition?

Part B   responds to congregations convinced that all service content should be projected on a screen. How do words work when projected like images?

Part C   considers what screens are, and are not, good for in performing the gospel in church. What should not be projected?

Part D   offers ideas on practical matters when projecting in church.

A technological revolution is taking place in the way the gospel is performed in liturgy. Popular culture, dominated since World War I by a sound-oriented 'radio' ethos of passive reception, shifted to a 'seeing' one as TV spread in the 60s and 70s, and today we live in the sound-and-sight dominated, inter-active age of the internet and computer games. The ubiquitous smartphone has brought a revolution in personal communication: just one device can play favourite songs, hold the Bible in several versions, and access manifold web resources for videos, podcasts—and prayers. Free time for many children today means computer games rather than reading, hobbies or playing outside. How does someone for whom computers and smartphones are second nature play their part in performing the gospel?

In churches, this major cultural shift is evidenced by a new piece of furniture: one or more large screens used to project service content (whether by data projector or television). Using microphones, screens and their associated computer-related technologies in Christian liturgy makes a lot of sense. As with earlier technologies, the issue is not whether these are 'good' or 'bad', but how best they may be employed to further the *performance* of authentic Christian worship. If people end up watching rather than joining in a service, something is out of kilter—worship is not just a spectator sport. Similarly, if a power blackout means that 'the service is off today, folks', something is very wrong.

In some large church buildings, such as St Andrew's Cathedral, Sydney, television screens have been used for many years to enable the congregation (especially people behind pillars) to see what is going on 'up front'. This does not of itself change the ways in which worship is traditionally performed, however: it just makes the 'up-front' action more accessible (whether at lectern, pulpit or holy table). Where both the 'live' performance and the screen can be seen at the same time, issues can arise—what does it mean to be looking at the *projected* action ('virtual' performance) rather than the action itself, for example? And what happens when the words used in a service are projected on screen rather than read from a book or pew sheet?

Part A Performing the gospel as media cultures shift

Technology inevitably affects how liturgy is performed, and how participation is affected. Until printing arrived, all manu-scripts were that—hand (*manus*)-written texts, available only to a few. In pre-printing times, only the leader was likely to have a copy of the service: others participated by listening, or repeating after the leader, or saying words known by heart. Even when printing came about, it took a long time before books were cheap enough for worshippers to have a copy of the Bible, prayer or hymnbook. And the possibility of a congregation producing its own services, songbook or pew sheet was unthinkable until photocopying technology made this possible.

Similar comments could be made about sound. Chanting began in the Middle Ages as a way of amplifying a reader's voice so all could hear. The four-part hymn tunes western Christians are familiar with took centuries to emerge, made possible in large part by the printing of musical scores and hymnbooks. Electric amplification, radio microphones, digital recording and the like are shifting the way we hear in church. Electronic keyboards that can replicate every musical instrument, along with inexpensive recording equipment, have seen an explosion in popular hymnody and its publication.

The 'radio times' culture of the 1930s–80s has given way to one in which visual media form the way people primarily experience their 'world'. Word-processing, music software and the internet mean that a 'worship resource' can be constructed and published in days rather than years, and without the 'censoring' by committees, theologians and editors that print publication involves. Hymn and prayer books are increasingly being replaced by electronic texts, which can easily be edited and circulated. This cultural shift has been more pronounced in Protestant than Roman Catholic circles. The latter tradition is 'at home' with the symbolic, and has a strong sense of liturgical commonality. Protestants, on the other hand, have long regarded 'words' and 'freedom' as crucial in Christian worship, so are generally more open to the changes in text and structure enabled by electronic media. This is seen most clearly in Pentecostal 'mega-churches', where projected images rather than fixed symbols have come to be the main form of 'interior decoration', along with radio-mikes (which allow speakers to move around) and amplified music.

Slides, TV shows or films were occasionally used 'on screen' in services in the mid-20th century, usually in the 'sermon slot'. Yet what was shown had to be brought in from outside: content could not be created locally. The *Religious Film Society* did big business in the 1950s–70s—remember 'Fact and Faith Films'? In the 1980s, overhead projectors (OHPs) began to proliferate in classrooms, and then in liturgy. They were used mainly to project song lyrics, often on hand-scrawled acetate sheets that got easily mixed up or put on upside down. Creative preachers might use layers of sheets to show the development of a message, or project pictures for a children's talk, but OHPs could only project static images, while preparing materials was time-consuming and called for some artistic ability.

Meanwhile, colour television replaced radio as the major technology of communication, bringing about the demise of most Sunday evening services. The 'radio culture' of church gradually began to feel out of kilter with the 'seeing' culture of daily home life. And, as western society loosened up in the 1970s, the 'do your own thing' ethos imbibed by baby boomers began to make its impact felt in church. Resistance to the perceived inflexible 'modernism' of church-approved rites and songs of yesteryear grew and spread. It was not surprising that OHPs were seen as a step towards more visual and flexible patterns of worship. But compared to TV they were lifeless.

The development of the graphics capacity of personal computers—most notably from the release of the Apple Macintosh and Microsoft Windows 3.1 in the early 90s—changed all this. Software such as PowerPoint allowed an averagely skilled user to produce graphics previously only available from a sign-writer. Clip Art followed (the 'religious' ones are still dreadful), and the web/internet emerged from the mid-90s. Digital cameras, scanners and data projectors came within the reach of ordinary citizens from 2000 or so. As a result, locally prepared, dynamic visual media for *performing* the gospel became possible, spread rapidly and proliferated, especially in schools.

Interestingly, the growth in use of visual technologies seems to be strongest in Christian traditions that have favoured 'ear-gate' over 'eye-gate', hearing words over seeing images. Evangelical Protestants and revivalist Pentecostals were quick to take up not only amplification, but also projection technologies. Radio mikes free the preacher to walk around, while miked-up singers can lead music without being drowned out by an amplified band. Christian music videos, graphics, YouTube performances and the like have seen an increasingly rapid dissemination of new resources. An amazing range of graphics, music and words, addresses and videos from just about every theological and politically (in)correct nuance is now available, many for free. Projection screens are (literally) the focal point for these resources being used to perform the gospel in liturgy.

By way of comparison, Eastern Orthodox churches are dominated by a screen, separating the building into two spaces, for the people and the clergy.[1] The screen (and sometimes the walls and ceiling

---

1   John Fenwick, *The Eastern Orthodox Liturgy* (Nottingham: Grove Worship Series 56, 1978) offers a readable overview of its distinctives.

spaces) faces the people with icons, hence its name, the *iconostasis*. These focus on Christ, and his mother, Mary *Theotòkos* (Mary the God-bearer), along with other biblical figures and saints across the ages. An icon is not a painting: each is 'written' as an act of tangible prayer, using precious materials, and its content and style is based on an earlier one. Also, Eastern Christians view three-dimensional images of spiritual realities as verging on idolatry. Icons are definitely not statues, but *two*-dimensional, inviting the eye of faith to have communion with whomever the icon depicts. Given this rich understanding of how the visual works in liturgy, it is hard to envisage a projection screen being used by the Orthodox—certainly not as a 'virtual' screen for icons. Yet just as technology has changed the highly 'radio–book' culture of Protestants, it may yet bring changes in the Orthodox tradition in new and unexpected ways. The ideal behind the *iconostasis* invites a deeper understanding of screens—a sacramental one.

Part B   The sacramental screen

How then should projection screens be considered in liturgical terms? Having a projector and screen is commonly seen as a sign of a congregation being 'contemporary', not 'out-of-date' by lacking that essential item for the church of tomorrow. One Anglican bishop in Melbourne, for example, encouraged churches in his region to apply for a grant to fund a projector and screen. Such enthusiasm can be motivated by post-modern desire to drop 'traditional' hymns and prayer books and replace them with 'contemporary' resources. Some—including some Anglicans—regard the use of a book in worship as not only a sign of being out-dated, but standing in the way of 'contemporary' worship. Which prompts the question: is a Bible allowed?

The flexibility of electronic media is one of its key advantages. Yet this also means that what it portrays is transient. Can it bear the weight of passing on ('traditioning') the gospel, for which the book, as a tangible object, is suited? Further, the adaptability of electronic media to new trends can also lead to a congregation's performance of the divine drama being dominated by the latest downloadable resource. Despite good intentions, and without realising that it is happening, we can lose touch with the long and deep Christian tradition of scriptural prayer and praise, so that our spiritual diet becomes impoverished. The opposite problem is when we become so familiar with what happens in church that our performance of the gospel becomes mere routine, and seems to have zero impact on liturgy or lifestyle ('seems to' since God's grace and love can never be limited.)

But becoming liturgical Lollards and rejecting the new technologies of mikes, computers and screens has little, if any, point—we live in a visual age, and there is a lot going for it. A better way is to view the new technologies in 'icon'ic terms and through sacramental eyes. Christian living revolves around a *person*, the living Word (*Logos*—not *rhema*, 'words'). The scriptures, sacraments, common prayer and common life are the Spirit's means of communicating Christ. Classical Christian theology emphasizes that these 'means of grace' must not be confused with the Lord they seek to communicate (idolatry). The same applies to screens and the like. In the centuries of oral and 'radio' cultures, the lectern (with its Bible) and pulpit functioned as outward and visible signs of God's life-giving grace, and as means for us to receive that grace (cf the Catechism definition of 'sacrament'). And they continue to do so. In an age dominated by eye alongside ear, the screen can helpfully be regarded as an item of church furniture which functions similarly—an outward and (very) visible sign of God's re-creative love and grace, helping God's people to participate in the divine drama of salvation.

But having affirmed the new technologies does not end the conversation.

Screens and words

Screens are commonly used in church to project words. But it's worth asking; where in daily life do we encounter words being projected on screen? When asked in a workshop, typical responses are 'in a classroom' or 'in a business presentation'. Does this assume that Christians meet primarily to hear lectures, or be informed of a church's business plans? And in increasingly visual and inter-active cultures, does putting many words on screen increase the already strong 'verbosity' of church culture?

Another way we encounter words on screen in daily life is as subtitles in foreign-language movies. When words appear on screen in church, what is the assumed 'world' we have entered? It is indeed 'foreign' in the sense that as Christians we live in exile in this age, while experiencing something of what it means to be 'citizens of heaven', God's new creation. But feeling worship is 'foreign' can also evoke the idea that Christian faith is irrelevant to the wider world in which we live. On the other hand, people hard of hearing (as I am) welcome sub-titles on DVDs and TV, foreign-language or not. So hearing-impaired parishioners may welcome words on screen in church—but do they also convey the subliminal message that worshippers are deaf to what is being proclaimed?

Screens are primarily a *visual* rather than *verbal* medium. When there are lots of words on a screen, this can reinforce the sense that church is 'wordy'. If the screen is never blank, quiet space goes missing, and leaders can feel that the service must go on without pause—which can convey the subliminal message that gaps for reflection are dangerous. And words 'work' on screen in a different way to words read from a book. People for whom reading is difficult don't link the sound of a word to its visual, written form.[2] In societies where few read ('oral' cultures), words are taken to heart by being memorized. The written word has a quasi-magical quality, especially when pronounced as a 'spell', words *doing* something ('performative language'). Saying 'Peace be with you' *does* something beyond what the words literally mean: they 'effect' an 'affective' greeting, so are often accompanied by an action. The same is true for 'performative' words that bless, laugh, groan, or shout 'wow' or '@#!*&' or 'hallelujah'. And this is how 'versicles and responses' work in church, enabling instinctive echoes from the heart—'and also with you', 'amen, sister', 'preach it brother', 'we lift them to the Lord'. Words like these do much more than just convey information: they have a 'symbolic' or 'sacramental' dimension.

Words on screen, however, are there mostly to communicate content. They function in an 'instrumental' more than 'symbolic' register. There is nothing wrong with that—lots of words in worship are there to communicate content. When this becomes the predominant mode, however, the 'feel' of a service can become wordy, functional, clinical. Words are 'spelled out' rather than being 'spell-binding', reduced to being 'bare signs' rather than possessing a sacramental character. Classically, words work in liturgy as a sacrament of sound—*audible* outward signs of inward

---

[2] An interesting question here is whether there are 'deep' philosophical / theological differences between alphabetic languages such as Hebrew, Greek, Latin and English, in which a word as a meaning unit is constructed from letters and syllables, and ideographic ones such as Egyptian or Minoan hieroglyphics and Chinese, in which a word is constructed from pictorial symbols. Do words on screen work differently for churches in which pictorial rather than alphabetic language is used?

and spiritual truth, and as the means by which we receive the grace these words offer.

The tensions involved are eased when the sacramental function of a screen in showing words is kept in mind. When the congregation says or sings words while standing, looking up at a screen can help the sense of *doing* them, and doing them *together*. And familiar song lyrics on a screen will continue to evoke heart-felt meanings, just as reading them from a book can. But when large slabs of text such as scripture readings are screened, especially when people are sitting, the danger arises of them being 'studied' rather than 'heard', and of making the service feel too 'wordy'.

In short, putting *some* types of words on screen is a good thing—but putting others can get in the way of people engaging with the living Word. Similarly, having some types of words available in printed form is a good thing: here, individuals can have personal access to them, and can adopt a variety of approaches to engaging with what they represent—active listening, drifting off, meditating, studying...

Putting screens in their place

The arrangement of a building used for Christian worship is very important. How does the furniture which reflects the gospel (lectern, font, holy table) assist/limit/distort our participation? Can everyone see and hear what matters? How are worshippers placed in relation to one another; and to leaders, readers and musicians? Can all sit, stand and kneel readily? How easy is it to move around—or are we trapped in our seats? In particular, how does the placement of a projection screen affect all this?

As a sacramental item, the screen (or screens) must be placed so that people can see it readily, or its purpose is defeated. But it is likely to be the dominant item of furniture: when the focus of a service is the screen rather than the symbols and ministers of the gospel, something is out of whack. A well-placed screen (with unobtrusive projector), however, can enable preaching, baptising, praying and presiding to be more clearly seen, and so enhance the personal ministry of the Word. On the other hand, seeing leaders larger than life on screen all the time can reinforce 'personality cult' ideas. It is a moot point whether or not it is helpful for a congregation to view a baptism 'live' or via a screen: might this focus too much on the individual candidate than on the act of baptising? Similarly, would a congregation seeing the laying on of hands in ordination 'close-up' on screen over-personalise what is a corporate act?

Installing a screen marks the greatest internal change in western church buildings since pews began to arrive in the 18th century. To protect people from over-zealous clergy (and vice versa), Anglican church law requires major changes in a church building to be approved by the bishop granting a 'faculty'. So a congregation has the right to insist that a faculty be sought before a screen is installed permanently—as does the parish priest. Situations may arise in which the request is turned down, or better design is sought, for example, in a heritage building. Whenever a church building is to be erected, renovated or renewed, the location of a screen should be taken as seriously as that for the lectern, font and holy table—it must 'fit' alongside these enduring symbols of the means of grace. And when not in use, it needs to be either 'invisible', or easily rolled up (preferably by remote control). Such requirements are likely to mean that professional advice will be needed.

One possibility is to have a section of wall made suitable for projection, for example, above and to one side of the main lectern/holy table sight-line, so that it is readily seen when in use but 'invisible' otherwise. Another is a retractable screen, able to be lowered and raised in seconds, so that it is only seen when in use: this can reduce the sense that the focus of a service is the screen rather than the symbols and ministers of the gospel. Some places use one or more large LCD screens: however they have the disadvantage of looking 'empty' when turned off, so an 'invisibility graphic' will be needed when the screen is not in use (see further below).

Part C   Screens and performing the gospel

The key question is this: in what ways does projecting content on screen enhance or diminish the *performance* of the gospel in Christian worship? A good place to begin is to consider how it affects our bodies.

Screens and the body in the body of Christ

To be seen, a screen needs to be placed above people's heads, which means that faces are lifted up when it is in use. This posture is ideal for hymns of praise or affirmation, and liturgical elements that make strong affirmations, such as 'Glory to God' or Creed. But is quite unsuitable for the confession of sins, for reflective singing, meditative or silent prayer—and hopeless when we are kneeling. A screen favours standing, allows seating, but to all intents and purposes excludes kneeling—and the type of words said or sung when kneeling. Some will delight in not having anything in their hands when standing, especially those who like to lift them. Others, however, will feel at ease holding a book or leaflet, feeling awkward about what to do with their hands when standing.

The scriptures do not lay down any one posture as compulsory. Many passages, however, call worshippers to adopt a posture of humility before God:

O come, let us worship and bow down,
let us kneel before the Lord, our Maker;
For he is our God, and we are the people of his pasture,
 and the sheep of his hand. (Psalm 95:6–7)

Further, our body posture will reflect something of what it means for each believer to be a member of Christ's body, the Church. Insisting that everyone must adopt the same posture is not helpful, for example, whether to kneel or stand to receive communion: Christian unity is about harmony rather than uniformity. Yet a church in which posture is merely a matter of individual preference has lost an important aspect of its oneness. It is well worth reflecting on how using a screen at particular times in a service can affect the unity we express and experience as the body of Christ made visible.

And every Christian has times when s/he just wants to sit up the back and avoid eager peace-givers or 'the cuppa': singing or speaking from a screen may make such 'anonymity' more difficult. Of course, allowing someone to remain 'anonymous' all the time raises questions about whether they are being treated as a 'member of Christ'. This goes well beyond using screens, but points up the possible consequences of a screen's use on the emotional boundaries and inclusiveness of a church. Sensitivity is needed: sitting to sing on occasion may be helpful, for example.

But what happens when a screen is used, and the power goes out? All is not lost—it is possible to perform the gospel without a screen—or books. After all, for most of church history neither was available to congregations, many of whom could not read anyway. Familiar items can be said or sung from memory—people may not be able to say the Lord's Prayer by themselves, for example, but will join in when said with others. Less familiar elements, such as confession of sin, can be voiced by one or more leaders (as provided in *BCP* Holy

Communion—a traditional role for a deacon), or a responsive form could be used (cf *APBA* pages 52-3 #5, or page 145). In *BCP* Morning and Evening Prayer, written for people who could not read, the confession was said phrase by phrase as they followed the minister, "saying after me". This can still work today for short forms of prayer, though it requires a strong sense of trust in the minister.

Seeing is believing

Screens are a **visual** rather than verbal medium. As noted above, in the Orthodox tradition the *iconostasis* screen sets several icons before the congregation: each is based on an earlier one, but once placed in church, an icon remains unchanging. In contemporary technological culture, however, it is moving images that are portrayed on screen, and now opened up to inter-active possibilities via computer gaming and the internet. Yet visual resources are absent from the scriptures, prayer and hymnbooks. So today's screens need new resources and new methods.

What then works well on a screen in church? The obvious answer is anything *visual*—graphics, pictures, diagrams, collages, photos—and preferably *moving:* video clips, YouTube, and so on. **A screen comes into its own when used visually more than verbally.** Rather than existing primarily to replace books, *visuals* should be the primary reason why a screen is used in church. Some 30 years ago, at an open-air Christmas carol service I first saw the possibilities of this: sketches from the Good News Bible were shown on an OHP during readings—it was a very effective way of engaging occasional worshippers with the story, using quite basic technology. Today, kindergarten and primary school teachers typically tell a story using a screen to show its images: a picture book is fine to read with a few children, but more of a challenge with twenty.

So, here are some ideas for using a screen visually in church:

- Pictures can welcome a congregation as it gathers, perhaps introducing a theme.
- A visual collage can accompany the introduction of topics for prayer—though during the actual praying, a blank screen allows personal engagement and closed eyes.
- Diagrams, using a few key words, can help people 'see' a sermon's shape.
- Children's talks can be accompanied by pictures, as if read from a storybook.
- A short video or film clip can be shown as part of the sermon: more than a minute or two and all else will seem 'pale', however, and more than one per service tends to make it feel like 'we're at the movies' rather than performing the gospel.
- Quiet music or singing during the administration of the holy communion can be accompanied by 'mood' screens or symbols (cup, loaf, wheat, people).

Screens are particularly helpful for special services. For example, the long Good Friday 'passion gospel', John 18–19, can be read in sections, with appropriate pictures faded in and out during significant periods of silence between them.

The internet provides a treasure of sites offering art for Sundays in the Christian year, many scripture passages, video clips, screen-friendly fonts and so on.

A note on screens at funerals

It has become common for slides of a person's life to be screened at funerals, sometimes as its main content ('Celebration of the life of N'). A Christian funeral, however, is in the first place an act of divine worship and respectful mourning. A eulogy has its proper place (cf #9 in the *APBA* funeral rite), and a projected picture of the person can be helpful. But projecting many pictures of the person and their life is better left to the 'wake' or a cuppa after the service. Funerals are not an occasion to put words on the screen, except in special circumstances. A service book including all that the congregation needs allows for a variety of participation—not everyone present will want to join in—and will be appreciated as a memento, especially if the person's photo and dates of birth and death are on the cover.

Screens on song: copyright, censorship, canon and communion

Probably the most common use for a screen is to project the words of songs, psalms and canticles (e.g. 'Glory to God'). This saves paper, calls for a song-strong 'heads-up' posture, and enables new material to be introduced easily. From the beginning of hymn-singing as we know it, with Isaac Watts and the Wesley brothers, western Christians used a hymn book from which to sing—until the arrival of the OHP.[3] Word processing and music software made fresh composition easy, and myriads of songs can now be found on the web—which raises new issues.

As regards copyright, earning money from writing prayers or hymn words runs strongly against the Christian tradition that texts

---

3   Until the mid-18th century, singing in church was mostly of psalms, whether 'chanted' from the Bible text, or 'metrical', i.e. rhymed and sung to folk-style tunes: the translations by Nate & Bray, and then Sternold & Hopkins, can be found bound with the *Book of Common Prayer*. Apart from a small number of hymns honoured by ancient use, singing from other than the words of scripture was regarded as sacrilegious. It is hard to appreciate today how revolutionary the work of the Methodist evangelists was viewed, though by the mid-19th century hymnbooks—with the notable exception of some Scottish Presbyterians—were accepted in most western Christian traditions.

for worship belong to the people of God rather than their 'authors'. Why should someone be paid for writing words for prayer and praise—especially because, like icons, they will be crafted from the work of earlier generations? Both time-honoured and newly-authored texts are to be respected: copyrighting liturgical texts for this reason is justifiable to protect their integrity. But the recent trend of congregations needing to fuss with licence renewals, rather than being trusted to treat with respect the words they sing and pray is not helpful.

In contrast, copyright for music composition, and the use of professionally-prepared graphics and photos, is a quite different matter. These form part of a trained person's livelihood, for which payment should be made: licence schemes for tunes and graphics form part of the obligation on Christian congregations to support those who labour for the gospel in this way.

Text copyright points up a deeper issue—the *lack* of censorship in the proliferation of words for use in worship, especially songs. When a hymnbook is produced, the group responsible scrutinises each potential text for its scriptural, theological and pastoral truth. Further, the range of hymns available in a book remains manageable, so that a common body of songs known across congregations forms. English-language hymnbooks change gradually over time, and each will reflect the emphases of the tradition on which it draws. But they pass on a 'rolling canon' of well-known hymns across the generations. The recent explosion of texts, due to the ease of their being written, distributed and presented, raises issues about the communication of God's truth—and its distortion—across the generations. Congregations can cluster around 'niche' religious fads more than singing 'in communion' with the broader Christian tradition. But this is getting beyond screens in church. Issues like this relate more to technology making an unprecedented range of sources available, than the manner in which they are presented, on screen or otherwise.

Screens on song: versification

A particular screen issue is the number of many words that can be seen at the one time. Typically, eight lines of text is the manageable limit. For psalms said together by the congregation, the main issue is watching where line breaks are made, which is fairly easy. 'Choir' reading, in which half those present speak and listen in turn—the way the Hebrew Bible sets out the psalms—is readily achieved by using different colours onscreen, or left and right justifying the text for the left and right side of the assembly to recite.

For longer texts, such as the lines in Creeds relating to Jesus Christ, the question is where best to place 'page breaks', that is, when a screen change happens. People have to react quickly to the new set of words, so the break best comes when a breath fits easily. Making one where there is a new sentence or change of subject is ideal, but for long sections a slow scroll can be used. This takes some skill for both the designer and operator, but once learnt is easily implemented.

With songs, however, usually only one verse can be shown at a time. Each verse is thus separated into a discrete 'meaning unit': the thread that joins a hymn's pearls is easily lost, as can be the gradual build-up of a theme, the unfolding of a story and so on. (Philosophically, screens over-do post-modern resistance to meta-narratives, the modernist assumption of an overall meaning that lies behind traditional versed hymns.) This is where singing from a printed text has a distinct (pre-modern/modern) advantage. When singing from a book or pew sheet, the eye is aware not only that the brain is processing verse three for the larynx to sing, but also in view are verses one and two, as well as those that follow. As noted above, however, a major advantage of projecting sung words on a screen is the positive effect this has on body posture. Singing from a screen fosters its sacramental function, as an outward and visible sign of the divine truth performed in song. So, given the concerns about versification noted above, should screens only be used for songs with just one verse, that is, 'choruses'? This would be needlessly restrictive—and choruses are short enough to be sung from memory, so that they don't need to be projected. A few techniques can help congregations get a sense of the 'verse development' of a hymn when projected on screen:

- Show two verses at a time, side-by-side or higher and lower, singing the left or higher one each time, marked by use of a border, darker colour, bold type, and so on. People will then sing each verse while being aware of the next, which appears as a starting-to-be-familiar text rather 'jumping' from a new screen.
- Place a number graphic on the top or bottom screen border, with the one that corresponds to the current verse being illuminated in some way—this also allows singers to know which is the last (often climatic) verse.
- Change the background gradually from verse to verse to reflect a song's developing mood/story—but resist the temptation to become manipulative.

Techniques like these call for more work in preparation—and they are as significant as the careful choice of songs to be sung. The effort put in will be rewarded, not only in more meaningful singing, but greater awareness in those who prepare the service of how what is sung furthers the performance of the gospel.

What about projecting the melody line of a hymn on screen? This is not really feasible: apart from further restricting the number of lines shown, the music line is hard to follow on screen except by those skilled in sight-reading. The day is already here when singers can have their own tablet on which a full music score can be shown. People singing from their own mobile phones may be pushing 'community' a bit far—but why not? Singing from a personal screen is functionally closer to using a hymnbook than a corporate screen.

Leading 'from above'

The clergy keenest on screens seem to be those who want to do away with books, in favour of 'freedom' in worship. That worshippers need no books when a screen is used can give the impression that they are 'free'. Their hands may be free, but in fact, using a screen calls for a high degree of detailed preparation, and thus a more controlled environment. It is much easier for a congregation to move away from a printed sheet or book, than from a service prepared in advance so the technology can do its job.

Once again, the point is not to demean technology: a computer-planned, screen-using service will mean a lot more preparation than just opening *APBA* and saying 'Our service begins on page 119' or whatever, and churning the liturgical prayer wheel. The point is that a *screen-oriented service concentrates power in the hands of those who prepare and lead it*. It is crucial that those responsible for the performance of the gospel in a congregation are aware of this—classically, the bishop who presides, and the presbyter/priests, to whom has been delegated the 'cure of souls', who typically do the preparing and leading.

A contrasting yet similar point concerns those who 'enable' the gospel to be performed—the *diakonoi* who operate the projector, raise/lower the screen, adjust microphone levels and so on. Understandably, these tasks are often allocated to people most at home with the technology—who face the temptation to believe they 'control' the liturgy, rather than serving God's people through their ministries. For major occasions a rehearsal will see them consulted, but such *diakonoi* should be part of preparing *every* service using technology. Operators will have good ideas about how best a screen could be used, e.g. to help communicate a particular message, or on a non-regular occasion (e.g. for the renewal of baptismal vows at Easter). And involving 'nerdy' believers, listening to their technical input, will assist their formation as liturgically skilled disciples of Christ.

Some screen 'no-noes'

What elements of a service ought then *not* to be projected on screen?

My first 'no-no' is projecting the text of scripture readings. Practically, a screen can hold only a small number of words that are large enough to be read easily. Further, readings on a screen increases the 'wordiness' of a service, and can make those with low reading skill or poor eyesight feel excluded. More significantly, the scriptures were written to be *heard* in church—performed—and so that worshippers, as limbs and organs of the body of Christ, might do so *together*. A scripture reading on screen militates against such corporate listening to the word of God. The Bible is not read aloud in liturgy to be 'studied' individually, let alone 'observed' from afar. Many congregations have pew Bibles, of course, and some bring their personal copy to church. Those who find it helpful to follow the text while it is read aloud can do so using a Bible, but putting the text on screen forces all into study rather than hearing mode. Best practice is to leave the screen blank while the scriptures are read: this allows those present to focus on hearing with their ears, rather than watching with their eyes.

A second 'no-no' is putting **responses** on screen. A feature of traditional Anglican worship, these are used even more widely today to encourage participation. Responses encourage memorisation, and the sense of personal interchange. Minister and people engage in *dialogue* with one another, reflecting the encounter between Christ and the people of God, not merely exchanging information. For example, to pronounce 'The peace *of the Lord* be with you' and to respond 'And also with you' is to take the bold step of being 'Christ' to one another (see John 20.19–26; 1 Corinthians 1.3; 2 Corinthians 1.3, 13.13). **The peace can only be offered by a person, not a screen—** and the same goes for 'Lift up your hearts'. In theological terms, the minister who presides represents God's initiative towards us—the technical term is *in persona Christ* (but not *in loco Christi*, in the place of Christ). Conversely, the people's response is enabled by those who bear the responsibility of being agents of Christ (*diakonoi*) through the Spirit.

People become familiar with responses by *using* them. Newer members, including the youngest, quickly become familiar with repeated responses, especially when they are associated with an action. Where a new response is to be used, a screen can be used to show the words before the service, and allow people to practice them until they become instinctive, a matter of heart as well as mind. For regulars, this may seem a little silly, but practicing familiar words a couple of times a year may well assist long-term worshippers as well as newcomers to understand and 'enter in' more.

Similar issues apply to 'performative' words—absolutions, blessings, dismissals and the like, where the words spoken *do* something beyond conveying information. There is no practical need to have them on screen, since the words are not spoken by the people: it is best 'blanked' at this point, so that the congregation's eyes are focused on the person speaking, rather than on watching syllables on a screen. In short, it is important to reflect on where in a service words can just 'happen', and where they are best read from a screen.

Which leads to a further observation: it is arguable that the Lord's Prayer should not be shown on screen. This allows worshippers to pray with eyes closed and heads bowed, and encourages them to know it by heart until it becomes a deep 'godly rut' in their spiritual road. It may well be desirable to have it on screen when many visitors are present—at a baptism, for example. But this is a matter of wisdom.

Words sung—and not

The general rule argued for thus far is this: *when using screens, maximise the visuals, minimise the words ... and leave it blank quite often.* But what words do work well on screen?

The best use of words on screen is to support congregational singing. The poetic nature of song lyrics, and that these words are *sung*, deepens their 'formative' role beyond their 'didactic' (teaching) role. Screens are also good for longish liturgical texts that everyone says together: psalms and creeds for example. Words used to give information have some place, for example, to indicate the scripture reference for a reading, or dot points for notices. Another useful role for a screen is to indicate transitions in the service, for example, 'Ministry of the Word'. Since these function as 'headings' in print terms, ideally they will have accompanying visuals/graphics.

But the general rule is—in liturgy, *minimise* the number of words projected on screen. Which leads to perhaps the most important 'rule'. **Any screen used should stay blank**—ideally by being invisible, not just blank—**for at least half of a service.** Corporate Christian worship is primarily inter-personal, a divine-human dialogue: when the screen is on, attention is focused there rather than on people or symbols. This rule applies not just to so-called 'contemporary' services, but across the Christian tradition, whether the service is highly liturgical, flexibly structured, locally composed or charismatic in style. Think: does a screen help or get in the way of people receiving communion? Laying on hands for healing? Speaking in tongues?

Once a permanent screen is in place in a church building, the temptation arises to have it on all the time, crowding out the responsive, reflective and active dimensions of corporate prayer and praise. Each month or so, it can be instructive to have a service in which a screen is deliberately not used. Worshippers can then realise how much they have committed to memory, different service structures can be tried, and other ways of leading. Of course, similar advice applies to a congregation whose noses never get out of a book.

Part D Screens in church—some practical matters

In 2000-2001 I was part of an online chat group of people developing electronic resources for Christian liturgy. With screens increasingly common, I was starting to reflect on how this affects worship—what you have read thus far forms most of my learning. I remember asking the group, "what principles do you think matter when liturgy is on screen?" I was surprised to find that the only responses were about practical matters—"Make sure that you use at least a 24 point font", "Check that the background colour does not clash with the word colour" and the like. No one seemed to think that there were any issues raised by replacing books and pew sheets with a screen. But practical matters are important.

First and foremost, **anything projected on screen needs to be of good resolution and presentation quality**. Those present will take for granted the standard of even the most banal telly programme.

Blurred or confusing images, unreadable text or overly busy contents distract eye, mind and heart. 'Screen noise' gets in the way of worshippers playing their part in performing the gospel.

With that said, here are some tips that aim to see screens used well in church.

Images

The brain takes in one image at a time, though it can do so quickly. When multiple images are to be projected, for example, to illustrate different points in a sermon, for example, or during the prayers, it is a good idea to have them come up one after the other, 'building' the picture overall.

Each image must be clear enough and large enough for any details that matter to be seen easily. And *why* the image is being shown must be obvious. It is distracting for a congregation to have to struggle to pick out a detail being discussed, or puzzle about the relevance of what is on the screen.

When showing moving images, a video clip for example, check that both the computer and projector, *and* their combination, have enough software and resolution grunt for images to project smoothly.

Fonts (how words and letters look)

Style: 'Serif' fonts, whose letters have little extensions (serifs)—Times Roman or Book Antiqua, for example—work well for reading printed material, but are less easily read on screen. 'Sans serif' (i.e. no extensions) fonts are better on screen: Arial, Cabrini, Helvetica or Universal, for example.

Size: 24 point is usually the minimum size that can be read easily on screen—resist the temptation to reduce the font size to pack the screen with words.

Colour: The foreground colour, the one used for words, must stand out clearly against the background colour *when projected*. What looks good on a computer monitor or laptop is not always the case when projected. Further, the lighting levels in the church building affect the visibility and contrast levels of what appears on a screen. *Please test the colour combination of text and background colours, as actually projected in the building where it will be used, before committing to them.*

Aesthetics (what pleases the eye)
Images and video clips should 'work' aesthetically—or not be used. But similar principles apply when it comes to words, the focus of this section.

Placement: Similar items should be placed in the same position on successive screens. Song words or a repeated graphic 'jumping around' between verses, for example, is distracting for worshippers. Consistency of placing can be achieved by having a template slide for each typical element in a service.

Combinations: When the combination of font, size and colour is pleasing to the eye, it will be easier to read and understand. Good design does not necessarily need a professional graphic designer—but there may well be one in the congregation glad to help.

It is also helpful to use the same combination of font style, size and colour for similar items in a service—song text, headings, and creed for example. This helps worshippers approach and engage instinctively with each element with a similar emotional response.

Lineation: Each new line said or sung by the congregation should reflect the natural breathing spots and sense of the phrase. This assists with the poetic 'feel' of the words, and helps people engage with their rhythm and follow their meaning sequence. The prayers in *APBA* offer good examples, especially the ones in **bold text**, while modern songbooks generally pay attention to this—following their layout usually works best.

Transitions: Smooth transition from one slide to the next assists the flow of a service. Making people wait to see the words of the next song verse is a definite no-no (and pity the musicians). Whoever operates the projector/computer needs to know every slide change, including when the screen is to be blanked. Their ministry will be appreciated most when it goes unnoticed.

Preparation

Teamwork: No performance can work well when those involved are not working together, no matter how small the production. Good teamwork is a pre-requisite for every drama to be effective, and especially so when celebrating the work of God among the people of God. Service leaders, people taking particular parts, musicians involved, those running sound and projection—each is called to perform their task as a ministry which helps the gospel be performed well, so that God is glorified, and the people of God built up in faith.

Rehearsal: It is good practice for the operator to do a 'cold run' of what is to be projected in a service, checking their changes with leaders and musicians. This can ensure that timing is understood, that slides or videos are in the right order—and a lookout kept for misspelt words, unintended double entendres, and issues with slide location or transition.

For special occasions, a full rehearsal is desirable: it is standard practice for weddings and ordinations, but should not be restricted to these. And a rehearsal provides a great opportunity for mutual prayer, learning and encouragement.

A 'screen audit'

If a screen is used regularly in your congregation, doing an occasional 'audit' of its use can see it used better. Two steps are involved.

1. A static audit

The first (easy) audit begins by having a few regular participants sit in different places in the building. For clergy and others usually 'up front', seeing how things look from a 'pew view' can be instructive. For each place, ask:

- Can the screen be seen easily? Can it be seen too easily, that is, does it dominate? How noticeable is it when blank?
- How does the screen relate to the pulpit, lectern, holy table and similar places from which leaders need to be seen and heard?
- After all involved have moved around to three different places, get together to reflect on your responses. Are there any recommendations for the parish council to consider?

2. A dynamic audit

This involves exploring similar questions during a service, with some who are normally 'up front' sitting among the congregation, and by having some 'regulars' take part from their usual place. In addition, questions like these should be explored:

- What was showing on the screen as participants entered? How well did it 'ease the way in' to the service, or not?
- For what parts of the service was the screen used primarily for images? Could they be seen easily? In what ways did they contribute, or not, to performing the gospel?
- For what parts of the service was the screen used primarily for words? Could the words be read clearly? Did the transitions make sense?

- For what parts of the service was the screen left blank? Why do you think this was done? How helpful, or not, was it to have the eyes directed elsewhere for a while?
- How did the use of the screen work, or not, to support the ministry of service leaders? In particular, how did it support key points in performing the gospel—preaching, praying, presiding, administering communion, healing ministries and the like?

After the service, those involved get together with clergy and others who played leading parts to reflect on their responses. Are there any recommendations for the clergy, worship committee, parish council or similar bodies to consider?

Conclusion: screens and learning

Projecting words on screens makes a lot of sense in education, whether in school, college, business or a sports centre. In Christian education, from Sunday school to theological college, computer-related technologies offer new possibilities for learning—the ready availability of on-line basic courses on Christian faith, to massive databases of primary documents, for example. However it is done, education for faith in Christ is an ongoing responsibility of every congregation, and technology can help.

But liturgy has a different ambience to education: it is not in the first place about *information* so much as *transformation*. Classically, Christian liturgy is structured according to the mission of God, who gathers us, addresses us and sends us out, having fed and inspired us for a life of applied prayer. The people of God are 'assembled' to be 're-membered' in the body of Christ, 're-formed' to live in the 'fellowship of the Holy Spirit'. Christian liturgy aims to embrace all the oddities in a congregation: educational processes, on the other hand, take account of each learner's particularities. **Using a screen as if liturgy is a class, board or locker room activity leads to overly didactic, unhelpfully verbose—and thus less including—services.**

Screens, mikes and amplified sounds are now part of everyday culture in much of today's world. Using them in Christian worship is both inevitable and desirable—but, as with older technologies, these new ones must serve the kingdom of God, not displace it. In particular, over-using, misusing and abusing screens obscures the reality that Christian worship is about *performance*. It seeks to shift the imagination more than direct the mind, to open eyes and ears rather than just entertain them, and so turn stony hearts into godly flesh. In more technical terms, Christian liturgy is about *formative* learning, which takes place in *evocative* more than *instructive* modes—which technology can further when used well. Typically, the performance of the gospel in Christian worship, whether as liturgy or lifestyle, communicates less through sentences than through parables and sacraments—for which Jesus set a firm precedent.

Chapter Eight
When we perform the gospel: times and seasons

Overview

Part A   reflects on how 'time' interweaves with Christian faith in the light of Christ.

Part B   explores the variety of ways in which time marked the life of Israel of old, and how these have been taken up in the Christian tradition.

Part C   considers the 'Christian year', and what it means in places like Australia where sports, public holidays and civic events dominate.

Part D   offers ways to help you reflect on how time shapes your living.

"When should we perform the gospel?" your minister asks from the pulpit. "All the time, of course," someone shouts, and people clap. Which is fair enough—living the gospel day by day, hour by hour, year by year, is our calling as Christians. As the body of Christ our 'when' of performing the gospel is most obviously on

Sunday, 'in church'. But Sundays in mid-January holidays are very different from mid-August winter ones, and the rhythm of the week is governed as much by shopping and sport. So how does time interact with Christian faith and life, both for us as individuals, and as churches?

Albert Einstein led us to speak of a 'space-time' universe. His 'Theory of General Relativity' posited that existence is not just 'in' time, but that space and time are interwoven aspects of reality. Reflecting on time is not a new idea: it has played a significant role for centuries; back to the philosophers Plato, Aristotle and many others.[1] In ordinary life we sense time as if we are moving through it—but the truth is more complex. Our experience shows this too: when bored, we can feel that a short time lasts and lasts, while an exciting hour seems to pass in a minute. And thinking about time brings us to a paradox: speaking of a 'beginning' to time assumes that it occurred in time itself.

Such ideas are neither foreign to the Christian tradition, nor Israel of old. As the Psalmist wrote of God, "a thousand years in your sight are like yesterday passing, or like one watch of the night" (Psalm 90.4). The royal philosopher of Israel famously observed, "For everything there is a season, and a time for every matter under heaven" (Ecclesiastes 3.1–8). Classical Christian reflection on the mystery of creation and beginnings owes much to Augustine of Hippo, who famously held that 'creation is *with* time, not *in* it'.[2]

How do these somewhat abstract reflections bear on *when* we perform the Gospel, especially, but not only, in church? A good place to begin (as always) is with Jesus Christ.

---

[1] For an overview of this and modern discussion is Ned Markosian, 'Time', in Edward N. Zalta (ed), *The Stanford Encyclopedia of Philosophy* (2016), https://plato.stanford.edu/archives/fall2016/entries/time/.

[2] See Augustine, *Confessions*, Book XI, written between 397 and 400AD.

Part A   Time in Christ

Life of the aeons/ages

Jesus marks the centre of how we date time: BC (before Christ) and AD (*anno domini*, Latin for "in the year of the Lord"). But we do not say AC (after Christ)—his life has no ending. Raised from the dead, and exalted to the Father, the Lord Jesus is beyond the power of death, 'truly alive', and offers 'eternal' life (literally 'life of the aeons/ages'). As John wrote, "God so loved the world that he sent his only Son, so that each one who believes on him should not perish, but might have *life of the ages*." (John 3:16)

'Eternal' life is commonly envisaged as 'life without end'. This is not the Christian hope or understanding—and endless living as we are would quickly become boring and dreary. Rather, Christian hope looks toward life renewed, lived in intimate relationship with God and with others. We are offered not so much an endless *quantity* of life in Christ, so much as a new *quality* of life. This 'life of the aeons' changes our priorities and relationships, and brings healing and forgiveness. It calls us to be agents of new life in Christ, anticipating the new creation, the "life of the world to come" (as the Nicene Creed concludes). This life is the *koinonia* (communion) of Father, Son and Spirit into which we are baptised.

The New Testament writers use two words for time. Ordinary time, experienced in a regular sequence of periods, is *chronos*, (clock time). Special time, giving opportunities for action or marking significant happenings, is *kairos* (a season or opportune time). Both are true of Christ. On the one hand, God's purpose was "set forward in Christ as a plan for the fullness of times" (*kairos*, Ephesians 1:10; see also Mark 1.15; Titus 1.3). On the other hand, "God sent forth his Son, born of a woman" only "when the fullness of time had come" (*chronos*, Galatians 4:4). The Lord Jesus, the Word of

God incarnate in our flesh, spent some 33 years bound up with our *chronos*, revealing the *kairos* of God's time-transcending love and intentions. There is a sharp paradox here: 'eternity' is revealed through a particular time in history. God's majesty transcends time, and its limitations. Yet it is because God came to occupy a particular place in time in Jesus Christ that we know this to be true. Because of Jesus, we realise that God is not abstractedly 'timeless'. Nor is God merely 'everlasting' in the sense of 'endless'.

Such ideas were debated in the ancient world, not least amongst Greek philosophers, who "posited timeless and temporal reality as different kinds of being ... and all meaning and value were located in timeless being", as Robert Jenson puts it.[3] If Christ brings eternity into time, fusing what is 'timeless' with what is 'temporal', then God must be a very different sort of being from what we typically imagine. Christian thinkers trained in the Greek philosophical tradition worked hard to transform such ideas in the light of Christ. Jenson makes this comment on the work of the great Greek Christian thinker Gregory of Nyssa:[4]

> The Greek deity is eternal in that in it circling time has its motionless centre. Gregory's God is eternal in that he envelops time, is ahead of and so moving before it. The Greeks' God stands still, so that we may ground moving things in him; Gregory's God keeps things moving.

The triune God is thus the Lord of time: not a mere timeless principle, but time's Creator, the "I am who I am" who works in, through and beyond time. This Lord calls us to share the 'life of the aeons' through a particular human life, lived in a specific time, enabled by

---

3   Robert Jenson, *The Triune Identity* (Philadelphia: Fortress, 1982) 60.
4   Jenson, 165.

the Holy Spirit (Luke 1.35, 3.22). So, whenever we perform the gospel the Holy Spirit draws deeper into the 'life of the ages'. In one way we are brought 'out of' ordinary *chronos* time, while in another way we are plunged into the depths of *kairos* time—just as Jesus was.

The Lord Jesus—Son of the Father

Even more, the boundless future of the risen Christ opens out the time-transcending life of the new creation—and the past. Time in Christ extends 'backwards': the Word that took our flesh in some way 'pre-existed' Jesus, as John's gospel implies: "In the beginning was the Word ... All things came to be through him, and without him nothing came to be" (John 1:1-3). Reflecting on this 'backwards' perspective can seem speculative, less relevant than our future 'life of the aeons' in Christ. But consider what it means to describe Jesus as 'son of God' (as the New Testament does). Understanding this in a 'literalistic' way means there was a point in time when God as 'father' sired Jesus as 'son'. So Arius, whose name is linked to the heresy involved, held that "there was a then when Christ was not" (this slogan was easily memorised in Greek). But if this son had a beginning, even if at the very start of time, then he is a creature—and to worship such a one as God would be idolatry.[5] More, as a creature, this 'son' could not be God with us, nor bring us to God, but would be like a senior angel: fine for angels, but not much help to humans.

Bishop Athanasius of Alexandria was a focal point for 'orthodox' belief during the Arian controversy. He delighted to point out that, just as figs beget figs (and in an organic way), horses beget horses (in an animal way), and humans beget humans (in a human way)—so God begets *God*, and in a *divine* manner. The Nicene Creed, which

---

5   This is the 'Arian' heresy, which involved a range of complex issues, though become politicised: see Charles Sherlock, *God on the Inside: trinitarian spirituality* (Canberra: Acorn, 1991) chapter eight.

formed out of the controversy, thus speaks of the Lord Jesus as *'eternally* begotten' of the Father. This does not mean that the 'Son' was constantly being 'sired' by the Father, but that they stand in a distinct, divine relationship. As the triune God transcends time, so does the life of God as 'Father' and 'Son'—joined in loving *koinonia* by the Holy Spirit.

"We are a long way from thinking about when we perform the gospel," you may be thinking. But the gospel is all bound up with the identity of the Lord Jesus Christ as truly human and truly God. We will never have a full understanding of this, but false ideas about Jesus distort the gospel. The Word of God incarnate in Jesus is not merely an 'appearance' of divinity in time, but the 'en-flesh-ment' and 'en-time-ment' of the in-the-beginning Word, the eternally begotten Son. As Karl Barth put it:

> If, according to Gal 4.4, Jesus Christ is the 'pleroma [fullness] of the time,' we have to remember that, according to Col. 2.9, 'in him dwelleth all the pleroma of the Godhead bodily.[6]

Earlier in the same passage Barth wrote:

> When I really give anyone my time, I thereby give him the last and most personal thing that I have to give, namely myself.[7]

A tangible gift, no matter how thoughtful, may well have

---

[6] Karl Barth, *Church Dogmatics I / II* (trans. G.W. Bromily and T.H.L. Parker, London: T & T Clark, 1956) 55. The whole of paragraph 14, 'God's Time and our Time' offers remarkable philosophical, scriptural and theological insights into time and eternity.

[7] Karl Barth, *Church Dogmatics I / II* (trans. G.W. Bromily and T.H.L. Parker, London: T & T Clark, 1956) 55. The whole of paragraph 14, 'God's Time and our Time' offers remarkable philosophical, scriptural and theological insights into time and eternity.

'belonged' to me, but is still 'outside' me. When I give someone my time, however, I share with them a portion of my life span, my own life. In sharing a particular time with us in Christ, God opened to us God's own self, the 'life of the aeons'. Amazingly, the triune God chooses and delights to have time for us. So when in daily life we share God's gift of time, we are following Christ's example, playing our part in performing the gospel.

Revelation, the last-placed book in the New Testament, speaks of Jesus and time in a striking way. Twice, once at the start and once near the end, it is *God* who says, "I am the Alpha and the Omega"—the "A and Z" (Revelation 1:8, 21:6). In the book's last chapter, however, *Jesus* takes up and expands the phrase, saying: "I am the A and Z, the first and the last, the beginning and the end" (Revelation 22:13). What was said of God as Lord of time is now placed on the lips of the risen Lord Jesus Christ. God as revealed in Jesus Christ is not 'timeless', but the Lord of time—'time-full'. God shared our time in Jesus Christ, and brings us to share eternity, the 'life of the ages', through the Holy Spirit. This Lord enters history in the Word "through whom all things were made"—time included—while transcending it.

The 'time-full' gospel we perform in time thus hinges around the conception, birth, life, death and especially the resurrection of Jesus. In being raised from death and exalted as Lord, Jesus overcame the barrier that keeps us slaves to time. But what does this mean for the way we perform the gospel as the body of Christ? To explore this we turn to examine how the scriptures speak of our experience of time.

Part B Time-patterns in the scriptures

Evenings, mornings and weeks

The rhythm of night and day is the basic unit of time in human experience. It also provides the fundamental shape for describing God's creative work in the Bible's opening chapter. Six times we read, "and there was evening and there was morning, the first ... sixth day" (Genesis 1.5,8,13,19,23,31). The basic utterance of Israel's faith, "Hear (sh^{e}ma') O Israel, the Lord our God the Lord is One" was commanded to be prayed "when you lie down and when you rise up" (Deuteronomy 6.4). Putting evening before morning seems to us rather odd. But in biblical terms, a 'day' runs from sunset of the 'eve' until the next sunset. Rest precedes activity, and we begin the 'day' by trusting ourselves to God's protection when we are helpless, in sleep.

The seventh day is not described like this, however. Each of the preceding 'days' has seen God at work. But "God rested on the seventh day from all the work ... So God blessed the seventh day and hallowed it" (Genesis 2:2-3). The seventh day, the *sabbath*, sets another rhythm in the created order, the week. It is not described in terms of 'evening and morning', but is left open-ended, pointing to the 'end'—the goal as well as conclusion—of creation, to "enter God's rest" (as Hebrews 4 argues).

Sabbath and week were fundamental to the life of Israel. The Commandments set this down directly: "Remember the sabbath day, to keep it holy: in it you shall do no manner of work". The two versions give different reasons for this—neither appealing to the rhythms of nature: "For in six days the LORD made heaven and earth, the sea, and all that is in them, but rested the seventh day" (Exodus 20.11), and "Remember that you were a slave in the land of Egypt, and the LORD your God brought you out from there" (Deuteronomy 5.15). The first grounds observance in God's creative work and rest; the second in the Lord's deliverance of the people from slavery (and goes on to include animals and foreigners in the requirement for rest).

As time went on, regulations about what 'rest' entails grew. The Pharisees of Jesus' time were scandalised by his behaviour on the sabbath, but his concern was God's re-creative intention. Jesus sharply attacked legalistic approaches that stood in the way of hungry people and animals being fed and disabled people being healed (for example, Matthew 12.1–12; Luke 13.10–14.5; John 5.1–18; 7.22–23; 9.1–16). "The sabbath was made for humanity, and not humanity for the sabbath," Jesus taught, adding "so the Son of Man is lord even of the sabbath" (Mark 2.27–28).

The week as a time-pattern thus derives from biblical teaching rather than patterns of nature; so matters in performing the gospel. It became observed in western societies as the Roman Empire adopted Christianity as the official religion. But it has not been the 'time-shape' of others: Roman, Greek, Asian and other civilisations have work–life patterns determined by religious and public holidays of varying length and placement. The seven-day week has spread by western economic arrangements and leisure practices. The 'weekend' is widely entrenched, with family and community activities, shopping and sports seen as desirable forms of 'recreation', protected by 'penalty rates' for people required to work then.[8]

Months and seasons

What then of time patterns that derive from natural cycles? The movements of the moon around the earth, and both around the

---

[8] The seven-day week was challenged in the French and Russian revolutions, indicating its deep significance: a fascinating account of Soviet revisions towards five and six day patterns, see www.cabinetmagazine.org/issues/61/wood.php

sun, determine the month and the year.[9] Human societies across the globe have structured time around the movements of sun and moon, including Israel of old. God made them to 'rule' day and night (Genesis 1.14–18), and each month began with special offerings beginning of each (Numbers 28.11–14). Seasons are the other natural time pattern observed among all temperate climate societies. In Israel they are seen as reflecting God's faithfulness to creatures' ongoing wellbeing: "As long as the earth endures, seedtime and harvest, cold and heat, summer and winter, day and night, shall not cease" (Genesis 8:22).[10]

Outside Israel, the cycles and seasons of nature typically led to development of 'nature religions', patterns of beliefs and behaviour designed to assure the ongoing provision of food against the uncertainties of life. That the lunar month corresponds approximately to women's menstrual cycle likewise shaped fertility rituals designed to ensure continuance of the human species. That is why Baal worship was fiercely rejected by the prophets of Israel: it put faith in human activities and invented deities rather than the Creator (see I Kings 18.20–29; Isaiah 44.910; Jeremiah 44). But 'fertility religion', relying on human ingenuity to 'control' nature, is as much a problem for modern as ancient societies—and highly dangerous for the wellbeing of human beings, our fellow creatures, and the earth itself.

So there are tensions in how we live with the rhythms of nature—the year, its seasons and months. The seven-day week is not 'natural', but

---

9   Lunar months vary between 27 and 29 days, depending on the earth's distance from the sun, and the angle of the earth's and moon's planes. Calendars based on the lunar month—for example Hebrew, traditional Chinese, Korean, Indian—each add days to fit twelve months into the 365.25 days of the year. The Julian calendar used since 1752 does this by assigning different day lengths to months, and including quadrennial and quadcentennial leap years.

10 Though only the two 'extreme' seasons are listed, elsewhere in the First Testament the other temperate seasons are noted, especially the times of rain (2 Samuel 11.1; Jeremiah 5.24; Hosea 6.3).

derives from God's creative gift of the sabbath. It is all of a piece with the 'Jubilee' ('trumpet blast') year—the fiftieth year after a week of weeks of years (Leviticus 25). Land was to be returned to its original clan, and 'slaves' (embonded servants) freed. We do not know how far this was practised, but it emphasised that we do not 'own' the land.

> The earth is the Lord's and all that is in it, the world, and those who live in it. (Psalm 24:1)

The land belongs to God, not humankind.[11] The Jubilee sets limits to 'private property' (see I Kings 21), and sees history as a journey of creation towards freedom. Fertility religions envisage history as 'cyclic', a series of endless returns to stability and security; Israel's faith sees the path of time as 'linear'. History is given meaning by successive events, shaped by the covenants with Abram and Sarah, with Moses, Joshua and David—moving towards the "new covenant" (Jeremiah 31.31-34) and creation's fulfilment in the "new heavens and earth" (Isaiah 66.22-23).

Israel's feasts—and our Christian inheritance from them—blend historic event with the seasons of nature. The Passover meal celebrates Israel's deliverance from slavery under Pharaoh, and is a springtime festival. Likewise, in Europe and North America today Easter is closely associated with spring—which has its dangers. That it falls in autumn in the southern hemisphere has the theological advantage of not reducing Christ's resurrection to a cycle of nature.

The feasts of Israel

The pattern of feasts in ancient Israel was pretty straightforward.

---

11 See further Walter Brueggemann, *The Land* (revised edition, Philadelphia: Fortress, 2002).

There were daily, sabbath and new moon offerings, plus two major 'groups' of festivals (summarised in Leviticus 23).[12]

The *spring* group falls in the first lunar month, Nisan (roughly September in the southern hemisphere, March in the northern):

Passover, marking the angel of death 'passing over' Israel, and Israel's 'passing over' the Red Sea (Exodus), falls on the 14th day.

Unleavened Bread follows immediately for eight days (inclusive) until the 22nd day, and includes the feast of First Fruits on the 16th day.

'Weeks' comes a week of weeks later (50 days, 'pentecost' in Greek): this marks the grain harvest and the giving of the Law to Moses.

The *autumn* group opens on the first day of the seventh month (roughly March in the southern hemisphere, September in the northern) with:

Trumpets (the pre-exilic New Year),[13] followed soon after by

Yom Kippur, the Day of Atonement on the 10th day,[14] and then

Booths or Tabernacles, when from the 15th day people lived in tents for a week—this combines the vintage harvest with remembering Israel's Exodus years in the wilderness.

---

12 Other relevant texts are Exodus 23.14-17; 34.18-23; Numbers 28-29; and Deuteronomy 16.1-7. Helmer Ringgren, *Israelite Religion* (trans. David Green, London: SPCK, 1969) 185-200 gives a full discussion.

13 The final form of Leviticus 23 took place in or after the Exile, and its numbering of months follows the Babylonian system: hence the post-exilic change in the New Year from the first to the seventh month.

14 *Yom Kippur* rites transcend the various types of sacrifice in Israel. These did not bring forgiveness, but gave the people of God rites of dedication, thanksgiving, communion with the Lord and humility. It is thus *Yom Kipper* that is the focus of Hebrews 9-11, not the wider sacrificial system. See Charles Sherlock, *Words and the Word* (Melbourne: Mosaic/Morningstar, 2013) chapter 7.

Each group holds together the celebration of God's work in nature and history—spring and Passover, autumn and Exodus: creation and redemption are seen as seamless facets of divine activity, while 'fertility religion' is avoided.[15] The biblical marking of 'time' thus integrates the 'cyclic' patterns of nature with the 'historical' acts of God's re-creative work (exemplified in Psalm 19).

The Christian year: performing the gospel in time

Harvest and similar festivals cannot set Easter or Christmas aside, but have their place in performing the gospel. Time-cycles derived from God's work in nature and history interact in the Christian year. In the early centuries three elements stand out:

- First was the shift of sabbath observance from Saturday to Sunday, the 'first day' of Christ's resurrection, and the 'eighth day' of the new creation. [16] Hints are found in the New Testament (Acts 20.7, 1 Corinthians 16.2, Revelation 1.10), but the clearest reference comes in the *Didache* XIV.1: "on the Lord's Day of the Lord come together and break bread and give thanks".[17]
- Second, and closely related to Sunday, was marking the 'paschal feast' (Easter) near the time of Passover, associated with baptisms.

---

15 After the return from Exile, the feasts of Purim ('lots', celebrating Israel's deliverance under Esther) and Dedication ('Hanukkah', 'lights', marking the cleansing of the Temple by the Maccabees after its desecration in 167 BC: see John 10.22) grew in significance.

16 Which is also why baptismal fonts, as the place of entry to the 'eighth day', are traditionally eight-sided.

17 *The Didache* ('The Teaching of the Twelve Apostles') is dated by scholars between 70 and 110AD. By 150AD Sunday is noted by Justin Martyr as "the day on which we all hold our common assembly, because it is the first day on which God, having wrought a change in the darkness and matter, made the world; and Jesus Christ our Saviour on the same day rose from the dead." (*First Apology*, §67)

- Third, the witness (*marturia*) to death of Christians saw the date of their 'victory' marked, leading to 'saints days' being included.[18]

After the Roman Empire first tolerated, and then made the Christian religion official, the Christian calendar took shape. Easter was extended 'backwards' by a time of preparation (Lent), and 'forwards' through to the day of Pentecost, when the Spirit came upon the Church (Acts 2). As in Israel, it has two main groups, based on the life and ministry of Christ:
- return, birth and identity (Advent–Christmas–Epiphany)
- temptation, passion and resurrection (Lent–Easter: Passover to Pentecost).

Just as Passover is related to spring in the First Testament, Easter is associated with the northern hemisphere spring. No liturgical *text* links Easter to spring, though the *events* are often related in the way churches are decorated. This Pasch–spring pairing reflects the integration of God's work in creation and re-creation—an integration also seen in the way Christian festivals are linked with the seasonal cycles of the sun:

March 25 is the approximate (northern) equinox, the opening of spring. The Church year marks it as the Annunciation to the Blessed Virgin Mary ('Lady Day'), the conception of Jesus, the "first-born of the new creation" (Colossians 1.15).[19]

June 24 is the approximate (northern) summer solstice, after which summer days shorten. The Church year marks it as the Birth

---

18   The persecutions in Rome by Nero (c. 64AD) and Domitian (c. 96AD), the testimony of the old man Polycarp at his trial (156AD), the bravery of Perpetua and her companions, and the witness of numerous faithful in the widespread persecutions of 250-257 and 303-313, burnt their way into Christian memory.

19   New Year's Day in Europe was March 25 until the calendar revisions of 1752 (whose omission of eleven days is a trap for unwary historians), when it returned to the Graeco-Roman practice of January 1.

of John the Baptist, "he must increase, I must decrease" as John said in relation to the "sun of righteousness, rising with healing in its wings".

September 29 is the approximate (northern) autumn equinox, the beginning of autumn. The Church year keeps it in honour of Michael and All Angels, spiritual protectors in darker times.

December 25 falls nine months after March 25, so the Church year marks it as the birth of Christ. Being the approximate (northern) winter solstice, in Europe's north it attracted 'pagan' rites to ensure the sun's return, but (contrary to popular thinking) Christmas was not observed in opposition, but because Christians knew about the typical length of pregnancy.

Christmas and saints' days were rejected by the 17th century Puritans, who objected to what they saw as 'popish practices' (appealing to Galatians 4.10). When some fled to New England, they left the Church year behind—which was also rejected, for anti-Christian reasons, in the French Revolution.

Western societies, while still retaining the week, saw a 'civil year' develop, with public holidays marking national events alongside Christmas and Easter, observed largely for their economic usefulness.[20] Beginning in 1960, the United Nations began to list 'International Decades' (e.g. to combat racism), 'International Years' (e.g. of youth), annual 'International weeks' (e.g. World Breastfeeding Week) and 'International Days' (of which there are now over 130: December 1, World AIDS Day, is one of the best known and observed). From a Christian perspective, these commemorations have been a welcome way of growing public awareness about important issues—though their sheer number may be diluting their effect.

---

20 The civil and Christian year continue to overlap in some places. Thus the English academic year starts (in September) with Michaelmas term, followed by Lent and Trinity terms.

Part C: Performing the gospel in today's time

Australia's civil calendar is increasingly shaped by public holidays, sporting events and 24-hour shopping. Southern hemisphere seasons are the inverse of those in England and the US—and much of Australia lies in tropical climes where they are unknown. In what ways do factors such as these affect the way Australian Christians mark the rhythms of time in performing the gospel? Let's start at the beginning, with the day.

The day

We live each day in the wake of electricity, from the morning alarm to artificial light, which extends the evening to any time that suits. In the scriptures, however, each day began at sunset: the Bible's opening chapter sets rest before busyness as our first experience of time (Genesis 1-2.4a). Graeco-Roman practice was more prosaic—each day began with its tasks (see Acts 4.3, 23.32). Israel's understanding continued in the early churches, with Sunday commencing on Saturday evening, especially at Easter (the 'vigil' service—see further below).[21] But this approach has all but disappeared—a remnant remains in having 'First Evensongs' for the major festivals (e.g. Christmas, Pentecost) and saints (All Saints, John the Baptist, Mary, Peter & Paul).

What might this mean for performing the gospel today? Many

---

21 Roger Beckwith notes that the main meal for first-century Jews, and the Passover meal in particular, was at nightfall. So, "When, in 1 Cor. 11.20, Pauls calls the combined meal [eucharist and agape] 'the Lord's Supper (*kuriakon deipnon*)' he is probably indicating that it was held at this hour. The Didache 14 speaks as if the combined meal is the first event of the Lord's Day ... so it may be that it was regularly held after nightfall." Roger Beckwith, *Daily and Weekly Worship: Jewish to Christian* (Alcuin/GROW Liturgical Study 1. Nottingham: Grove, 1987). Augustine held a similar view (Ep 36, *ad Casulanum*) as did John Cassian (*Institutes* 2.18).

Christian parents give a night-time blessing to their children as the light goes out—this can evoke the biblical notion of 'day' as beginning with rest.[22] But the more typical focus of evening prayers concerns surviving the dangers of the dark rather than beginning the day with rest. In the traditional late night service before sleep, Compline, the emphasis falls on 'Lighten our darkness'. Its contemporary form in *APBA* and other modern books is called 'Prayer at the End of the Day': how would you feel if it were called 'Prayer at the Opening of the Day'?

Thinking of the day in terms of rest before activity sets God's grace before our human endeavours—and as enabling them. Yet the post-electricity assumption that the day begins at dawn has positives. As we wake, we make a 'fresh start', and can take the opportunity to offer the day to God, praying that we may 'walk in the light' with Christ. Performing the gospel by offering thanks and prayer each evening and morning (in either order) grounds our living in grace, and empowers it.

Sunday and the seven-day week

What then of Sunday, when Christ was raised from the dead in the pre-dawn hours? As noted above, in the early churches it quickly attracted the 'sabbath' concept of a day of rest, along with that of gathering to encounter, listen to and eat with the risen Lord. But Sunday was an ordinary workday: gatherings took place in the early morning, before work. It only "became a day of rest after 321 when Constantine closed the law courts and stopped the crafts working

---

22   This text was over my bed as a child — later over our son's, and now our granddaughter's bed:
      And now I lay me down to sleep—I pray you, Lord, my life to keep.
      If I should die before I wake, I pray you, my life to take.
      If I should live another day, I pray you, Lord, to guide my way.

on it".²³ English law protected the observance of Sunday, defended as a work-free day by 'The Lord's Day Observance Society'.²⁴ Jewish and Christian practice thus led to the 'seven-day week', even though each day's name derives from the Norse pantheon. The 'weekend' became a staple part of society, with 'penalty rates' guarding against Australian workers being exploited. But pressures on governments to loosen shopping hours, especially in 'tourist areas', have seen Sunday now observed more as a day for sport, eating out and shopping rather than church-going.

How do we perform the gospel on Sundays in today's 'deregulated' societies? It is useful to remember that, if the first dozen or so generations of Christians coped with the pressures of a 'non-observing' society as regards Sunday, and learnt to adapt to its cycles of time, so can modern Christians. The Roman Catholic Church, for example, in the 1960s introduced regular Saturday evening 'vigil' services for people who could not be 'in church' on Sundays

Sunday is the day of new creation inaugurated by Christ's resurrection—the 'eighth' as well as 'first' day. It is always a day of joy, never displaced by other feasts: "the day that the Lord has made—we shall rejoice and be glad in it" (Psalm 118.24). So there are 47 days from Ash Wednesday to Easter Day, not 40—Sundays are never 'of' but 'in' Lent. Performing the gospel each Sunday 'in church' thus enables Christians to engage with their risen and ascended Lord: we listen and respond to Christ the Word of God, offer our thanks, prayers and confessions through "our advocate with the Father" (I John 2.1), and encounter our living Lord in holy communion.

---

23   Peter Cobb, "The History of the Christian year", in Cheslyn Jones, Geoffrey Wainwright and Edward Yarnold sj (edd), *The Study of Liturgy* (London: SPCK, 1978) 405.

24   This society was founded in England in 1831. In 1920 it united with the *Working Men's Lord's Day Rest Association*, then in 1953 with the *Lord's Day Observance Association of Scotland*, and in 1965 with the *Imperial Alliance for the Defence of Sunday*. It is now *Day One Christian Ministries*: www.dayone.org.uk.

Sunday and sabbath

But how does Sunday relate to the seventh day of creation, the sabbath? As creatures made in "the image and likeness of God" (Genesis 1.26), we are called to follow God's example, and 'rest' from our labours at the beginning of each day and the end of each week. Sunday, the day of new creation, is the first day of the week, not Monday, when work resumes. This 'sabbatical lifestyle' is the antidote to being overloaded with busyness; it gives 'shape' to living for those without the routines of employment. Further, a 'day off' stops us from thinking we are indispensable: for one day a week we entrust our responsibilities to others. But does our 'sabbath' need to be Sunday? 'Seventh Day' Christians reject the shift of 'sabbath' from Saturday to Sunday.[25] They face the challenge of seeking to gather on a day even more engaged by shopping, sport

---

25   Seventh Day Christians argue that the three New Testament texts that are taken to refer to Sunday as a day for Christians to gather for worship are ambiguous:

a)   Acts 20.7 states: "on the first day of the week, when we had gathered to break bread". Was this the usual day for such a meeting– or when Paul happened to be present in Troas as he journeyed?

b)   Paul wrote: "On the first day of every week, each of you is to put aside and save whatever extra you earn" (1 Corinthians 16.1). Was this the usual day for churches to meet—or payday in Corinth?

c)   John states: "I was in the spirit on the Lord's day" (Revelation 1.10). Was he in church, or was this the day that his vision happened to come?

Taken as a whole, especially given early writings which specify Sunday as the day for Christians to gather (e.g. *The Didache*), and universal practice, the three texts better read as referring to a very early (Corinthians was written c. 51AD) and growing practice of Sunday observance—that it is now "the Lord's day" in Revelation supports this conclusion. Ignatius of Antioch, writing to the Magnesians around 115AD, sees Christians as "no longer observing the Sabbath, but living in the observance of the Lord's day, on which also our life has sprung up again by him and by his death" (9). For details, see the article by Peter Cobb cited above, and Roger Beckwith and Walter Scott, *This is the Day: the Biblical Doctrine of the Christian Sunday in its Jewish and Early Church Setting* (London: Marshall, Morgan and Scott, 1978).

and entertainment, while missing the opportunity to meet with other Christians on the day of resurrection.

All Christians can agree that Saturday remains 'sabbath' in biblical terms, not Sunday. But there are lots of good reasons for keeping Sunday 'special', with a sabbatical flavour: as a boy of scholarly disposition, never doing homework on Sundays kept it as a day of freedom. Households can link re-creative activities with communal worship, in which people who live by themselves can join. Opportunities for ongoing learning, informal conversation and small group sharing can take place.

But the seventh and first days have different foci: the first centres on Easter, the Lord's day; the seventh is the day of rest. We are called to perform the gospel in both ways in our personal, family and church living. Which raises the questions: to what degree should disagreements over Sunday or Saturday be church dividing?

The Christian year's Easter ('Paschal') cycle

The Christian year revolves around Easter—THE Sunday of Sundays. Just as what it means to be a Jew is inextricably tied up with Passover, what it means to be a Christian is inseparable from Easter, the Christian passover ('paschal') feast. There are ideas aplenty around keeping Easter today, from classical texts to internet sites. But some issues arise about principled practice.

Season: spring, autumn or tropical?

Easter (and Passover) falls in spring in the temperate northern hemisphere. As noted above, overdoing this can lead to Christ's resurrection being seen as just illuminating a cycle of nature, rather than God's decisive intervention in history. In contrast, the southern hemisphere experience of autumnal Easter emphasises God's paschal transformation of nature, and fits the subdued tone of Lent. And if you live in the tropics—well seasonal change is about rain and humidity more than temperature. But wherever you live in western society today, chocolate consumption (originating from the eggs decorated by Eastern Christians to mark Easter) is front and centre in media coverage. Enjoying an Easter egg hunt is fine as an incidental part of enjoying performing the gospel—but the gospel is about more than the cycle of nature.

Holy Week: re-enacting or re-membering?[26]

Expanding the celebration of Easter to include the events of Christ's final earthly week began early in the church's life, especially in Jerusalem.[27] In medieval practice, performances that recount the story of Holy Week engaged a population for whom neither reading nor books were available. This slowly shaped its being observed as a re-enactment of Christ's last week, of which the Oberammergau Passion Play is one of the most famous. Understanding Holy Week as re-enacting the passion remains popular among contemporary Christians: palm processions, the Good Friday plays, or 'stations of the cross', Easter dawn services on hillsides or the beach, for example. Drama is the typical element of such events: it is their time-setting that brings out the 'when' of performing the gospel.

But there are dangers here. Christ's saving work was 'once for all' (Hebrews 9.26–28): it can and must be commemorated, but cannot be repeated. At least in the popular mind, the medieval eucharist was seen as a re-enactment of Christ's sacrifice. The Reformers saw this as a blasphemy that, for the sake of the gospel, had to be

---

26 Peter Akehurst, *Keeping Holy Week* (Nottingham: Grove, 1976) is an excellent overview of the issues involved.

27 Egeria's description of Jerusalem rites around 380AD strongly influenced how others came to observe Holy Week. John *Wilkinson, Egeria's Travels (Oxford: Aris & Phillips, 2006) is the most recent translation.*

rejected. The English Reformers sought to retain what was good of their medieval inheritance: this included Holy Week, which was retained but also reformed. So in the *Book of Common Prayer*, 'The Sunday next before Easter' is called that, not 'Palm Sunday' and the Gospel is Matthew 27, Christ's trial and crucifixion, not the 'triumphal entry' (Matthew 21). In *APBA* and other modern prayer books it is 'Passion' Sunday, setting before us the story as a whole as we approach Holy Week. Yet human nature loves to enact a story: starting the service with a procession of palms into the building can be an effective way by which all take part in performing the gospel without compromising the once-for-all work of Christ.

Similar comments could be made about Maundy ('new commandment') Thursday and Good (God's) Friday. We do not gather to re-enact the unique ministry of the Lord Jesus, but to re-engage with it—to be 're-membered' in Christ. Sharing a simple meal on the Thursday evening during which eucharist is celebrated quietly, or having a stark cross brought into church for all to acknowledge in some way—symbolic actions such as these can be 'effectual means of grace' in helping us enter into the deep mystery of Holy Week.[28] But to be authentic performances of the gospel, they need to be experienced as various facets of our commemorating the 'once-for-all' work of Christ.

Holy Saturday: day of victory or rest?

Holy Saturday, in between Good Friday and Easter Day, can be a puzzle. Seeing Christ's work as a victory over Satan, sin, death and evil is how many Christians experience his saving work. In dramatising the story, some came to see Christ, having descended

---

28 Australian Anglicans have access to services that include such elements in forms acceptable to all, though some had been rejected in 1548, as Reformation got under way. They are available at www.anglican.org.au/governance/commissions/pages/liturgy.aspx.

to the dead,[29] as gaining victory by defeating Satan on Holy Saturday—the 'harrowing of hell'. The danger here is thinking in 'might is right' terms, rather than the New Testament emphasis on Christ overcoming these evils through suffering, 'absorbing' them and so rendering them harmless for believers.[30] Christ's last word, according to John, is *tetelestai* ('finished'). He *dies* victorious, having taken on all that could be thrown at him. Matthew's gospel states:

> Jesus cried again with a loud voice and breathed his last. At that moment the curtain of the temple was torn in two, from top to bottom. The earth shook, and the rocks were split. The tombs also were opened, and many bodies of the saints who had fallen asleep were raised. (Matthew 27:50-52)

Christ's death opened access to God, and saw the earth open to release those imprisoned in its depths. However literal this description is, it places the victory of Christ in his suffering and dying, not in a post-death test of strength. Holy Saturday is not the day of Christ's going into battle with the forces of darkness—it is the great Sabbath, the day of divine rest, after death has been

---

29 This (late) phrase in the Apostles' Creed, *descendit ad inferos* (descended to the underworld) was translated as 'descended into hell' in the *Book of Common Prayer*. In Hebrew thought, Hades, Sheol or the Pit was the place of the departed, a lifeless place but not one of punishment (see Psalms 88, 142.8 etc.). Considerable debate took place in the Reformation as to the meaning of the phrase, as evidenced in it receiving separate treatment in (abbreviated) Article III of the Thirty-Nine Articles

30 Only two New Testament texts portray Christ's ministry principally in 'victory' terms, Colossians 2.15 and Hebrews 2.14, but both do so in terms of his redemptive suffering. Likewise, though the ascended Lord is pictured as a warrior in Revelation (19.11-16), the over-riding image is of Christ as "the Lamb who was slain" (5.1-13; 6.1-14; 7.7-14; 8.1; 13.8; 14.1-4; 15.3; 17.14; 19.7-9; 21.9-22.3) who conquered by his blood being shed, the calling also of Christian witnesses (12.11).

overcome. As God rested after the work of creation, so Christ rests after the work of redemption, of re-creation.

How then are we to perform the 'paschal' gospel on the 'in-between' day of Holy Saturday? Yes, some of it will be filled with busy preparations for Easter Day—placing furniture, arranging the best flowers of the year and so on. But finding ways to keep it in the spirit of resting with Christ is the 'better part'.

One feast or several?

The technical name for Holy Week's concluding days is 'Triduum' (Latin for 'of three days'). 'Churchy' names are not always helpful, but this one points up a significant issue: do we keep them as a string of separate commemorations, or as integrated facets of the one act of God? The way this question is framed shows my response—as God is One, this greatest of Christian festivals should be a unitive, not fragmented celebration. In the early centuries just one (long) service took place, from Saturday evening through to Easter morning.[31] Separate rites for each day of Holy Week developed over time, reflecting our human love of story telling—performing the gospel indeed. No problem arises unless we slip into 're-enactment' thinking. As we Christians walk through the various facets of the 'paschal mystery' in Holy Week, we are 're-membered' in Christ into the 'life of the aeons', the communion of Father, Son and Spirit into whom we are baptised.

---

31 Trevor Lloyd, in *Celebrating Lent, Holy Week and Easter* (Nottingham: Grove, 1985) notes the useful distinction made by A. Scheer between *passio-pascha* and *transitus-pascha* traditions. The former (early) tradition focussed on the cross and Passover lamb, commemorated in one integrated celebration — the Easter Vigil, observed continuously by Eastern Christians, and revived in the West over the past century or so; the latter (later) tradition, with an Exodus 14 focus, expanded the celebration into a series of commemorations. Lloyd comments that "The *transitus* feeling is that of having arrived; the *passio* feeling is that of being about to go out." Official Anglican liturgies retain the *transitus* shape, but with a *passio* ethos.

Fifty is more than forty

Easter's fifty days are more than Lent's forty (or 46). Easter is not just a one-day matter: it is celebrated for a longer time than any other season of the Christian year. Following the calendar of Israel of old, Easter concludes with Pentecost, a week of weeks plus one day—a Jubilee of days, calling us to live in anticipation of the new creation, which Christ's being raised from death, began to usher in. So our performing of the unfathomable gospel over Easter is 'stretched', giving opportunity to explore the various New Testament accounts. Easter draws to its (never-ending) conclusion at Pentecost, when Israel gave thanks for the giving of the Law at Sinai. Our performance of the gospel on this Jubilee day celebrates the coming of the Holy Spirit, without whom we would not be performing the gospel in the first place. This is a day for unbridled joy—perhaps even risking come 'charismatic' behaviour. It is a fitting time to join together with Christians of other traditions, to mark the birthday of the body of Christ on earth, giving joint witness to the gospel we share.

The Christian Year: the Advent–Christmas–Epiphany cycle

Advent: beginning from the end

Why does the Christian year start with Advent (Latin for 'arrival')? Advent set before us the scriptures' vision of the 'end' of all things. Why not start with creation, the 'genesis' of all that is, or with Christmas, the 'genesis' of Jesus Christ (Matthew 1.1)?

In medieval times, the day of judgment was portrayed in churches by images displaying the sharp contrasts of heaven and hell. Protestant 'dispensationalists' focus on the return ('second arrival/coming') of Christ, speculating over the 'rapture' and 'tribulation'. But a focus on 'judgement day' or the 'millennium' is not why Advent begins the Christian year. Indeed, they might be reasons to see Advent as *ending* it.

More commonly (and positively), some see Advent as preparing for Christmas. The prophecies of Isaiah are read, for example: but their message is primarily about the end of all things, not the incarnation in isolation. Indeed, it is 'getting ready for Christmas' approaches to Advent that lie at the spiritual root of the 'shopping days left' mentality, viewing December as the climax of the retail year, 'ChristXma$'. The slide from preparing for Christ to be "born in our hearts today" to "have we sent a card to every business contact and got a gift for every relative?" is slippery.[32]

So why *does* Advent begin the Christian year? Jesus teaches us to pray: "Your kingdom come, your will be done, on earth as it is in heaven." Here we pray to live from God's future backwards. We pray to live the 'kingdom' or 'rule' of God now, to live 'on earth' as citizens of the new creation ('heaven'). This is made possible by the Holy Spirit, who brings God's future into our present, as the 'down-payment' of God's future (2 Corinthians 5.5). The alternative is to live from the past forwards. But the past is drenched in sin and its ramifications, all the dark things from which Christ's blood liberates fallen creation, reconciling 'all things, things in heaven and on earth' (Colossians 1:20).

Advent begins the Christian year because it calls us to perform the gospel from God's future backwards, rather than from our human past forwards. It is a time to do the serious work of re-visioning our living with heads gladly in the clouds, seeing all things in the light of the Lord Jesus' reign. We perform the gospel in Advent by basking in the 'blessed hope' of the full presence of Christ, our judge and vindicator. We stand in awe of the age-old prophets, who saw these things from afar, and brought fierce indictment against all

---

32 An ancient tradition of turning towards Christmas in the final eight days ('octave') of Advent is reflected in modern lectionaries (including that issued with *APBA*), with daily 'O' prayers (O wisdom…).

who practiced oppression and lived unjustly. It is a time to perform the gospel with serious joy. Only then can we truly welcome the first 'advent' of our Lord, the amazing gift of God's eternal Word en-fleshed by the Holy Spirit in Mary's womb.

Christmas and Epiphany

Christmas is the best-known Christian festival, and resources aplenty exist to draw on in performing the gospel then. But why twelve days—and do they come before or after December 25? Among Eastern Christians, the emphasis falls on the incarnation as a *doctrinal* truth: January 6 is Christmas, explicating what the birth of the Saviour means. In the West, on the other hand, telling the story is the great delight, and this begins on December 25, nine months after Jesus was conceived. As with Holy Week, English traditions blend both approaches, specifying 'twelve days of Christmas' from December 25 to January 6, Epiphany, 'showing meaning' day. Most Australians today, however—Christians included—think Christmas ends by noon on December 25, and that the twelve days precede it, to encourage hectic shopping.

How can we 'stretch' our performing the gospel around the Christmas–New Year period? One way is to take the idea of 'epiphany' seriously, exploring what Christ means to us through his 'signs'. Both East and West now mark the first Sunday after January 6 as 'Baptism of the Lord', the beginning of his public ministry: on this day Greek Christians 'bless the waters', with television coverage.

The second Sunday marks Jesus' first 'sign', the wedding at Cana.[33] The *Revised Common Lectionary*, now adopted widely across the Anglican and other Communions, seeks to give Epiphany a clear shape as the 'season of signs', from Baptism to Transfiguration (observed on the Last Sunday before Lent).

In Australia, however, January—and Epiphany—is holiday time. Using the 'signs' Jesus performed in holiday-type ways (as beach mission teams do) offers possibilities. In this way the seasons of the Christian and civil year can be integrated in performing the gospel in ways that are true to scripture, and make sense in our modern context.

Much more could be said about other feasts, including some of special relevance to Australians and New Zealanders, such as April 25. But that is for other resources.[34] Paul's words to the Corinthians speak directly to when we perform the gospel:

> We urge also not to accept the grace of God in vain. For he says, "At an acceptable time I have listened to you, and on a day of salvation I have helped you." See, now is the acceptable time; see, now is the day of salvation. (2 Corinthians 6.1–2)

---

[33] In the *Book of Common Prayer* Epiphany was a 'filler' season. The last three Sundays before Lent looked forward to Easter: Septuagesima, Sexagesima and Quadragesima (i.e. roughly 70, 60 and 40 days before it). The number of other Sundays depends on the date of Easter: In BCP, extra ones were taken from the final Sundays of the year (which would then not be needed). The revision of the Christian year in the 1970s, in the wake of the Liturgical and Vatican II, numbers Sundays in 'Ordinary time' sequentially (Propers 1—34), so that Sundays after Pentecost basically take up where Epiphany ones left off.

[34] Charles Sherlock, *Australian Anglicans Remember* (Melbourne: Broughton, 2015) offers resources for Australian-specific days. See www.anglican.org.nz/Resources/Lectionary-and-Worship/For-All-the-Saints/For-All-the-Saints for information on other saint's day in the Christian year.

Part D   Time to perform

1. Think about your typical day. When do you feel that it starts and ends?
    What opportunities do you have, individually and with others, to pray, read the scriptures, to perform the gospel through serving others? How do these relate to the life of your local church?
2. 'Jesus Christ is the centre of time as we date it.'
    'God is not so much time-less as time-full'.
    'God had time for us in Jesus Christ.'
    What do you make of these theological claims? In what way(s), if any, do they help you think/live as a Christian in time?
3. Think back over the past year.
    What major events stood out in your personal life (e.g. a special birthday)?
    In the life of your local community? In your local church? Take one item from each category, and consider how it related to the civil or Christian year. In what way(s), if any, was the gospel performed or lived?
    How might some aspect of the gospel have been performed—or done better?
4. What does a typical Sunday look like in your household and local congregation?
    After reading this chapter, do you have any plans to live it differently? If so, what are they, and why have you made them? Will you share them with others?
5. What major festivals of the Christian year stand out in your own life?
    In the life of your local congregation?

How do they relate to one another?
6. This chapter has raised issues about performing the gospel by 're-enactment' and/or by 're-membering'. How does this distinction help you—if at all?

Chapter Nine
Common prayer? Planning to perform the gospel

Overview

Part A reflects on how 'common prayer' is best sustained today, in the light of the main 'plots' of classical Christian worship. Understanding these can be quite liberating.

Part B offers insights into planning for common prayer in today's post-modern environment, using some examples from *A Prayer Book for Australia*.

Part C explores how good planning enables effective performance of the gospel, especially across cultural and church boundaries.

Part D outlines how to undertake a 'worship audit'. Highly recommended!

"You have been approached about helping arrange a dramatic performance in church…" That is the opening sentence of this book. Chapter by chapter, different aspects of what it means to 'perform the gospel' have been explored—in daily life, special spaces, leading, hearing, singing, seeing and when. But how does it all hang together, especially for a typical Sunday service? What basic 'shape' of a performance best conveys the gospel?

Before going further, a reminder of other points made in the opening chapter is necessary. In speaking of Christian worship as 'performance', the key focus is on what *God* is doing. Those who exercise the ministry of the gospel in Word and sacrament are indeed to *perform*, using their God-given skills to the fullest. Their own personality must serve the part they are called to play, not dominate or displace it. That said, it is tempting to think that the performers are just the ministers and musicians, while the audience is the congregation, who join in only now and then. But **performing the gospel is the calling of every Christian**, whether in daily life or 'in church': how each person participates may differ, but all are 'performers'.

The writing of this final chapter began on a cruise ship. Passengers came from a dozen or more English-speaking nations (and others), and several Christian traditions. What type of service for a Sunday on board best sustains 'common prayer'? By the time you have finished this chapter, you will have some idea of how we responded to this challenge. Interestingly, when the ship's Captain led services, it followed Morning Prayer from the *Book of Common Prayer* (1662)—a wonderfully rich scriptural diet, but unfamiliar to quite a few passengers. And how many hymns are there to choose from that most will know?

Should regular Sunday services work towards 'deepening godly ruts' (the ministry of familiar forms) or 'empowering revival' (the spontaneity of newness)? What place do liturgical texts and well-known songs play—and do these restrict freedom or shape it? And what about 'traditional' words? Tradition—the process of 'handing over' something—is both critiqued and valued in the New Testament. It can be a 'torch' for passing on the gospel (1 Corinthians 15:1-3) or a 'fossil' that imprisons or distorts God's truth (Mark 7:1-13). How does our performance of the gospel work as 'torch' but not 'fossil'?

As recently as 50 years ago, most Christian services in English—whether Anglican, Baptist, Church of Christ, Lutheran, Methodist, Presbyterian, Roman Catholic, Salvation Army (note the alphabetical order)—week by week followed similar structures and used similar words. Television, social mobility, democratic ideals, electronic media—the 'post-modern condition' that breathes the air of diversity and variety—has shifted the ground towards an increasing variety of liturgical practice. Further, as church and society have drifted apart in the West, most congregations today consist of 'regulars'—visitors are noticed. This combination of cultural shifts and tighter congregational identity has seen Sunday services become more and more localised, to the point where visitors from other churches, even from the same tradition, can feel lost. And while the charismatic movement and 'contemporary worship' music styles have loosened things up nicely, less and less songs and texts are held in common across English-speaking Christians.

So, what basic 'shapes' or 'plots' support authentic performance of the gospel? How free can or should 'common prayer' be in the midst of the variety experienced today?

Part A   Common words, common structure

Anglicans tend to think of 'common prayer' as the contents of the *Book of Common Prayer*, but the concept is much wider. It is an ethos, a sense of corporate prayer that crosses boundaries of place, culture, language, church traditions and even communions. It is more than a narrowly Anglican phenomenon, but embraces the prayer life of all who own the name of Christ. But in today's world of endless choices, how is such a unifying vision to be experienced in a local congregation? In some places, little change—perhaps beyond using modern English—has happened, leading to dull services with barely a spark of divine imagination. In others, however, adaptation has gone on for decades, so that idiosyncratic local patterns have emerged, unfamiliar to people from other churches. How then is common prayer to be sustained across the body of Christ in the post-modern cultural air that western Christians breathe today?

Common words

Until only 50 or so years ago, pretty much all the words in a service—beyond the readings and sermon—were in common across the Anglican world. Indeed, the *Book of Common Prayer* forbade anyone but the minister to speak in public services, and (beyond preaching) he was tightly restricted in what could be said. The advantage of this regime, especially since most people went to church at least a few times each year, was that everyone had a shared vocabulary and experience of worship. This was heightened by the *King James Bible* being the only English version in use, and the growth of congregational singing from the early 1800s, as hymnbooks began to appear. But the Anglican (and wider Christian) world steadily changed, through missionary work, the Industrial Revolution, better education, immigration, and the effect of mass media. In the world of the twentieth century, both the 'olde

English' of the words of hymns and the *Book of Common Prayer*, and the inflexibility of its services, saw pressures to change grow, and modern-language prayer books issued.

Having the words of a service the same across congregations made some sense in past ages (though Christians like John Bunyan who opposed this policy were persecuted). Today it is an idea that belongs to history. How then is the notion of common prayer sustained when it comes to the words used? A strategy increasingly adopted across the range of English-speaking churches is to adopt common wording for items that relate to Christian identity. These include the Lord's prayer, Apostles' and Nicene creeds, familiar psalms and hymns, responses such as 'Lift up your hearts / we lift them to the Lord!' and the like. A person who knows such texts with deep familiarity goes beyond just reading the words to using them in ways that embrace mind and spirit. They become 'heart-felt', enabling those present in worship to pray *together*, 'in common'. For English speakers, the *English Language Liturgical Consultation* has produced agreed modern-language texts, many of which are used in *APBA*. In this way common words form part of common prayer.

But this does not resolve all the issues. In particular, agreement on the wording of the Lord's prayer is yet to be found. Roman Catholics and some Protestants continue to use a 'traditional' form—'Our Father, who art in heaven...', though with different pronouns and endings ('doxology').[1] Most worshipping Anglicans and mainline Protestants, however, use the ELLC version, 'Our Father in heaven...', though 'Save us from the time of trial' (ELLC) is sometimes left as 'Lead us not into temptation' (for example, in the Church of England).

---

1 BCP has 'Our Father *which* art in heaven' (implying that the Father is 'at least' personal. i.e more than 'a person'); 'them' rather than 'those' who trespass against us; and ending "for thine is the kingdom, the power and the glory". Roman Catholics use 'who' and 'those', with the ending (sometimes after a response), "for the kingdom, the power and the glory are yours".

People from the wider public may not know any version, or a 'traditional' form at best. At a civic service or funeral, for example, or when different Christian traditions meet together, a useful practice is to encourage people to pray using the English (or other language) form they are most familiar with. Indeed, such disciplined variety can be a model for avoiding undue uniformity being imposed, while sustaining the sense of praying together in heart and mind.

Common structure

Even more significant to common prayer today, however, is seeking a common structure for public worship. A familiar structure helps people sense 'where we are' in a service, yet allows for considerable flexibility without losing a gospel-focused shape. When, for example, the wording of the intercessions is different from what people are used to, they can still know 'where they are' in the service overall. Of course a service can be taken so badly that no structure can be detected, and no one knows where they are. Too many—or too few—directions, chatty commentary, leaving things out without warning and so on are typical problems.

But what does a gospel-focused 'shape' look like? Two basic patterns have emerged in western Christian traditions, complemented by one identified by cultural anthropology.[2]

The office shape

The first derives from daily Morning and Evening Prayer—the 'office' shape. (The name derives from the Latin *officium*, 'duty';

---

[2] The use of 'shape' bears similarities here to that of Gregory Dix, in *The Shape of the Liturgy* (London: Dacre Press, Adam and Charles Black, 2nd Edition, 1945). Dix's brilliant analysis concerns the shape of the eucharistic action—take, give thanks, break, share: this, he argues, is what is in common across the earliest Christian churches, rather than common words or doctrine. His thesis has been qualified, but remains a basic strategy of modern revision.

the commitment to daily prayer made in Christian monastic communities and by clergy.) In outline, this consists of psalms and songs framing readings from scripture, with intercessions. On Sundays, such a 'Service of the Word' often begins with confession and absolution, includes a confession of faith, and is typically followed by a sermon. From the people's point of view, the climax towards which this shape moves is preaching.

Eucharistic shape

The second shape is 'eucharistic', with two main parts. The first includes preparation, then readings from the scriptures climaxed with one from the gospels, responded to in creed, sermon, and intercessions. This 'synaxis' or 'ante-communion' leads into the second part: preparation for communion, the great thanksgiving prayer, receiving the bread and wine, and being sent out.[3] These two parts of a gospel-shaped Sunday service are sometimes spoken of as the 'two tables'—the table of the Word and the table of the Lord—or (as Augustine of Hippo loved to say) the Word 'audible' (heard) and 'visible' (seen). Even so, from the people's point of view, the climax towards which this shape moves is receiving communion.

A significant difference between these two shapes (as distinct from their contents and climaxes) is the way in which the scriptures are *heard*. Instruction in and meditation upon the scriptures is to the fore in the 'office'; biblically grounded gospel proclamation is the keynote in the eucharist. These two approaches are not opposed, however, but complementary (as the images of the two tables, or Word heard and seen, suggest). The standard Sunday service in the *Book of Common Prayer* (1662)

---

[3] Holy Communion Outline Order (*APBA* page 813) shows this structure on a single page. In terms of the argument below, the 'doing' section is filled out with separate headings from the Peace to Communion.

combines Morning Prayer, Litany and Holy Communion—office, prayers, preaching and communion. But with few parishioners being communicants at the Reformation, Morning Prayer (with sermon added) came to be the most common Anglican Sunday service until the mid-20th century (with similar 'Services of the Word' among other Protestant traditions). Over the past 50 years, liturgical revision has these three elements recombined into an integrated rite, whose structure is shown by headings.

Pilgrimage: and liminality

Some services do not quite 'fit' neatly into either structure, however—community services like Anzac or Remembrance Day for example, and especially funerals, and public vigils after a tragedy. A third shape from the Christian tradition that serves well here is 'pilgrimage', in which those involved journey together from one place to another (whether literally or symbolically). One example is an ecumenical 'stations of the Cross' service on Good Friday: following the story of Christ's passion, Christians walk (perhaps singing on the way) together to several 'stations' where scripture is read, reflection is made and prayers offered. A pilgrimage structure is good when dedicating a church, as people move around the furniture that symbolises the gospel—font, prayer desk, lectern, pulpit and holy table. Similarly, an anniversary service can be a pilgrimage marking a congregation's various stages of life.

Related to this are insights from 'rites of passage/liminal' analysis. These arose in cultural anthropology to clarify what is going on when human beings mark key transitions in life by using rituals.⁴ A community group faces a situation of challenge by 'separating' from regular life in order to cross a dangerous boundary or threshold (limen) in safety, before resuming daily living as people 're-incorporated' in an adjusted identity. Thus marriage rites overall can be seen as a process of separation (engagement), wedding (limen) and honeymoon (re-incorporation); more closely in a buck's/hen's night; wedding; reception: and the wedding service itself is shaped by the couple making separate entrances; exchanging vows; and exiting as 'Mr and Mrs'.

Rites of passage analysis is particularly helpful in planning events that relate to birth, maturity, marriage and death (whether individual or community 'dyings'). Typically these will involve people from beyond the Church—thanksgiving for a child, weddings, funerals, anniversaries of events that have shaped a community's life. Liminal theory has obvious application in such situations. But it also has relevance to transitions in Christian life, notably baptism, confirmation and renewal services, and ordinations.⁵ Services like these mark stages of Christian growth and commitment—rites of passage 'in Christ'. Pilgrimage structures integrate rites of passage concepts with performing the Gospel, maximising opportunities to bring committed Christians and others together in shared experience of God's grace and love.

A clear example of the pilgrimage structure is the Funeral service in *APBA*. Provision is made for significant symbolic rites 'Before the

---

4 The work of Arnold van Gennep is basic to liminality theory: the Wikipedia article 'Rite of passage' offers a succinct account. See further Victor Turner, *The Ritual Process* (London: Penguin, 1969).

5 It is important to note that, while the baptism of an infant is often thought of as a 'birth-right' in popular culture, baptism is a 'new birth' rite from darkness to light, symbolizing our being buried in Christ to be raised to new life. The service of 'Thanksgiving for a Child' (which includes naming) is included in *APBA* in order to provide a distinct birth rite, which may be used in its own right or in association with baptism.

Funeral'; the funeral service; burial or interment. Liminal theory is also reflected in the funeral service itself, which is shaped as a pilgrimage of several stages. After the gathering, which establishes the funeral as an act of Christian worship, the **'story' of the person** who has died can be told; psalmody marks the transition to the **'story' of God's work** in giving and redeeming life, through scripture and sermon; and **both 'stories' join** in the prayers and farewell, before they separate as the body is taken out and the congregation turns to resume daily life. In this way the truths of typical human responses to grief, and the gospel of Christ's life-transforming ministry, are performed in ways that seek to respect and integrate them.

Conclusion

This section has argued that common words assist in sustaining the sense of communion across the body of Christ, notably words that cross the spectrum of Christian identity. But too many common words, even sound biblical words, can feel like uniformity in today's more flexible social cultures. That is one reason why prayer books over the past half-century include phrases like "in these or similar words", and offer a variety of options. In this cultural setting, the concept of a common structure forms another way by which 'common prayer' can be sustained. Alongside both approaches, liminality theory, seen most clearly in pilgrimage structures, offers a way of thinking about liturgy that fosters the embracing of human culture when the gospel is performed in public, beyond the usual boundaries of church life.

Now, what might all this look like in practice?

Part B   The shape of God's mission

How is 'common prayer' sustained across the post-modern contexts in which English-speaking Christians live today? The argument so far suggests that common words are important, but more, that common structures—illuminated by insights from cultural anthropology—offer a principled way forward. Two basic 'shapes' employed in Christian liturgy over the centuries were sketched. But what might the 'shape' of a service that performs the gospel on a typical Sunday these days look like? Perhaps not surprisingly, given the research and creative thought put in by scholars and churches over the past century, considerable agreement is found across the western Christian world: *gathering, listening, praying, doing, going*. Behind this structure lies the conviction that it corresponds to the 'shape' of the mission of God, as revealed in the scriptures.

Being gathered to being sent

The *'gathering* to *going'* shape undergirds God's giving of the first covenant ('First Testament'), as described in Exodus. The people of Israel, rescued from slavery in Egypt, having wandered in the wilderness for a generation, were gathered by God at Mount Sinai to listen to the 'ten words' of the covenant, as a "kingdom of priests" (Exodus 19.1-20.17; cf Deuteronomy 5.1-22; 6.1-9). The people responded as Moses both spoke and wrote down God's words in the covenant: "All that the LORD has spoken we will do, and we will be obedient" (Exodus 24.3, 7—cf Deuteronomy 5.23-29). Moses then sprinkled them with the blood of the covenant, before setting off with Aaron and the elders of the people to go up the mountain, where "they beheld God, and they ate and drank" (Exodus 24.11). Through this covenant with this new nation, God would fulfil the promise to Abraham and Sarah that "in you all the families of the earth shall be blessed" (Genesis 12:3).

In sum, being **gathered** by God at Sinai to **listen** to the words of the covenant, to offer the three-dimensional **prayers** of dedication and or well-being 'peace' offerings (Exodus 20.18-26; 23.14-19), to **celebrate** the covenant and **live it out** in fairness (Exodus 21.1-22.27; 23.1-9) and harmony with the land (Exodus 23.10)—this was Israel's calling, their 'worship' of God as "a people consecrated to me" (Exodus 23.31). Tragically, it was a calling that they had already failed (Exodus 16-17; Deuteronomy 1.19-45), and would do so even before Moses came back down from the mountain (Exodus 32)—and would do so time and again (as the books of Judges through 2 Chronicles spell out). But God continued faithful, and century by century sustained the covenant in the face of betrayal and disaster. As things went from bad to worse, the prophets looked to a 'new covenant' (Jeremiah 31.31-34), enabled by the 'servant of God' who, through costly witness and suffering, would be a 'light to the nations' (Isaiah 42.1,6; 49.6), calling the people to "Arise, shine, for your light has come!" (Isaiah 60.1), drawing all the nations to their light.

It comes as no surprise that a similar 'shape' undergirds the New Covenant/Testament. Jesus the Christ is identified as God's obedient servant (Matthew 12.17-21; Acts 8.26-35) through whose ministry believers—whether Jew or pagan—become "a chosen race, a royal priesthood, a holy nation, God's own people" (1 Peter 2.9, echoing Exodus 19.6). Jesus called people to **gather** around him as disciples, to **listen** to his teaching, and to follow his example of **prayer** and holy living. He assured them of his living presence as they obeyed his commend to "**do this** for my remembrance", and commissioned them to **go out** into all the world. This continues to be the pattern for the worship offered by Christian disciples, both in life-style and liturgy. Its shape—gather, listen, pray, do, go—begins with God's call, attends to God's word, responds in prayer and action (especially in the holy communion) and issues in being sent out to perform the gospel. It is the shape of God's mission.

This shape illustrated

Many modern prayer books have adopted this 'gather/listen/pray/do/go' structure. Australian Anglicans can see it in each of the Sunday services in *A Prayer Book for Australia (1995)*. Whether or not this is the book your church follows, it offers a useful example of seeking to perform the gospel in a mission-shaped ethos of disciplined Christian freedom. The Commission that drew together its 'Liturgical resources' (the book's sub-title) was aware of the 'shape' ideas sketched above. It employed them as part of its commitment to having a consistency of approach (theological, liturgical, linguistic and social) across the book, so it could be used by all Anglicans (and more besides).

Gather: in God's Name

What title should be used for the first part of a service? In the initial draft of services for *APBA*, 'Gathering of the People' was the heading used. This reflects the biblical picture of the 'people of God' meaning those whom God has called out to be 'church'—literally assembly, *ek-klesia*, from *ek* (out) and *kaleo* (call). But it was soon realised that many would read this today as a gathering that *we the people* do. Further, those gathered in Christ are baptised "into the Name of Father, Son and Holy Spirit" (Matthew 28.19). So with both these ideas in mind, 'Gathering in God's Name' emerged. God gathers us together as people baptised "in God's Name", now assembling ('churching') to engage with God and one another in performing the gospel.

Sometimes it is good for a service to be held outdoors—at a parish camp, at dawn on Easter morning, or for a wedding. When the weather suits it, a congregation's usual service can take place in a public place—a park, gym, street, cinema, cafe—so other community members can see what 'church' is like. On occasions like these, taking care over the 'gathering rite' (as liturgists describe it) is particularly important. It should help people feel at home in a new setting, set out the framework for what is to happen—and not least, clarify that participants have been gathered to worship God.

Listen: the Ministry of the Word

The focus of all Christian worship is the Lord Jesus Christ. The 'Ministry of the Word' thus means far more than just reading and hearing words—or even performing them. It is the living Word, Jesus Christ, who speaks to us through the scriptures and their exposition (cf Luke 24.27, 32). Such a 'Ministry of the Word' demands response, which can take place through silence, creed, sermon and/or discussion.

The words employed in this ministry are typically said by a single voice. But using more than one reader for a narrative text can bring out the movements in the story: setting the Palm Sunday gospel as a dramatic reading is often done, but it could happen even more often. Likewise, two voices sharing a reading from a New Testament letter can ease the density of some passages, or clarify the way the argument develops. There are many possibilities: but what matters is the sense that it is *Christ* who performs the gospel in our midst as the scriptures are attended to. In the eucharist, this ministry of Christ is symbolised by our standing to hear the gospel (see Chapter Five, 'Stand up. Stand up for Jesus.').

Pray: the Prayers of the People/Ministry of Prayer

Our response to the ministry of the Word moves into the great privilege of praying for the world, for the church, for those we know, and for ourselves (cf 1 Timothy 2:1), aware of the great communion of saints whose example and prayers support ours (cf Revelation 8.3-4). Such a 'Ministry of Prayer' involves more than individual Christians offering private prayers at the same time. It is 'The Prayers of the People' (as some titles express it), a *corporate* act of 'common prayer', our praying *together*. Whoever leads this part of performing the gospel—whether one or several voices—does well to keep this in mind in preparing for this ministry. But this will not mean that the prayers are bland, 'politically correct' offerings. Rather, they will gather together what has been heard in the Ministry of the Word with what lies on our hearts from the news and pastoral needs. In this way God's people will offer their thanks and petitions according to the will of God.

Anglican—and many other—prayer books offer a wealth of prayers, thanksgivings and blessings. These can be used with confidence, since their contents are true, and they have been shaped by generations of use.[6] 'Traditional' Christians sometimes assume that only such 'official' prayers should be used in church. On the other hand, 'democratic' believers tend to think that only prayers prepared for this occasion—perhaps offered off the cuff rather than written down—are 'real' praying. Both extremes are unhelpful: to be truly 'prayers of the people', the best path is to draw on sources that join the prayers of the present with those of the past—and future—people of God.

Do: 'this for the remembrance of me'

The command of the Lord Jesus during his 'last supper' with the disciples, 'do this for the remembrance of me', is probably the best-kept command ever issued by anyone. Gregory Dix, in discussing

---

[6] In *APBA*, see 'Prayers for Various Occasions' (pages 180-222). The Index of Prayers at the end of the full ('red') book (pages 838-843) includes the prayers of the day and week, and those found in all services in *APBA*.

'The Performance of the Liturgy', makes the point that Christ did not command 'say' but 'do' this for his *anamnesis*. "If you believe that the liturgy is primarily a thing 'said', your part in it if you are a layman is to 'hear'." But "the apostolic and primitive church regarded the eucharist as primarily an *action*, something 'done', not something 'said' … and that this action was *corporate*, the united joint action of the whole church."[7]

It must be acknowledged that over the centuries the eucharist has been misused, corrupted and become a cause of division.[8] But that is no excuse for its being ignored or made suspect. In the taking of the bread and wine, the offering of thanks for all God has done in Christ, the breaking of the bread and sharing of the bread and wine—what following Dix, scholars call the 'four-fold shape'—Christian churches perform the gospel in a tangible way, in Christ's living presence 'proclaiming his death until he comes' (1 Corinthians 11.26).

Over the past half-century, across the Christian spectrum there has been a renewal in how the eucharist is celebrated. It is now the main Sunday service in most congregations. But 'doing' what Christ commands is not restricted to holy communion services, or to baptism, the other major 'doing' rite—let alone our Christian worship in daily life. The Ministry of the Word and the Prayers of the People call for active response in any and every performance of the gospel. So in *APBA*, Morning and Evening Prayer (Second Order) provide for such 'doing' through the laying on of hands and similar tangible actions. Likewise the service of Praise, Prayer and Proclamation drives towards 'Confession of Sin' (and absolution)

---

7   Dix, *Shape* pages 14–15.

8   An accessible summary of Christian belief regarding the eucharist, made in the face of historical division, is the first Agreed Statement of the *Anglican-Roman Catholic International Commission* (ARCIC), 'Eucharistic Doctrine', available at www.prounione.urbe.it/dia-int/arcic/doc/e_arcic_eucharist.html.

as our responsive 'doing'. Every service of Christian worship can incorporate a 'doing', an active response to the gospel being performed.

But all Christian services that attend to the 'shape' of God's mission conclude with the sending out.

Go: the Sending out of God's people

'Dismissal' is the technical term for the last part of a Christian service—and means far more than an end-of-term service at school. In this Christ calls us to go out to perform the gospel in our lifestyle. As the eucharist has been revised over the last 50 years, words have been added which echo the 'great commissions' that conclude the Gospels: "go in peace to love and serve the Lord", "go in the peace of Christ" or similar. As Jesus sent out the first disciples, so Christ sends believers out today to perform 'divine service' in God's world—but only *after* they have received God's blessing.

'Sending' by Christ is epitomised in the words of blessing and dismissal. But this section invites being filled out to strengthen the link between performing the gospel in Christian liturgy and Christian living. In the eucharist, our self-offering in response to Christ's feeding us in communion marks the transition from 'doing' to 'sending', as we ask God to send us out "in the power of the Spirit". In any service, eucharist or not, 'sending' is the appropriate time to mark anniversaries (with prayer for the year ahead), to bless those who are moving on, or have special needs, to commission people for new ministries and so on.

The most common—and perhaps most abused—part of 'sending' is the Notices. Yes, they can be too long, unduly chatty or just repeat what is on the pew sheet. *APBA* places them *before* the blessing and dismissal, integrating them into the service rather than being an 'afterword'. The Notices signal particular ways in which the gospel will be performed in the activities of the community in the days ahead—by *every* Christian, not just clergy.

Overall, the basic structure of Sunday (and several other) services in *APBA* looks like this:

Gathering in God's Name
The Ministry of the Word
The Ministry of Prayer/Prayers of the People
Doing
The Sending out of God's people

This structure is not the only one possible for Christian worship. But since it is based on the shape of God's mission, a Sunday service without each of these elements would be significantly impoverished. As week by week passes, a common structure such as this enables the gospel to be performed in ways that promote 'common prayer', adapted flexibly to different needs, times and circumstances.

Behind this concept of a five-part shape is the importance of disciplined flexibility. Each part matters—but trying to make each one as significant as the others in any one service is likely to lead to spiritual ingestion. Each occasion calls for varying emphasis on different parts. In a baptism, for example, the gathering could include introducing the candidate and sponsors, and the 'doing' will be the natural focus. But the prayers can be minimal, trusting that baptism itself is a way of bringing all of life before God. An image that captures this flexibility is playing a concertina or accordion: it only works by being expanded and contracted. So it is with performing the gospel in liturgy. When each part in the shape of God's mission is expanded and contracted in relation to the context, the Spirit will breathe all the more fully in all present.

Part C   Planning to perform the Gospel

And so we come to the last Part of this book. The big question left is—what are good ways to bring together a service in which the gospel is performed authentically, and so that the people present are engaged by it? The outline that follows sets out some useful steps: only on special occasions will each step need to be considered, but having an overall process in mind means that 'regular' services will be prepared with care.

One preliminary point: it is assumed that the service is presided over by a priest or authorised minister, and that several people are involved in preparing and taking active parts. That reminder is needed again—*performing the gospel is the calling of every Christian*. The principle is that 'corporate worship should be corporately led', especially given the 'democratic' culture of today's Western societies (see Chapter Three). There are occasions when, for good reasons, the minister takes the whole service: if it is you, hopefully you will know how to adapt what follows.

1. Discerning the context

It might sound obvious, but it helps to start by acknowledging what cannot be changed and must be accepted. **What are the 'givens'?** There is no point in becoming frustrated about these. Just identify them and get on with the preparation.

For example, where will the service be held? What furniture is significant—and how flexible is it? Who is available to take active parts? Is a particular liturgy to be used? Who will be the congregation, and what is their life-setting? What language style is a 'given', on a scale from 'chatty' to 'formal'? What creativity is *possible* (as well as desirable— freshness is important for each performance of the gospel, but overdoing creativity can distract from what matters, and use too much energy).

Consider these examples:

- An ordination in a cathedral
  The liturgy will be tightly scripted, there is little opportunity to re-arrange furniture, and the bishop will preside. The congregation will be drawn from several churches, and will include friends and family of the candidates, for whom it is a vitally important time, some of whom may not be churchgoers. Hymns that everyone knows may be few in number. However, people with performance and musical skills will be available, which should ensure that all is done well, and that all present can engage with the service. Much of what happens is a 'given', but there are opportunities in the dramatic parts of the service—processions, examination, ordination, communion— for creative approaches that highlight what matters. Since the service is likely to be longer than usual, these can break up a 'mono-cultural' ethos that fosters boredom.

- A eucharist held in the bush at the end of a parish camp
  Here there are very few givens beyond the basic liturgy and readings. Indeed, some things that are taken for granted on a Sunday in church will need to be supplied—Bible, seating, bread, wine and table, music and so on. The challenge is the *lack* of givens—which is also an opportunity to be creative (without becoming so different from 'the usual' that people are lost). How will priest and people be arranged, especially if some have physical difficulties? Can all hear and see? Will people be too hot or cold? Will flies make a beeline for the wine? And what will be the best way for all to join in? Lugging

a pile of books into the bush feels out of sync with the setting, so service sheets are useful. But those present might know their parts, and the music could employ well-known hymns, Taizé chants or listening to singers or a recording.

- An ecumenical service of healing in a hospital chapel.
  The significant 'given' here is those who will be present. Some will not be in the best of health, and participants will come from a range of churches (or none). The chapel will be plain, the time available may be fixed, and hospital staff will need to be present. The service will need to be fairly short, and not involve much movement: those present are likely to be looking to be led rather than be active. While remaining a performance of the gospel of Christ, service content will need to be contextually sensitive, for example, with pew sheets using large (14+ point) type. Singing might be a challenge, but symbols (possibly including anointing) can provide creative opportunities.

- An inter-denominational service on a cruise ship
  Time (maximum 30 minutes), the ship's 'happy holiday' ethos, and a congregation from different churches meeting in a large theatre, are the 'givens'. Those who come are familiar with church of some sort, however, and like singing. We planned a service around two scripture readings (from the lectionary), written intercessions—read by others—plus psalm, Lord's prayer and short reflection. Two hymns set to well-known tunes were included (the ship provides a pianist), plus the (trinitarian) sailors' hymn, 'Eternal Father, strong to save', which it is traditional to have. All the people's words fitted on one A4 page, folded to make an A5 booklet. This

'shape' has worked well on several occasions—a key factor is service leaders and cruise staff trusting one another.

On board over Christmas one year, we were asked to take a 'midnight mass' ("or the Catholics will complain", as the cruise director put it). Careful preparation saw this work out well, with another minister preaching, and other passengers helping distribute communion as well as reading. The service only started after midnight, but a large and appreciative congregation came, including some crew members, and no one seemed to mind that it took 45 minutes.

Of course many 'traditional' buildings have fixed furniture that makes seeing and moving difficult: here the 'givens' can feel oppressive. At the other extreme is a congregation that meets in a place where everything has to be set up each time—a school hall, for example—where the sheer physical labour involved makes any 'given' seem a treasure.

St Paul's (Anglican) Cathedral in Bendigo had to be closed in 2007, and the parish hall was set up for regular use (which meant a lot of busy Saturday afternoons). Over the next year or so, the seating faced different walls at different times, and the main furniture was placed in a variety of ways, so that the congregation could explore a range of patterns before returning (not 'going back') to the cathedral when it re-opened. Special occasions such as the annual legal service called for arrangements different from those for Sunday morning. For a funeral, the placement of the coffin, and where family members were seated, needed to be taken into account. The first Easter morning after the closure, the main service—robes, choir, bishop and all, with people sitting on deck-chairs and rugs—was held on top of the Coles car park across the road, including adults being baptised.

By now you will have got the idea. The point is to be aware of the *context* in which the gospel will be performed on this occasion—and avoid frustration about the impossible!

2. Sketching the substance

The substance of any performance of the gospel involves several key elements.

First cab off the rank are the Bible **readings** (see Chapter Five). They may have already been set, for example, from the lectionary or by the bishop. If the choice is open, two or more readings should be chosen—making sure that the scriptures are not being 'used'. In planning the distinctive content of the service, including activities, work from these texts in the first place, rather than a general 'theme'.

Next will be the **season** of the Christian year, or **special occasion** (funeral, anniversary), and the liturgical resources associated with it—colours, flowers and symbols (e.g. Advent candles) and the overall 'tone' of the service (quiet in Lent, joyful in Easter)

What is the **shape and style** of the service? Eucharist? Song-focused? Family service? (Whatever it is, recall the overall 'shape' sketched above: *gather/listen/pray/do/go*.) How will this affect the way the scriptures, liturgical resources and activities are engaged?[9]

Who is available to do what? The focal ministries of presiding and preaching may be already in place, and there may be a roster for welcoming, readers, children's ministry, musicians, intercessors, administering communion and the like. (If last-minute roster switches keep happening, it's probably time for the roster to be re-thought) Keep an eye out for those who might be overlooked, or people whose skills may not be obvious, or who are hesitant to

---

9   www.bettergatherings.com is a practical, interactive website from the Anglican Diocese of Sydney that offers 'templates' from *BCP*, *AAPB* and Sydney sources to assist planning. Its positive 'Sydney Anglican' theological stance is oriented to encouraging congregations who are suspicious of 'liturgy' to take it seriously.

'volunteer'. Everything should be done well—which does *not* mean people changing their natural accent to a 'parsonic' one. But it might call for some training and/or rehearsal.

3. Shaping the content

Whether or not the service relies on one person (e.g. at many funerals) or a small group, with all above work in mind, start shaping its content by reading the scripture passages aloud. Spend a little time listening to what each person 'hears'. Reflect together on how this ties in with the season, context, congregation and the wider world. If possible, agree on a motif or image that might weave its way through the service, and focus what participants 'take away'. But don't dictate to the presider and preacher what they must do and say. Conversely, look to the 'experts' to clear the ground, not fill and fence it.

The above steps take first place ahead of whatever 'prayer book' is used, and how 'set down' the liturgy appears to be. This book assumes that *APBA* or something like it provides the framework and common words for the service, but 'shaping the content' from the scriptures outwards matters whatever the church context. Indeed, the less liturgical 'givens', the more important this approach becomes, lest what is performed is shaped more by 'what people want' or 'what will ensure a happy occasion' than the gospel.

With this preparation done, now is the time to work on the music to be used—hymns, song-sets (e.g. before the service proper starts, during communion), anthems. As was observed in Chapter Six, music matters enormously to the *affective* dimension of performing the gospel. In some places, it will be the type of singing used in each part of a service that gives it shape—and not only in Pentecostal circles. When I was studying in the US, a Black scholar explained that in many Afro-American congregations with a heritage of low literacy, several different song styles are used, from chorales to 'shouters', each of which has its 'right place' in a service. But just as in 'liturgical' churches, shaping the content is about attending to the scriptures, so that it is indeed the gospel that is performed.

4. Working on the detail

With the overall shape and sense of the service gelling, practical matters need to be agreed upon. How will participants be positioned? What movements are they expected to make—and what issues might need to be sorted to let this happen? By whom will the scriptures be read, and how? What musical accompaniment is available? By whom and how will the Ministry of Prayer be undertaken? How will communion be administered, and by whom?

Reviewing the service overall, three questions can be helpful:

- What overall 'tone' is appropriate—and what would be unhelpful?
- What practical problems might become opportunities?
- What 'comfort zones' must be respected—or should be crossed?

This stage concludes by having a detailed plan ('running sheet') drawn up. It will include **who is responsible** for what; what **preparation** tasks are needed; and who will engage any **'surprises'** that might come up in the service (and they will). For regular services, a template that can be adapted for each occasion saves time and energy.

Committing the occasion to God in prayer will have been on people's minds and hearts, but now is a useful time to do this together. Which leads into the next step.

5. Final preparation and rehearsing

By now it is time to let those named on the 'running sheet' get on with their work; trusted that they will do so carefully and prayerfully.

For most regular Sunday services, a meeting 15 to 30 minutes before the start time is usually sufficient to check that all is in readiness, and pray together briefly.

But for larger occasions, especially when something special is planned, or when people will be up front who are not used to it (e.g. weddings and ordinations), a rehearsal makes sense. Since this may take as long as the service itself, it is best arranged on a different day.

6. Reviewing and planning

When the service is over, that is not the end of things—review and reflection are important (see the next section). *But leave critique of the service until at least the following day.* Write down things that disturbed you so that you will have accurate recall. Trust God that, whatever faults, poor performance or even heretical ideas have occurred, the gospel has gone out and God's people have been fed so they can live it out.

No theatre company worth its salt would run a show time and again without ongoing review. The same should be true for a church, whose 'performance' is crucially important. For special occasions such as an ordination, responsibility for review will rest with the bishop or diocesan leaders, but expecting one to happen can encourage its taking place.

Note: funerals and weddings do not lend themselves to particular review, but whether or not a church is approached for more will soon let you know what the funeral directors and wedding planners think of its ministry.

Arranging a regular time to review regular services is particularly helpful (but not on the same day). A meeting of those involved every 4-6 weeks is sufficient—doing so over a meal, or coffee and cake, will help. Identifying what worked well might be seen as fairly easy, but it is encouraging, and helps discern where the Spirit is at work. Admitting what did not go quite as planned can be harder, but can also be a growth point, and identify where skills can be sharpened. Learning can be consolidated, and a look ahead made to the weeks coming up. But this is not the place for following up lack of preparation, poor performance or disagreements: these are best dealt with by the parish priest in private.

Most importantly, review can help people sense what *integrating* the various aspects of performing the gospel means. Why did a particular service 'hang together'? How did its 'flow' lead people to live out the kingdom of God more fully in daily life?

Part D   Taking a 'worship audit'

Mark Earey, an English liturgical scholar and practitioner, some years ago penned *Worship Audit. Making Good Worship Better* (Nottingham: Grove Worship Series 133, 1995). It remains an excellent brief introduction to reviewing a congregation's regular worship. What follows are questions raised in his booklet. He asks:

> What does *God* think of this act of worship?
> What do *'we'* (regular participants) think of it?
> What do *'they'* (visitors) think of it?

Mark includes a questionnaire that can be used to assess the second and third questions. You might like to prepare one for your situation. Mark's sections are these:

A   Tell us a bit about yourself (relation to this congregation; time there; age; gender)

B   Before the service started (welcome; atmosphere)

C   During the service (service book usability; leadership; 'hanging together'; symbols)

D   Music (fitting in; mix of styles; familiarity; how helpful for praising God)

E   Sermon, readings and prayers (how clear/understandable; how thought-provoking; how the Bible was read; helpfulness of prayers; silence for reflection; life connection)

F   General (what does 'reverence' mean for you? how others experienced the service)

Mark suggests that a small group summarise the responses made, taking care to watch confidences. Main outcomes can then be considered in a variety of small groups, with the aim of encouraging better understanding and participation in worship, and possibly leading to recommendations to the minister and Parish Council.

Yet in all this 'busy work', Mark keeps the focus on the first question: what does *God* think of our worship? He emphasises the importance in the scriptures of:

- *sacrifice* "Is our corporate worship the *focus* of the offering of our whole selves and lives (Romans 12.1ff) or a *replacement* for it?";

- *integrity* "Does our church life (indeed our very *act* of worship itself) scream 'injustice, hatred, unforgiveness, envy, bitterness, racism ...'?"; and

- *worshipping in Spirit and truth* "How do we hold together the life of the Spirit and the truth of the gospel?".

Mark concludes by noting that he is a keen 'transport spotter'. With this in mind he asks:

Is our worship like a tram, running on fixed lines—but unable to adapt? Or like a bus, able to go anywhere—but prone to truth taking second place to experience? Or like a trolley bus, flexible but taking power from overhead lines, and not at the mercy of the driver or passengers!

And I would want to add—where does this act of worship *take* participants as they go out to perform the gospel in their lifestyles and living?

Further reading

Introduction

Chan, Simon, *Liturgical Theology. The Church as Worshipping Community* (Downers Grove: IVP, 2006)

Dawn, Marva A., *A Royal "Waste" of Time* (Grand Rapids: Eerdmans, 1999)

Stringer, Martin, *A Sociological History of Christian Worship* (Cambridge: CUP, 2005) Chapter 7, 'The globalisation of Christian worship 180-2000'

Webber, Robert E., *Worship is a Verb* (Waco: Word, 1985): a lively introduction to Christian liturgy from the 'ground up', with a strong emphasis on worship as doing and action.

White, Susan J., *Groundwork of Christian Worship* (Peterborough: Epworth, 1997)

Chapter 1

Articles 'Liturgy', 'Worship', in Davies. J.G. (ed), in *The New Dictionary of Liturgy and Worship* (London: SCM, 1986)

Article 'Worship' in Marshall, I. Howard et alia (edd), *The New Bible Dictionary* (Third edition, Leicester: IVP, 1996)

Article 'Worship' in Richardson, Alan (ed), *Theological Word Book to the Bible* (London: SCM, 1962)

Day, Juliette and Gordon-Taylor, Benjamin (edd), *The Study of Liturgy and Worship. An Alcuin Study Guide* (London: SPCK, 2013), especially chapters 1-3 (Worship, liturgy and ritual), and 19-21 (ethics, mission and culture)

Galbraith, Douglas G. (ed), *Worship in the Wide Red Land* (Melbourne: JBRE, 1981) chapter 1

McGowan, Andrew, *Ancient Christian Worship. Early Church Practices in Social, Historical and Theological Context* (Grand Rapids: Baker, 2014) chapter one

Sherlock, Charles, "From 'mate upstairs' to 'spirituality sponsor: God images in Australian Society", in Peter Malone (ed), *Developing an Australian Theology* (Homebush: St Paul's, 1999)

Sherlock, Charles, 'The Anglican Church of Australia', in Charles Hefling & Cynthia Shattuck (edd), *The Oxford Guide to the Book of Common Prayer. A Worldwide Survey* (Oxford: OUP, 2006) 324-332

Tripp, D.H, 'Worship and the Pastoral Office', in Jones, Cheslyn, Wainwright, Geoffrey and Yarnold, Edmund sj (edd), *The Study of Liturgy* (London: SPCK, 1978) 510-532

Young, Frances, *The Art of Performance* (London: Darton, Longman and Todd, 1980)

Willimon, William, *The Service of God. How Worship an Ethics are Related* (Nashville: Abingdon, 1983) chapters 1-3

Chapter 2

Giles, Richard, *Re-pitching the Tent. The Definitive Guide to Reordering Your Church* (Canterbury Press, 2004)

Irvine, Christopher, 'Space', in Day, Juliette and Gordon-Taylor, Benjamin (edd), *The Study of Liturgy and Worship* (London: Alcuin / SPCK, 2013), 102-112

Mauck, M., *Shaping a House for the Church* (Chicago: Liturgy Training Publications, 1990)

White, J.F., *Introduction to Christian Worship* (Nashville: Abingdon, 1981, 1990) chapter III

White, Kenneth, *Shrines for the Saints*, and *Centres for the Servants* (Bramcote: Grove Liturgy Series 3 and 4, 1975)

Chapter 3

Many of the Grove Worship series booklets are relevant to this chapter—too many to list.

Barnett, James, *The Diaconate: Full and Equal Order* (New York: Seabury, 1981) chapter six (on the history of orders)

Burnham, Andrew, *Guidelines for the Liturgical Ministry of Deacons*, and *The Deacon at the Eucharist* (London: Church Union, 1992): these relate to the Church of England.

Collins, John, *Are All Christian Ministers?* (Melbourne: EJ Dwyer/ Harper Collins, 1992): examines the scriptural data on ministry with 'democratic' issues in mind (and argues for 'No').

Green, Robin, *Only Connect: worship and liturgy from the perspective of pastoral care* (London: DLT, 1987): gives profound insights into how worship relates to different sorts of people.

Hovda, Robert, *Strong, Loving and Wise. Presiding in Liturgy* (Collegeville MN: Liturgical Press, 1976): a classic text on presiding in mainstream liturgical traditions.

Webber, Robert, *Worship Old and New* (Grand Rapids: Zondervan, 1994) part IV: offers a range of perspectives on performing Christian liturgy with 'contemporary' issues in mind.

Willimon, William, *Worship as Pastoral Care* (Nashville; Abingdon, 1979): employs pastoral psychology to explore how the way that liturgy is led and understood shapes Christian life.

Chapter 5

Brown, David, *Introducing the Three Year Lectionary for Sundays* (Melbourne: JBCE, 1982)

Douglas, J.D. (ed), *The Illustrated Bible Dictionary* (Volumes I–III, IVP, 1998): also available on DVD.

Fee, Gordon D., and Stuart, Douglas, *How to read the Bible for all its worth* (Third Edition, Zondervan, 2002)

Sherlock, Charles, *Words and the Word: case studies in using scripture today* (Morningstar/Mosaic, 2013): especially chapters 1–3.

Paul White, *Reading the Bible Aloud* (Lancer, 1980)

Chapter 6

Bales, David, and Miller, Herb, "We Are Singing the Right Hymns ... Aren't We?" *Church Effectiveness Nuggets* Volume 32 (2007). http://bishopperryinstitute.org.au/uploads/ChurchEffectivenessNuggets-Volume32.pdf

Begbie, Jeremy S., *Resounding Truth: Christian Wisdom in the World of Music* (Grand Rapids, Michigan: Baker Academic, 2007)

Brown, Frank Burch, *Inclusive yet Discerning: Navigating Worship Artfully* (Grand Rapids, Michigan: Eerdmans, 2009): explores the ways we think about the arts in worship, arguing for the development of an 'ecumenical taste'.

Brown, Rosalind, *How hymns shape our lives* (Cambridge: Grove Books, 2001)

Cole, David, "Hymns and Meaning." *St Mark's Review* (Autumn 1991) 14–17: a short, penetrating treatment of how music and text work together in song.

Cooke, Victoria, *Understanding songs of renewal* (Cambridge: Grove Books, 2001)

Faulkner, Quentin, *Wiser Than Despair—the Evolution of Ideas in the Relationship of Music and the Christian Church* (Westport, CT:

Greenwood Press, 1996): a comprehensive survey of the history, culture and the music of the Church.

Harrison, Anne, *Sing it again—the place of short songs in worship* (Cambridge: Grove Books, 2003)

Hawn, C Michael, "Streams of Song: An Overview of Congregational Song in the Twenty-First Century." *The Hymn* 61/1 (Winter 2010) https://babel.hathitrust.org/cgi/pt?id=mdp.39015080918306;view=1up;seq=1

Hull, Kenneth R., "Text, Music, and Meaning in Congregational Song." *The Hymn* 53/1 (January 2002), 14–27 https://babel.hathitrust.org/cgi/pt?id=mdp.39015054346070;view=1up;seq=7

Johansson, Calvin M., *Music & Ministry: A Biblical Counterpoint* (2nd edition, Peabody, MA: Hendrickson, 1998)

Magee, Fay, "Examining Contemporary Congregational Song— Beyond Sung Theology" (Melbourne: MA Thesis, University of Divinity, 2012) http://repository.divinity.edu.au/id/eprint/1240

Postman, Neil, *Amusing Ourselves to Death—Public Discourse in the Age of Show Business* (London: Methuen, 1986)

Ramshaw, Gail, "Words Worth Singing." *The Hymn* 46/2 (April 1995) 16–19 https://babel.hathitrust.org/cgi/pt?id=mdp.39015033625891;view=1up;seq=97

Routley, Erik, *Christian Hymns Observed* (London: Mowbray, 1983): a short and insightful book from the great hymnologist of the twentieth century.

Saliers, Don E., *Music and Theology* (Nashville: Abingdon Press, 2007): short and helpful book on what the title describes.

Smith, Elizabeth J., "Crafting and Singing Hymns in Australia." In *Christian Worship in Australia: Inculturating the Liturgical Tradition*, edited by Stephen Burns and Anita Monro (Strathfield NSW: St Paul's, 2009)

Ward, Pete, *Selling Worship—How what we sing has changed the Church* (Milton Keynes: Paternoster, 2005)

Wren, Brian, *Praying Twice: The Music and Words of Congregational Song* (Louisville, KY: Westminster John Knox Press, 2000): probably the most significant and extensive investigation of the contemporary usage of congregational song.

Wilson-Dickson, Andrew, *The Story of Christian Music—from Gregorian Chant to Black Gospel; an Authoritative Illustrated Guide to all the Major Traditions of Music for Worship* (Oxford: Lion, 2003): a good coffee table reference book giving background to the world of church music.

Chapter 8

A Prayer Book for Australia (Melbourne: Broughton 1995), The Calendar (pages 451ff)

Akehurst, Peter, *Keeping Holy Week* (Nottingham: Grove, 1976): a practical guide based in careful reflection on what 're-enactment' involves.

Barth, Karl, *Church Dogmatics I/II* (trans. G.W. Bromiley and T.H.L Parker, London: T & T Clark, 1956) paragraph 14 (over 50 pages): a classic theological discussion of 'time'.

Robert Jenson, *The Triune Identity* (Philadelphia: Fortress, 1982) chapter three: explores how early Christian fathers adapted Greek philosophy in the light of scripture.

Lloyd, Trevor *Celebrating Lent, Holy Week and Easter* (Nottingham: Grove, 1985): follows up Akers, but with a wider focus on Lent.

Sherlock, Charles, *Australian Anglicans Remember* (Melbourne: Broughton, 2015): gives information and liturgical resources on the people and events in the *APBA* Calendar not in *BCP*.

White, James, *Introduction to Christian Worship* (Nashville: Abingdon, 1981) chapter II: discusses 'The Language of Time'.

www.anglican.org.nz/Resources/Lectionary-and-Worship/For-All-the-Saints/For-All-the-Saints
This website gives information on hundreds of saints and festivals.

Chapter 9

Day, Juliette and Gordon-Taylor, Benjamin (edd), *The Study of Liturgy and Worship. An Alcuin Guide* (London: SPCK, 2013): 22 wise essays by scholars grouped in four sections—Foundations (worship, liturgy, ritual etc.); Elements (language, proclamation, music, space etc.); Event (initiation, eucharist, marriage etc.) and Dimensions (ethics, mission, culture, ecumenism). This is a first-rate survey of 21st century learning about Christian liturgy and life.

Earey, Mark, *Worship Audit* (Grove Worship series #133): short, first-rate and practical aid to 'auditing' Sunday services.

ELLC, *Praying Together* (London: SPCK, 1988): agreed translations in contemporary English of prayers, creeds and songs used across the Christian tradition, with commentary.

Perry, Michael, *Preparing for Worship* (London: Marshall Pickering, 1995): excellent analysis of the elements of regular services, plus indexes to a wide range of songs.

Sherlock, Charles, *A Pastoral Handbook for Anglicans* (Acorn, 2000): includes ideas for baptisms, weddings and funerals, set in a theological framework for pastoral ministry.

Turner, Victor, The Ritual Process (London: Penguin, 1969): classic introduction to liminal theory, applied to ritual processes.

Young, Frances, The Art of Performance: *Towards A Theology of Holy Scripture* (London: Darton, Longman and Todd, 1990): a classic on *performing*—rather than theorising about—the scriptures, with similarities to the approach of the current book.

Webber, Robert, *Worship Old and New* (Grand Rapid: Zondervan, Revised Edition 1995) Chapter IV (the second half of the book): a highly readable approach to the issues of this chapter by a scholar from the mainstream Evangelical tradition in the USA.

Websites offering creative liturgical resources

ELLC texts: http://englishtexts.org/Portals/11/Assets/praying.pdf.

Australian Anglican resources: www.anglican.org.au/liturgy (still growing!)

Anglican Diocese of Sydney: www.bettergatherings.com This site offers 'templates' from *BCP*, *AAPB* and Sydney sources to encourage congregations who are suspicious of 'liturgy' to take it seriously.

For Australian Roman Catholics (and others): www.liturgyritualprayer.com

'New Patterns for Worship'—a wealth of ideas from the Church of England: https://www.churchofengland.org/prayer-worship/worship/texts/newpatterns.asp

From a creative Baptist pastor in Melbourne: www.laughingbird.net/LaughingBird/Welcome.html

From the Evangelical Lutheran Church of Canada—'Lift up your hearts': www.elic.com

www.ingramcontent.com/pod-product-compliance
Lightning Source LLC
Chambersburg PA
CBHW030436300426
44112CB00009B/1035